PRAISE FOR
COMMONPLACES: LOCI COMMUNES 1521

Melanchthon's *Loci Communes* are presented here in an appropriate and suitable manner: introduction and footnotes help to understand this founding text of Lutheran theology. Teachers as well as students in the field of Reformation will profit from this revised version.

—Prof. Dr. Volker Leppin
Eberhard Karls Universität Tübingen

This book takes us back to the early stages and to the heart of the Reformation, so it is just wonderful that it has now once again become so accessible. The translation is as fresh as the content of the *Loci* of 1521 and that makes it just the kind of material we need for teaching and learning. Melanchthon's book has been fundamental for church and theology in the Lutheran as well as the Calvinist tradition. And both will see through this new edition how relevant this reformer and his work still are today.

—Herman Selderhuis
Director Refo500
Professor of Church History
Theological University Apeldoorn

Christian Preus provides helpful historical and theological contextualization to the *Loci Communes* of Philip Melanchthon in his introduction. With the text itself, he gives us a clear, modern translation that both improves on the work of past translators and also includes judicious scholarly commentary. This is a welcome and useful tool for modern students of the Reformation.

—Dr. Günter Frank
Director of the European Melanchthon Academy

What better recommendation could one have for a book than Luther's praise of his colleague Philip Melanchthon's *Topics On Theological*

Matters, his *Loci Communes* of 1521: his friend's treatment of these "commonplaces" of Paul's letter to the Romans was "divine." Melanchthon incorporated Luther's distinction of Law and Gospel into the basic outline of scriptural truth in this work, which initiated the Lutheran dogmatic tradition. This handbook, intended as a guide for reading Scripture, almost five hundred years old, will aid twenty-first century readers in understanding Scripture and sharing this biblical faith with others.

—Robert Kolb
Missions professor of systematic theology emeritus
Concordia Seminary, Saint Louis

The lucidity that marked the first version of Melanchthon's *Loci Communes* is captured in this expert translation by a scholar equally expert in the nuances of humanist Latin and the principles of evangelical theology. Preus brings modern readers into contact with Melanchthon's brilliant early work, augmenting his clear translation with helpful annotations and the perfect introduction to Melanchthon's life and thought.

—Ralph Keen
Schmitt Professor of History
University of Illinois at Chicago

COMMONPLACES

LOCI COMMUNES 1521

COMMONPLACES

LOCI COMMUNES 1521

PHILIP MELANCHTHON

TRANSLATED WITH INTRODUCTION AND NOTES
BY CHRISTIAN PREUS

CONCORDIA PUBLISHING HOUSE · SAINT LOUIS

About the cover: Philip Melanchthon's crest depicts a serpent lifted up on a cross, a symbol that alludes to Numbers 21:4–9, where looking at a bronze serpent lifted up on a pole saved the people from venomous snake bites. Jesus Christ applied this story to Himself in His discussion with Nicodemus (John 3:14–15): "As Moses lifted up the serpent in the wilderness, so must the Son of Man be lifted up, that whoever believes in him may have eternal life." Melanchthon's use of this crest dates back to 1519. Beginning in 1526, it adorned printings of Melanchthon's writings.

Copyright © 2014 by Concordia Publishing House
3558 S. Jefferson Ave., St. Louis, MO 63118–3968
1-800-325-3040 • www.cph.org

Scripture quotations are translation of translator.

This work uses the SBL Greek Unicode font developed by the Font Foundation under the leadership of the Society of Biblical Literature. For further information on this font or on becoming a Font Foundation member, see http://www.sbl-site.org/educational/biblicalfonts.aspx.

Cover image: Courtesy of the Pitts Theology Library, Candler School of Theology, Emory University.

Manufactured in the United States of America

Library of Congress Cataloging-in-Publication Data

Melanchthon, Philipp, 1497-1560.

[Loci communes rerum theologicarum. English]

Commonplaces : Loci communes 1521 / Philip Melanchthon ; translated with introduction and notes by Christian Preus.

pages cm

Includes index.

ISBN 978-0-7586-4445-9

1. Lutheran Church--Doctrines--Early works to 1800. 2. Theology, Doctrinal--Early works to 1800. I. Preus, Christian, 1909-2000. II. Title.

BR338.L6313 2014

230'.41--dc23   2013042575

2 3 4 5 6 7 8 9 10   22 21 20 19 18 17

CONTENTS

ABBREVIATIONS

AE   Luther, Martin. *Luther's Works.* American Edition. Vols. 1–30: Edited by Jaroslav Pelikan. St. Louis: Concordia, 1955–76. Vols. 31–55: Edited by Helmut Lehmann. Philadelphia/Minneapolis: Muhlenberg/ Fortress, 1957–86. Vols. 56–75: Edited by Christopher Boyd Brown. St. Louis: Concordia, 2009–.

AC   The Augsburg Confession

Ap   Apology of the Augsburg Confession

AS   *Erasmus von Rotterdam: Ausgewählte Schriften.* 8 vols. Edited by Werner Welzig. Darmstadt: Wissenschaftliche Buchgesellschaft, 1967.

CR   *Corpus Reformatorum: Philippi Melanchthonis Opera quae supersunt Omnia.* 28 vols. Edited by C. G. Bretschneider. Halle: Schwetschke, 1834–60.

G   Jean Gerson. *Œuvres completes.* 10 vols. Edited by Palémon Glorieux. Paris: Desclée et Cie, 1960–73.

Maurer   Wilhelm Maurer, *Der Junge Melanchthon.* 2 vols. Göttingen: Vandenhoeck & Ruprecht, 1969.

MPG   *Patrologiae cursus completus: Series Graece.* 161 vols. Edited by Jacques-Paul Migne. Paris, 1859–1963.

MPL   *Patrologiae cursus completus: Series Latina.* 221 vols. Edited by Jacques-Paul Migne. Paris, 1859–1963.

Pöhlmann   Horst Georg Pöhlmann, trans. and ed. *Loci Communes 1521*. Gütersloh: Gütersloher Verlagshaus, 1997.

SA   *Melanchthons Werke in Auswahl.* 7 vols. Edited by Robert Stupperich. Gütersloh: C Bertelsmann Verlag, 1951–52.

SD   Solid Declaration of the Formula of Concord

WA   *D. Martin Luthers Werke: Kritische Gesamtausgabe,* 73 vols. in 85. Weimar: Hermann Böhlau, 1883–.

WA Br   *D. Martin Luthers Werke: Briefwechsel.* 18 vols. Weimar: Hermann Böhlau, 1930–.

WA TR   *D. Martin Luthers Werke: Tischreden.* 6 vols. Weimar: Hermann Böhlau, 1912–21.

INTRODUCTION

Philip Melanchthon's *Loci Communes* (*Common Topics*) of 1521 reflects the fusion of humanist and theologian. With the eloquence and philological acumen of a humanist, Melanchthon derides the inconsistencies and subtleties that he finds so objectionable in the writings of the Scholastics and arranges a summary of Christian theology in good, rhetorical fashion around clear and concise passages of Scripture. But with the fervor of a theologian, he takes the confession of Martin Luther as his own, parting ways with his humanist roots and insisting that canonical Scripture alone with its radical message of sin and grace, Law and Gospel, captivity and freedom, be the source and norm of a Christian's confession and life.

With this influential work, published in the tumultuous year of 1521, as Luther, the Reformation's Elijah, was hidden in Wartburg, Melanchthon, the grammarian and classicist, made his debut as theologian and emerged as Wittenberg's Elisha. In the years leading up to 1521, Melanchthon had shined as a star of humanism in Germany and was compared to Erasmus, whose critical edition of the Greek New Testament, among many other works, had made him world renowned.[1] In keeping with his humanist roots, Melanchthon had articulated the Gospel in largely ethical terms up to 1519, seeing Christ as the perfect moral example and speaking in generalities about God's grace.[2]

Melanchthon's theological breakthrough in these early years was his realization of the utter incapacity of fallen man to come to God by his own powers.[3] Melanchthon's acceptance of this aspect of Luther's theological anthropology meant his rejection of humanist theology

---

[1] Clyde Manschreck, *Melanchthon: The Quiet Reformer* (New York: Abingdon Press, 1958), 41.

[2] This stress is seen as late as 1520 in his address on Paul and the Scholastics, for which see below p. 7. Cf. Michael Rogness, *Philip Melanchthon: Reformer Without Honor* (Minneapolis: Augsburg, 1969), 10.

[3] See Wolfgang Matz, *Der befreite Mensch: Die Willenslehre in der Theologie Philipp Melanchthons* (Göttingen: Vandenhoeck and Ruprecht, 2001), 27–38; and below, pp. 5–6.

and its stress on man's natural, ethical potential.[4] If man is utterly dead in his sins, his only hope for salvation and life must be completely out of his own hands. If all human powers are thoroughly bound in sin, he cannot do good in God's eyes. God's grace alone frees him from the shackles of his slavery. And as Luther had articulated more and more clearly in the years leading up to 1521, the ground and reason for God's grace is found in Christ alone, who became man, suffered, died, and rose again to safeguard God's mercy to the human race. God's grace is not based in our obedience to God's Law. Rather, God's Law shows the sinner how sinful he is and would lead him to despair were he not to hear the gracious promise of the forgiveness of sins for Christ's sake. So these topics—sin, grace, Law, and Gospel—are the central topics of the Christian faith, the central themes of Scripture, and the central focus and experience of the Christian life. This is the thesis of Melanchthon's *Common Topics* of 1521.

To place the *Loci Communes* of 1521 in their proper context, I will first offer a brief survey of Melanchthon's life up to 1521, then address the three theological and intellectual movements most influential on this, Melanchthon's first major theological work—Scholasticism, humanism, and the theology of Martin Luther.

THE LIFE OF PHILIP MELANCHTHON (1497–1521)

Philip Melanchthon was born Philip Schwarzerd on February 16, 1497, in Bretten, the son of a well-off armorer, Georg Schwarzerd. His father died when he was 11 years old, poisoned by well water that had left him incapacitated for years. After his father's death, Philip's mother sent him to Pforzheim, where Philip's maternal grandmother lived, to attend the prestigious Latin school there. Through his grandmother, Philip became close to the famous humanist scholar John Reuchlin, his grandmother's brother and therefore Philip's own granduncle. In typical humanist fashion and under the influence of his

---

[4] Of course, Melanchthon himself remained a humanist, in the sense of a philologist. Not all humanists (especially after the start of the Reformation) held to a theology of works or of "free will." Even before the Reformation, the humanist Laurentius Valla held to a bondage of the will based on divine predestination (see p. 31 below). For Erasmus's derision of Valla, see p. 31, n. 40 below. Cf. Timothy Wengert, *Human Freedom, Christian Righteousness* (Oxford: Oxford University Press, 1998), 5–11.

granduncle, Philip hellenized his last name and began to be called Melanchthon ("black earth").

Philip excelled in Latin and Greek and in short time was ready to graduate to university studies. In October 1509, at the age of twelve, he began his studies at the University of Heidelberg. Within two years he had completed his Bachelor of Arts and immediately began his studies for the Master of Arts. When a year later he had completed the requirements for this degree also, his application was denied by the faculty, who cited his young age and childlike appearance as their reason. The rejection, however, was fortuitous. Melanchthon's humanist learning had already surpassed that of many of his professors at Heidelberg, which possessed a more conservative faculty still working with Scholastic models of linguistics, logic, and philosophy in the tradition of the *via antiqua*.[5] Urged by his granduncle Reuchlin, Melanchthon decided to seek his Master of Arts at the University of Tübingen, a university of a slightly more humanist bent and with professors following the *via moderna*. In Tübingen, Melanchthon flourished. Despite taking up with fervor the pseudoscience of astrology, with which he continued to be enamored his entire life, he supplemented his university studies with private readings in theology and the classics. He took special interest in Ciceronian rhetoric, Aristotelian logic (which he wanted to redeem from Scholastic corruption), and Scripture. On January 25, 1514, he obtained his Master of Arts and was certified to teach at the university.

Melanchthon was known as an energetic teacher from the start. As he taught, he continued his humanist studies, becoming more and more involved in the movement and identifying with such men as Reuchlin and Erasmus in opposition to Scholasticism. The Hebrew scholar Reuchlin, in fact, was already in quite the controversy due to his defense of Jewish literature (and therefore Jews) against a Dominican campaign seeking imperial approval to confiscate and destroy all Jewish literature in the Empire on the grounds that they were anti-Christian. Melanchthon saw firsthand that many of the old guard in academia—including even the faculty at the University of

---

[5] The term *via antiqua* refers to the "old way" of doing Scholastic theology, which posits the reality of abstract concepts (realism). The *via moderna* or "new way" denies the reality of abstract concepts, positing that they are merely names used to designate a class of concretions (nominalism).

Paris—were willing to undermine the study of Hebrew and advances in humanist learning because of uninformed prejudices and under the guise of ill-conceived inquisitions. Melanchthon's preface to Reuchlin's *Letters of Famous Men* demonstrates that at the early age of seventeen he was well on his way to becoming a famous and recognized humanist scholar.[6]

As a professor, Melanchthon was hard at work both teaching and publishing. Besides translating some classical works, he compiled a new edition of the comedian Terence in 1516, setting his plays to meter for the first time, and published his Greek grammar in 1518, a much used and quite popular primer, a major boon for humanist studies in Northern Europe. He taught rhetoric based on classical models and lectured on classical authors such as Livy and Virgil. Moved by the controversies of the day and a convinced humanist, Melanchthon also turned to theological study. The theology of the humanists was in large part a kind of practical ethic as opposed to the complicated Aristotelian system of the Scholastics.

Still, Melanchthon had to deal with the old guard of conservative Scholasticism even at Tübingen. More and more Melanchthon was viewed by the faculty there as a modern innovator, a dangerous and subversive teacher. In contrast, his reputation as a scholar among the humanists was growing all around Northern Europe—even in England, where his Greek grammar was received with enthusiasm. Melanchthon knew he had to leave Tübingen and began to seek where he could teach in a freer atmosphere. A position at Ingolstadt opened up, but, when offered the job, Melanchthon turned it down. His granduncle, John Reuchlin, had advised against accepting the position, thinking that Melanchthon would have the same kind of troubles there as at Tübingen.

Thus Melanchthon was almost as overjoyed as his granduncle when the latter informed Melanchthon that he had secured a position for him to be professor of Greek at the University of Wittenberg, a small university newly founded in 1502, but anxious to be a representative of the new learning and quickly growing in fame because of Martin Luther. The Elector of Saxony, Frederick the Wise, had asked Reuchlin who would best be suited for the position, and

---

[6] *CR* 1:5–6. Reuchlin shows in this work, by publishing his correspondence with the most eminent scholars of Europe, that he himself was being slandered by despisers of learning.

Reuchlin had informed him that among Germans Melanchthon was a humanist second only to Erasmus.[7] Despite opposition from Luther, who preferred a different candidate, the Elector chose Melanchthon. On August 25, 1518, Melanchthon arrived in Wittenberg, a small and unimpressive town in comparison with Heidelberg and Tübingen.

To Luther and his colleagues in Wittenberg, Melanchthon's small, boyish appearance was underwhelming and disappointing. But when Melanchthon gave his inaugural address a few days after his arrival, Luther realized that appearances had been deceiving. The address was entitled *On Reforming the Studies of the Youth.*[8] After hearing Melanchthon speak of educational reform, how by study of the classics in their original languages, by going back to the sources, including especially a fresh look at the works of Aristotle, students could be taught to pursue true philosophy, philology, rhetoric, and dialectic, and not the stale traditions of men pawned off as knowledge, Luther was convinced that Melanchthon was a gift from God, a true godsend for the University of Wittenberg. And he was right. Within two years of Melanchthon's arrival, the student population had tripled, in large part due to the fame of the young humanist.[9]

Melanchthon's inaugural oration shows that upon his arrival in Wittenberg his concerns were more educational and ethical than theological. But the next years would prove to be transformational. At first, Melanchthon taught exclusively in the classics, lecturing on Homer and other Greek and Latin authors. His works published in 1518 and the early months of 1519 reflect less Reformation theology than the humanism of Erasmus.[10] But as Melanchthon studied more Scripture and, in turn, read and listened to Luther more, he began to adopt his colleague's theology as his own, convinced that it was the theology of Scripture and that Scripture was the only reliable source of Christian doctrine. The turning point in this first stage of Melanchthon's theological development was his attendance at the

---

[7] *CR* 1:34.

[8] *De corrigendis adulescentiae studiis* (*SA* 3:29–42).

[9] Manschreck, *Melanchthon*, 43.

[10] See the discussion of Erasmian theology in Melanchthon's *Rhetoric* in Martin Greschat, *Philippe Melanchthon: Théologien, Pédagogue et Humaniste (1497–1560)* (Paris: Presses Universitaires de France, 2011), 23.

debate in Leipzig between John Eck, a theologian of Scholastic bent from the University of Ingolstadt, and Martin Luther.

In June and July of 1519, Luther and his colleague Andreas Carlstadt debated with Eck—Carlstadt over the bondage of the will, and Luther over papal supremacy, purgatory, and indulgences. Although only a spectator, Melanchthon was soon drawn into the debate. He had written a letter to his friend John Oecolampadius describing the debate and giving some slight criticisms of Eck along with lavish praise of Luther. Eck, upon reading the letter, responded with a vitriolic attack on the "grammarian" who dared offer his judgment against a doctor of theology.[11] The critique stung, as can be seen even two years later in the *Common Topics*.[12] But while he received insult from the Scholastic theologian Eck, he received the constant encouragement of Luther. In a reply of August to Eck, Melanchthon argued that Scripture was the only reliable norm for Christian doctrine.[13] A short time later, Melanchthon defended his baccalaureate theses, submitted in fulfillment of the Bachelor of Theology at the University of Wittenberg. Here he clearly argues that human nature cannot love God of itself and that Christian righteousness consists in the gracious declaration of God. He subordinates the authority of councils to Scripture and rejects the binding authority of the doctrine of transubstantiation.[14] His theses on faith, written within a year after his baccalaureate theses, clearly teach that sinners are justified through faith, and anticipate many doctrinal points in the *Common Topics*.[15] The same developing thoughts on faith, justification, the Law, and grace can be seen in the forerunners of the *Common Topics* of 1521, the *Theological Introduction to the Epistle of Paul to the Romans* of 1519 and *The Chief Points or Topics of Theology* of 1520.[16] We will return to these works shortly.

In embracing the teachings of the Reformation, Melanchthon was alienating himself from humanist doctrine, especially the teaching that man's righteousness resides in his own actions and not in the

---

[11] See p. 31, n. 40 below.

[12] See pp. 31–32 below.

[13] *Defensio Phil. Melanchthonis contra Joh. Eckium* (*SA* 1:12–22).

[14] *SA* 1:24–5.

[15] *CR* 1:125–127, and note (p. 125) the scholarly debate on the dating of these theses.

[16] *CR* 21:49–60; 11–48. See p. 19, n. 3 below.

gracious imputation of God. More than this, the humanists, at first allies with the Scholastic-battling Luther, were uncomfortable with the rough and gritty language of Luther and the unrest in Europe that surrounded his preaching and writing.[17] Reuchlin urged Melanchthon to leave Wittenberg and join the faculty of Ingolstadt, promising that Eck would forgive him and bear no grudge. After Melanchthon kindly refused, Reuchlin never spoke to him again. Melanchthon lost a father figure in Reuchlin (and the promised inheritance of a very valuable library), but gained a father in Luther.[18]

Beginning in 1519, Melanchthon began to teach theology at the University of Wittenberg. He began an intense study of Paul's epistles, especially his Letter to the Romans. It was from these studies and lectures that Melanchthon's *Common Topics* of 1521 arose. In his address on Paul and the Scholastics in January 1520, we can see the fruits of these studies. In this speech, Melanchthon mixes the eloquent rhetoric of Erasmus, along with some key Erasmian themes and phrases, with the Law/Gospel paradigm of Luther. On the one hand, he stresses Christ as the greatest exemplar of virtue and the author of happiness, and on the other he articulates the condemnation of the Law and the gracious pardoning of the Gospel in the free forgiveness of sins.[19] Moreover, Melanchthon's polemic against the Scholastics is no longer from a purely humanist perspective. He opposes them not because they are despisers of higher learning and the classics, but because they are enemies of Paul, who has expressed the Gospel with the greatest clarity. In Luther's fashion, Melanchthon attacks philosophy itself, which teaches only the external righteousness of outward actions and posits that practice makes perfect. Melanchthon insists that even as an ape will always be an ape, no matter how he practices, so by practice man cannot change his nature. The grace of God is needed, and this grace is the forgiveness of sins. Still, in this speech of 1520 Melanchthon concentrates more on the transformational, ethical results of God's grace in Christ than on the

---

[17] See Erasmus's letter to Melanchthon of 1520: "Those who support Luther—and almost all good men support Luther—would prefer that he had written some things with more civility and moderation. But this admonition is too late now. I see that the matter is tending toward public discord" (*CR* 1:205–6).

[18] In an emotional letter of May 1521, Melanchthon refers to Luther as his "dearest father" (*CR* 1:389–90).

[19] Cf. Maurer 2:121; Rogness, *Melanchthon*, 10–12.

forgiveness of sins. By giving his grace of forgiveness, God transforms the Christian so that he delights in obeying the Law.[20] Though this concentration would continue to be important for Melanchthon, he would give more attention to the centrality of forgiveness in his *Common Topics* of 1521.[21]

The turbulent year of 1520 would see Melanchthon drawing closer and closer to Luther, and Luther articulating the Gospel more clearly than ever. Luther's three great tracts of that year, *To the Christian Nobility of the German Nation*, *The Babylonian Captivity of the Church*, and *On Christian Freedom*, set forth with clarity the corruption of the Roman Catholic Church and the need for reform, so that the Gospel could be preached in its purity and the Sacraments administered according to their institution. If Luther was not already the hero of Germany, these works guaranteed his popularity despite Rome's strenuous objections. Melanchthon's references to these works in his *Common Topics* of 1521 show his enthusiastic agreement with them.[22]

On June 15, 1520, Luther was threatened with excommunication by the papal bull *Exsurge Domine*, in which many of his teachings were condemned as heresy. Ordered to recant within sixty days of receipt of the bull, Luther, with Melanchthon at his side, burned the papal bull publicly on December 10, 1520. To this the pope responded with another bull, *Decet Romanum Pontificem*, by which he formally excommunicated Luther on January 3, 1521. A short five months later, the decision of the emperor was published at the Diet of Worms against Luther, naming him a heretic and an outlaw. But Luther had already left Worms and was whisked away to hiding in Wartburg. Melanchthon was left alone in Wittenberg, without his Elijah.

It was in this period that the *Common Topics* was published. The polemical tone of the work is therefore understandable, as is Melanchthon's utter devotion to Luther and the Lutheran cause. Luther had made it clear to Melanchthon in letters from Wartburg that he could die knowing that Melanchthon would articulate the Gospel

---

[20] An English translation of Melanchthon's oration is available in Charles L. Hill, trans., *Melanchthon: Selected Writings* (Minneapolis: Augsburg, 1962), 31–56.

[21] See below, p. 108: "Is not the forgiveness of sins the chief message of the Gospel and the preaching of the New Testament?"

[22] See below, pp. 121, 170, n. 5.

better than he, that Elisha had surpassed Elijah.[23] Not knowing the future, Luther had passed his mantle on to the twenty-four-year old Melanchthon as his spokesman in Wittenberg. The unqualified and excessive praise that Luther heaps upon Melanchthon's *Common Topics* of 1521 speaks to how closely Melanchthon had followed his "dearest father."[24] But at the same time it speaks to Luther's acknowledgement of Melanchthon's unmatched ability to articulate and defend the Gospel clearly, convincingly, and in good order.

Melanchthon decided to publish his *Common Topics* of 1521 after an incomplete version, meant only for presenting the doctrine of Paul's Epistle to the Romans in a systematic way to his students, was published without his consent. This document, which Melanchthon calls his *lucubratiuncula* or "nighttime studies" was entitled *The Chief Points or Topics of Theology*. As Melanchthon explains in his prefatory epistle to the *Common Topics*, the work is short and obviously incomplete. Before the illicit publication of *The Chief Points*, Melanchthon had also composed in 1519 his *Theological Introduction to the Epistle of Paul to the Romans*, also a result of his lectures on Romans. This work condemned philosophy and Scholasticism in no uncertain terms and offered the content of Romans as an alternative to the philosophical presentation of Peter Lombard, whose *Sentences* had been used for centuries to teach theology in the universities.[25] Thus the *Common Topics* of 1521 resulted from an intense study of Paul, and above all, of Romans. This explains the constant reference to Romans throughout the work.

Before we leave this section, a brief explanation of the term *Common Topics* is needed. The Latin *Loci Communes* is a translation of the Greek *topoi koinoi* and finds its origin in Aristotle. But Aristotle's conception of the "common topic" is far from Melanchthon's. Whereas Melanchthon thinks of common topics in Ciceronian terms, namely as indices or guides showing where to find the material whereby to defend a proposition, Aristotle thought of common topics as propositions common to dialectical investigation. The difference is important, because it underlines Melanchthon's

---

[23] WA Br 2:348.

[24] *CR* 1:389–90. For Luther's praise of the *Loci Communes* of 1521 as "worthy not only of immortality but also of the Church's canon," see AE 33:16; WA 18:601.

[25] *CR* 21:49.

rhetorical approach to theological method, especially in this first edition of his *Loci*. The subject matter of theology is already present in Scripture. The job of the theologian is to learn the common topics of Scripture, the doctrinal veins of Scripture, so that he may be driven further into Scripture to confirm what Scripture expresses clearly elsewhere.[26] Whereas Scholastic theology argued technical theological points using logical syllogisms and complex dialectic, Melanchthon sees his job as showing what the clear Scriptures simply say. He does this rhetorically, that is, by gathering together several key subjects or topics that Scripture treats in abundance.[27] In this sense, as Melanchthon himself insists more than once in this work, the *Common Topics* of 1521 is more a hermeneutical handbook than a dogmatic treatise.

THEOLOGICAL CONTEXT
OF THE *COMMON TOPICS* OF 1521

Scholasticism was the theological movement, beginning in the twelfth century and lasting up to the Reformation, that stressed the systematic articulation of Christian doctrine through dialectic and logical inference and deduction. In its critical examination and organization of the statements of the ecclesiastical fathers, Scholasticism applied Aristotelian logic and Platonic categories to develop logically defensible systems of Christian theology. Scholasticism dominated the universities of Europe and coincided with their invention and growth. In the early sixteenth century, humanists decried its sterility and Luther its theology.

Melanchthon's criticism of Scholasticism in the *Common Topics* of 1521 centers upon a few prominent Scholastic theologians, but includes a condemnation of the Scholastic method in general. First of these Scholastics is Peter Lombard (c. 1100–60), whose *Four Books of Sentences* was used in the universities to teach Scholastic method and doctrine for centuries. In his *Sentences*, Lombard arranges Christian teaching under doctrinal headings, working from God and his attributes to the Church and her sacraments. The work consists

---

[26] See especially p. 20 below.

[27] For further discussion of the term *loci communes* see Quirinus Breen, "The Terms 'Loci Communes' and 'Loci' in Melanchthon," *Church History* 16 (1947): 197–209.

largely of quotations from Augustine and other Church Fathers. The significance of the work is not only in its content but also in its later use as a stepping stone for further development of Scholastic distinctions and theological divisions. The work was used as a textbook from its writing in the mid-twelfth century, and many major Scholastic theologians from that time on wrote commentaries on it. Luther himself began his career as a professor teaching and commenting on the *Sentences*, and Melanchthon studied them to earn his Bachelor of Theology. This work of early Scholasticism begins to arrange doctrine according to logical categories and introduces philosophical distinctions to explain theological problems, but is not excessively involved in Aristotelian or Platonic categories. Melanchthon's chief complaint against Lombard is that he cites the Fathers instead of Scripture.[28]

More objectionable to Melanchthon were later Scholastics, preeminent among whom was Thomas Aquinas (1225–74), a commenter on the *Sentences* who cites Aristotle as if he were citing Scripture. Aquinas defined and articulated Christian doctrine in Aristotelian categories, and his famous magnum opus, the *Summa Theologica*, gave philosophical articulation to such theological doctrines as original sin, man's free will, and the sacrifice of the mass—hotly debated articles for Luther and Melanchthon in 1521. Even more inimical to Reformation doctrine was the teaching of the late Scholastic Gabriel Biel (c. 1420–95), who had been a professor at Tübingen, Melanchthon's alma mater, and whom Luther had studied at length. Biel, a nominalist, so stressed the ability of the free will that he asserted man's power to fulfill the Law of God even outside the Holy Spirit—though he posited this only as a theoretical ability.[29]

Melanchthon was opposed to this Scholasticism both because he was a humanist and because he was a firm supporter of Lutheran theology. The humanist objection to Scholasticism is summed up well in Melanchthon's inaugural address to the faculty of the University of Wittenberg in 1518:

> Certain men, led either by the wantonness of their natures or by love of argument, fell upon Aristotle, whom, already obscure and rather complex in the Greek, they found

---

[28] See p. 22 below.

[29] See below, p. 51, n. 29.

translated into Latin in mutilated and mangled form, so that he rivaled the raving conjectures of Sibyl. Yet imperceptive men fastened onto this version of Aristotle. Gradually the better disciplines were neglected, we lost knowledge of Greek, and in general bad things began to be taught instead of good things. From this state of things proceeded Thomas, Scotus, Durand, Francis, Dominic, and others—a gang more numerous than the descendants of Cadmus. In addition, it came about that not only were the ancients despised in favor of the study of novelties, but if any of them survived in that time, they were banished from memory and thus perished, so that one wonders whether those authors of sophistries did anything more harmful than that in their insanity they allowed so many thousands of ancient writings to be utterly neglected. To such men was then all at once committed the authority of human and divine law, and from their decrees the youth was educated.[30]

The humanist motto *ad fontes*, "to the sources," is clearly seen in this programmatic address, and a little further on, Melanchthon will connect the failure to study the ancients with the deterioration of ecclesiastical rites and Christian morals.[31] Upon his arrival at Wittenberg, this was the thoroughly humanist goal of Melanchthon: to reform the educational system and thereby to reform the morals of people and Church.

More than anyone else, Melanchthon owes his humanist training to his granduncle.[32] From his earliest studies at Pforzheim, Melanchthon had come under the influence of this talented and enthusiastic humanist. Reuchlin's continued patronage, encouragement, and support followed Melanchthon through his mastery of Latin and introduction to the classics at Pforzheim to his university studies at Heidelberg and Tübingen. And by Reuchlin's commendation, Melanchthon received his professorship at Wittenberg. Reuchlin himself embodied the type of humanism that

---

[30] *SA* 3:32.

[31] *SA* 3:33: "This failure destroyed the truly Christian rites and morals of the Church."

[32] See Maurer 1:171.

Melanchthon would embrace, a return to philology and the study of ancient literature.

Though many other humanists influenced Melanchthon through friendship, teaching, or writing, Erasmus stands out among them. In the years following his arrival at Wittenberg, Melanchthon is often characterized as being "between Erasmus and Luther."[33] Above all, it is Erasmus's championing of rhetoric that influenced Melanchthon. This is seen clearly in Melanchthon's adoption of the *loci communes* method of biblical interpretation. It was Erasmus who recommended that such a method be used in interpreting Scripture.[34] Erasmus had employed it himself, but as Melanchthon notes, found only ethical topics.[35] This is, of course, perfectly in line with Erasmus's brand of humanism, which emphasized the potential of the human spirit and therefore the ethical righteousness of the free will—ironically making Erasmian humanism the theological ally of Scholasticism. So, while adopting Erasmus's rhetorical method, Melanchthon uses it to show that Scripture rejects the idea of the human spirit's natural potential. According to Melanchthon, the *loci communes* of Scripture are the doctrines of sin, Law, grace, and Gospel. These are also the common topics of Martin Luther.

It is hard to overstate Luther's influence on Melanchthon's *Loci Communes* of 1521. Melanchthon constantly refers to Luther. Even when he makes no explicit reference to Luther and his works, the stamp of Luther's theology is clearly imprinted. In fact, the *Loci Communes* of 1521 is, in large part, a digest of the early Luther's theology: a strong condemnation of papal and Scholastic claims regarding the freedom of the will;[36] the articulation of the Law as God's condemnation of the guilty sinner and of the Gospel as God's favor toward undeserving sinners with no regard to human merit;[37] the insistence that a Christian can be sure of his salvation;[38] that the sacraments have been given for this assurance;[39] a rejection of popes

---

[33] Maurer 2:27–42.

[34] See below, p. 19, n. 2 and p. 22, n. 12.

[35] See p. 25 below.

[36] See p. 30, n. 36 and p. 32, n. 45 below.

[37] See p. 47, n. 23; p. 69, n. 17; and p. 70, n. 20 below.

[38] See p. 142, n. 23 below.

[39] See p. 54, n. 36; p. 88, n. 60; p. 167, n. 2; and p. 177, n. 14 below.

and councils as authoritative sources of doctrine; and the championing of Scripture as the pure and unadulterated Word of God.[40]

But Melanchthon is not merely digesting Luther. Melanchthon's arrangement of Christian doctrine according to common topics is, of itself, a valuable contribution to the Lutheran cause, but he also has his own theological emphases. So Melanchthon's division of man into two parts, the affections and the intellect, is developed in line with Paul's language in Romans to explain how man cannot turn to God through his own powers.[41] So also, Melanchthon does not back down from his humanist emphasis on the ethical life of a Christian. While justification by faith in God's mercy for Christ's sake is his main stress, Melanchthon will not speak of justification outside of its connection with the renewal of the convert's senses and the incipient sanctification of a life directed toward God.[42] While these and other emphases are not in conflict with Luther's theology (Luther had spoken of the sinful "affections" overpowering the intellect and was concerned with the sanctified life), Melanchthon makes them his own and articulates them with his characteristic order and precision.

Melanchthon benefited from his humanistic studies and his association with Luther, and these influences can be clearly seen in his *Loci Communes* of 1521. But it would be wrong to relegate Scholasticism's influence on Melanchthon merely to the negative realm. Despite his constant condemnation of it in this work, Melanchthon adopted many Scholastic formulations. Working with Aristotle, he was able to adapt Scholastic classifications to his own use, as when he speaks of sin as *energia* (energy/active force, as opposed to mere potential) to stress its depth and culpability.[43] In later editions of his *Loci*, Melanchthon would largely eliminate his invective against the Scholastics and adopt more and more of their terminology and classifications.

---

[40] See p. 21, n. 6 below.

[41] See pp. 26–60 below.

[42] See pp. 138–47 below, and esp. p. 140: "There is no reason to separate one from the other."

[43] See below, p. 38, and n. 2.

EDITIONS OF THE *LOCI*

From their publication in December 1521, the *Loci* were wildly popular. The work was read enthusiastically even in Rome, until a Franciscan monk realized who its author was and copies of the book were banned.[44] For Lutherans it would come to unseat and replace Peter Lombard's *Sentences* as the doctrinal textbook for university study of systematic theology. And as Melanchthon continued to edit it throughout his life, it became more and more a book of systematic theology than the guide to Scripture that this first edition claims for itself. Concurrent with this change from biblical guide to systematic (or Scholastic) treatment of doctrinal topics were different stresses, additions, and outright alterations in doctrine.

Scholars divide the editions of Melanchthon's *Loci* into three periods. The first is from its first publication, translated in this volume, to its first major recension in 1535. The second period includes all the editions from the 1535 publication to its final major revision in 1543. This final version saw its last revision and edition in 1559, a year before Melanchthon's death. By the time Melanchthon had finished his revisions, the *Loci* were almost four times the size of the original *Loci Communes* of 1521. Moreover, the name of the work had changed. While the term *Loci* remained, the word *Communes* was dropped in favor of *Praecipui* (*Chief*), reflecting a departure from the rhetorical aim of the first edition and a movement toward the dialectical arrangement of Scholasticism.[45]

The teaching of the Anabaptist and radical reformers (Zwingli, Carlstadt, et al.), denying the bodily presence of Christ in the Lord's Supper, and in the case of some Anabaptists, questioning the doctrine of the Trinity, forced Melanchthon to deal thoroughly with the doctrine of God and the creation of man in his later editions—topics left out of his 1521 original. Other major changes in the later editions are due to Melanchthon's concern to disavow the charge of determinism—that man is predestined by God to a certain end, with no regard for human merit or demerit. So, while Melanchthon clearly teaches the utter bondage of the will to sin and the devil in this first edition, in his last edition he teaches that there must be some reason

---

[44] Manschreck, *Melanchthon*, 88.
[45] Breen, "Loci communes," 203.

in man why one is saved and another damned.[46] These changes and many others, along with the scholastic treatment of the subject matter, make the later editions of the *Loci* works of a different kind. A comparison of the *Loci* of 1521 and the *Loci* of 1559 shows the evolution in the thought and outlook of Melanchthon throughout the course of the Reformation. Still, Luther highly praised these later editions, including that of 1543,[47] and Martin Chemnitz and other leading Lutheran theologians used the last edition to teach their students and as a basis for their own dogmatic works.[48]

Despite Melanchthon's continued revisions, the *Loci Communes* of 1521 stands as a complete work of biblical theology. It is meant as an introduction to biblical theology and thus as an introduction to the Bible, its study and interpretation. As such the *Loci Communes* of 1521 is the beginning not only of the Lutheran systematic tradition but also of the Lutheran hermeneutical tradition. The Lutheran principles of biblical interpretation—that Scripture interprets Scripture, that the literal, grammatical sense of Scripture is the basis for all interpretation, that Scripture is united in its message of Law and Gospel, that Scripture is clear, that it is the source and norm of all Christian teaching and the formative power in the Christian's life—all of these are found in this influential and seminal work. It speaks to us today as forcefully as it did to its first readers in the turbulent years of the early Reformation.

THE TRANSLATION

The text has been translated from the *Corpus Reformatorum*.[49] I have aimed at readability without sacrificing a faithful rendering of the text. As with every translation, some interpretation is inevitable. No translation can be a replacement for the original text, and in the spirit of Melanchthon I recommend that those who are able reference the

---

[46] For a full treatment of the evolution of Melanchthon's teaching on the will throughout his editions of the *Loci*, see Matz, *Der befreite Mensch*.

[47] WA TR 5:205.

[48] See Martin Chemnitz, *Loci Theologici*, trans. J.A.O. Preus (St. Louis: Concordia, 1989).

[49] *CR* 21:81–228. The Latin may also be found with German notes in Hans Engelland, ed., *Melanchthons Werke in Auswahl*, vol. 2.1 (Gütersloh: C Bertelsmann Verlag, 1952).

Latin, which is more beautiful than this translator could replicate in the English language.

This translation is the third in the English language. The first by Charles Leander Hill, while a major boon and a praiseworthy achievement at the time of its publication, is literal to the point of difficulty and, at times, obscure. His introduction and notes, read with discernment of modern scholarship, are still valuable.[50] The translation of Pauck is quite readable with few errors, but is, inconveniently for many, bound up with Bucer's *On the Kingdom of Christ*.[51] Pauck's commentary is also sparse and in large part reduplicated from the German notes in the Latin edition of *Melanchthons Werke*. A more recent German translation of the *Loci Communes* of 1521 by Horst George Pöhlmann, with an informative and scholarly commentary, is available for those who can read German and are interested in further study of the context and theology of the *Loci Communes* of 1521.[52]

I have tried in this volume not to burden the reader with too many notes, but at the same time to give the necessary background for a better understanding of the text. In line with the introduction given above, I have included citations and quotations from Scholastic theologians, humanists, and Luther in order to show their influence on Melanchthon and his work. I have also referenced later Lutheran tradition and confessional writings when appropriate. It is my prayer that this edition and translation will profit the pastor, scholar, and layman interested in the theology and history of the early Reformation and in the Lutheran tradition of dogmatic and exegetical theology.

Thanks are due to my father, Pastor Rolf Preus, for his helpful comments and suggestions throughout the process of translation and commentary.

---

[50] Charles Leander Hill, *The Loci Communes of Philip Melanchthon* (Boston: Meador Publishing Co., 1944).

[51] Wilhelm Pauck, ed., *Melanchthon and Bucer*, vol. 19 of *The Library of Christian Classics* (Philadelphia: Westminster, 1969).

[52] Horst George Pöhlmann, ed., *Philipp Melanchthon: Loci Communes 1521 Lateinisch-Deutsch* (Gütersloh: Gütersloher Verlagshaus, 1997).

COMMON TOPICS OF THEOLOGY
OR THEOLOGICAL OUTLINE

1521

DEDICATORY EPISTLE

To Dr. Tileman Plettener,[1] a man as pious as he is learned, Philip Melanchthon sends his greetings.

When we were preparing to teach Paul's Epistle to the Romans last year, we methodically arranged its various contents under the most common theological topics.[2] This study was meant only to give a very rough treatment of the subject and proofs of Paul's argument to the students whom I was teaching privately (*privatim*).[3] But

---

[1] Tileman Plettener taught in Stolberg before enrolling at the University of Wittenberg in 1520, accompanying his two friends, the counts Wolfgang and Ludwig of Stolberg. Wolfgang was elected rector of the University of Wittenberg the following year, and Plettener became vice-rector at the beginning of the summer semester, 1521. Plettener earned his doctorate in theology at Wittenberg together with Justus Jonas on October 14, 1521.

[2] Melanchthon writes in a letter of April 17, 1520: "I followed the plan of the orators, who recommend that we treat disciplines (*artes*) with common topics" (*CR* 1:158–9). Erasmus, in his *Manner or Method of Arriving at True Theology in a Compendium* of 1519, had recommended a similar method of creating a compendium for theology (*AS* 3:117–495; cf. Maurer 2:140). Melanchthon later credited the rhetorical treatise of Rudolf Agricola (1444–85) as an influence on his use of common topics, writing that Erasmus and Agricola "have written best" on this method of arrangement (*CR* 20:696). Melanchthon was first introduced to Agricola's work when he was a University student in Heidelberg (*CR* 3:673; cf. Peter Mack, "Melanchthon," in *Renaissance argument: Valla and Agricola in the tradition of rhetoric and dialectic* [Leiden: Brill, 1993], 320–33).

[3] Melanchthon is likely referring to his private school. In addition to his lectures at the University, Melanchthon also held classes in his house, and the school that formed there became known as his *schola privata* or private school. There he taught Latin and Greek grammar, and in 1519 lectured on the Epistle of Paul to the Romans (*CR* 21:5; cf. Maurer 2:103–15, 139–40). From his lectures on Romans were written the *Theological Introduction to the Epistle of Paul to the Romans* in 1519 (*CR* 21:49–60), and in 1520 *The Chief Points or Topics of Theology* (*CR* 21:11–48). These

someone—I don't know who—published it.[4] Whoever did publish it showed more zeal than sense. Of course, I wrote in such a way that it is difficult to understand what I mean without constant reference to Paul's epistle. Now I cannot take back the little book since it is all but officially published, and so I thought it would be best to rework and revise it. For many places required more precise arguments and much of it needed revision.

Now to the substance of the matter. I here present the chief topics of Christian doctrine, so that the youth may know what they should especially look for in the Scriptures and so that they may realize how obscenely those have strayed in all things theological who have handed down to us Aristotelian sophistries instead of the teaching of Christ.[5] But we treat everything sparingly and briefly, because we are making an index rather than a commentary. For we are merely compiling a catalogue of topics that the reader should consult as he makes his way through divine Scripture, and we are teaching with only a few words the foundations of all Christian doctrine.

I am not doing this to distract students away from the Scriptures into obscure and difficult arguments, but rather to attract them, if possible, to the Scriptures. In fact, I do not generally approve of commentaries—not even those of the ancients. The last thing I want is to draw anyone away from studying the canonical Scriptures with too long a writing. Rather, I could wish nothing more than that all Christians, if possible, were thoroughly versed in divine Scriptures alone and wholly transformed into their nature. For since in them

---

works, though incomplete and in the form of outlines, were enthusiastically received (cf. Pöhlmann, 8).

[4] Some of Melanchthon's students published his notes on Romans without his consent. The work referred to is *The Chief Points* of 1520. Though some have taken Melanchthon to be referring to the *Theological Introduction* of 1519 (e.g., Maurer 2:103–4), *The Chief Points* must be the proper referent, since this work rather than the *Theological Introduction* most resembles the *Loci* and could easily be revised into the *Loci* that we have (cf. *CR* 21:7; *SA* 2:2).

[5] *Aristotelian sophistries.* The reference is to the scholastic tradition that began in the twelfth century and relied heavily on Aristotle to systematize Christian doctrine. Melanchthon here echoes the polemics of Luther. Luther's frequent condemnation of Aristotle and the scholastic tradition is summed up neatly in Thesis 29 of his *Heidelberg Disputation* (1518): "Whoever wishes to philosophize in Aristotle without danger must first become completely foolish in Christ" (WA 1:355; AE 31:41). See also Luther's *Disputation against Scholastic Theology* of 1517 (WA 1:221–28; AE 31:9–16).

divinity has expressed its purest image, it cannot be known more surely or more intensely from any other source. Whoever seeks the nature of Christianity from a source other than canonical Scripture deceives himself.[6]

How far are the commentaries from the purity of Scripture![7] In the latter you will find nothing undignified; in the former how many things that depend on philosophy and the suppositions of human reason, things diametrically opposed to the judgment of the Spirit! The writers failed to suppress their human nature (τὸ ψυχικὸν) so as to breathe only spiritual things (πνευματικὰ). If you take away all the absurd allegories of Origen, together with the forest of his philosophical opinions, how little will be left?[8] And yet the Greeks almost unanimously follow this author. And of the Latin fathers, Ambrose and Jerome, who are supposed to be pillars, chase after him.[9] After these authors, it is almost the case that the more recent the writer, the more corrupt he is, until finally Christian doctrine has been degraded to sophistic nonsense, and it is hard to say whether it is more impious or stupid.[10] In a word, it cannot but happen that human writings often mislead even the careful reader.

---

[6] Melanchthon had written two tracts in 1521 championing the cause of Scripture against the Scholastic tradition. His pseudonymous *Oration of Didymus Faventinus for the Theologian Martin Luther against Thomas Placentinus* and his *Philip Melanchthon's Defense of Luther against the Mad Decree of the Parisian Theologians* both maintained that Scripture was the sole source of Christian doctrine and lambasted the scholastic tradition (*SA* 1:56–162). In the latter he writes, "But what could be clearer than that neither the universities, nor the holy fathers, nor the councils can establish articles of faith?" (*SA* 1:145).

[7] Melanchthon has in mind the commentaries on Peter Lombard's *Four Books of Sentences*. Hundreds of Scholastic theologians commented on Lombard's *Sentences*. No book, besides Scripture itself, has had more commentaries devoted to it.

[8] Origen of Alexandria (c. 184–254) was a Christian Neoplatonist famous for his allegorizing of the Old Testament. Contained in this condemnation of Origen is a veiled criticism of Erasmus, who calls the exegesis of Origen a "river of gold" (*AS* 3:158) and consistently praises him (cf. Timothy Wengert, *Human Freedom, Christian Righteousness* [Oxford: Oxford University Press, 1998], 59).

[9] Cf. Galatians 2:9. For Jerome's spirited defense and panegyric of Origen see his *Epistle* 33 (*MPL* 22:446–48); cf. Ambrose, who mimics Origen in his *Epistle* 63, stating, "The Old Testament is a well, deep and quite dark, from which you can draw water only with difficulty" (*MPL* 16:1210). For most of the Church Fathers, the alleged obscurity of the Old Testament necessitated its allegorical interpretation.

[10] Cf. Melanchthon's *Defense against the Parisian Theologians* (1521): "The Gospel has been obscured, faith erased, a teaching of works accepted, and instead of a

But if knowledge of sacred matters is indeed prophecy and a kind of inspiration, why do we not embrace this type of literature, through which the Spirit flows? Or has God not accomplished all things through his Word? For the Spirit, or as 1 John [2:27] says, the Anointing, will teach by means of the Scriptures many things that the greatest exertion of the human mind could not attain. We are determined to do nothing else but help in some way the studies of those who want to be versed in the Scriptures. If my little book does not seem to achieve this, may it be destroyed outright, for it is not my concern what the public thinks of a public work.

COMMON TOPICS OF THEOLOGY
OR THEOLOGICAL OUTLINE[11]

Individual disciplines customarily have certain topics with which each discipline can be summarized. These topics serve as the scope according to which we should direct all of our studies.[12] In theology, we see that the ancients also followed this way of doing things, though sparingly and with moderation. More recent theologians, such as John of Damascus and Peter Lombard, have done so senselessly. For John of Damascus is an excessive philosophizer,[13] and Lombard preferred to collect human opinions rather than record the judgment of Scripture.[14] And though, as I said before, I do not want students to

---

Christian people, we are a people not even of the Law, but of Aristotelian morals, and contrary to every intent of the Spirit Christianity has been turned into a philosophical way of life" (SA 1:143).

[11] Hypotyposis, translated here as "Outline," is taken from Greek and means "illustration," "model," "example," or "outline." The term is used to stress the rhetorical nature of the work—to give an outline for studying the Scriptures (cf. Quirinus Breen, "The Terms 'Loci Communes' and 'Loci' in Melanchthon," Church History 16 [1947]: 197–209, esp. 203).

[12] Cf. Erasmus, Manner or Method (1519): "Doctrines, having been drawn from the Gospels first of all, then also from the apostolic epistles, should be taught after being arranged into a summary or compendium, so that the theologian has everywhere certain scopes, to which he may compare what he is reading" (AS 3:170).

[13] John of Damascus (c. 676–749) was a Greek theologian from Damascus in Syria. His rather philosophical dogmatic work, On the Orthodox Faith (MPG 94:789–1228), was received in the West and influenced the Scholastic tradition, especially in the works of Peter Lombard and Thomas Aquinas.

[14] Peter Lombard (c. 1100–60) was a Scholastic theologian who taught at Notre Dame in Paris. His magnum opus, the Four Books of Sentences, was used for

dwell on summaries of this sort,[15] still I think it is almost necessary to point out, at least, on what topics the sum of theology depends. In this way, one can understand where he should direct his studies.

Now the following, in general, are the chief topics of theology:

God	The Fruits of Grace
His Unity	Faith
His Trinity	Hope
Creation	Love
Man, Human Powers	Predestination
Sin	The Sacramental Signs
The Fruits of Sin, Vices	Human Estates
Punishments	Magistrates
The Law	Bishops
The Promises	Damnation
Renewal through Christ	Blessedness
Grace	

Just as there are some subjects among these that are completely incomprehensible, so there are some that Christ wants every Christian to know most intimately. We should adore the mysteries of divinity, not investigate them. In fact, as many saints have experienced for themselves, great danger necessarily accompanies the inspection of these mysteries. God almighty clothed his Son in flesh to draw us away from contemplating his majesty and toward contemplating our flesh, and thus our weakness.[16] So also Paul writes to the Corinthians

---

centuries to teach Catholic doctrine in the schools. The work consists largely of systematically organized quotations from the Fathers, especially Augustine.

[15] The term *summae* (sg. *summa*), translated "summaries" here, applied to the dogmatic works of medieval theologians, such as Peter Lombard's *Sentences* or Thomas Aquinas's (1225–74) *Summa Theologica*. Melanchthon's attack on sophistry and Scholasticism in large part centers on these two works, which still in the sixteenth century were the main theological textbooks in the schools.

[16] Cf. Luther, *Heidelberg Disputation* (1518), who after quoting 1 Corinthians 1:21 writes, "It is neither sufficient nor profitable for anyone to know God in his glory and majesty unless he knows him in the humility and shame of the cross" (WA 1:362; AE 31:52–3). Melanchthon, by calling God *optimus maximus* ("best and greatest," translated "almighty" above), is contrasting the majesty that we should not

that God wanted to be known in a new way—through the foolishness of preaching, since in his wisdom he could not be known through wisdom [1 Corinthians 1:21].

Moreover, there is no reason for me to exert much effort on those majestic topics about God, his unity, his Trinity, the mystery of creation, or the manner of his incarnation.[17] I ask you, what have these Scholastic theologians accomplished over so many centuries as they concentrated only on these topics? Have they not become vain in their disputes, as Paul says,[18] while they talk nonsense their whole lives through about universals, formalities, connotations, and other vacuous terms?[19] And their foolishness could be forgiven if those stupid arguments had not meanwhile obscured the Gospel and the benefits of Christ. Now if I wanted to display my genius unnecessarily, I could easily destroy the arguments that they offer in support of their teachings and show how many of them seem better to support various heresies than catholic doctrine.

But whoever is ignorant of the other topics—the power of sin, the Law, grace—I do not know how I can call him a Christian.[20] For through these topics Christ is properly known, if it is true that to know Christ is to know his benefits, and not, as *they* teach, to contemplate his natures and the modes of his incarnation. Unless you know why Christ took on flesh and was crucified, what is the profit of knowing historical facts about him? Or is it enough for a doctor to

---

investigate with the weakness imposed upon the Son of God, which Christians must know intimately.

[17] Melanchthon does not treat God as a topic in this work, but adds the articles of God and creation to his later editions. The exclusion of topics on God and creation does not reflect Melanchthon's view of their importance, but rather the scope of his work—to correct the Scholastics on the topics of sin, Law, and grace (cf. Maurer 2:140).

[18] Romans 1:21.

[19] Melanchthon is dismissing the centuries-long debate between realism and nominalism as irrelevant to the proclamation of the Gospel. Realism taught that abstractions had reality or form and thus spoke of "formalities," while nominalism taught that abstract concepts were merely names (*nomina*) and thus concentrated on semantic concerns and "connotations." In his *Defense against the Parisian Theologians* (1521), Melanchthon accuses the Parisian Scholastics of caring about nothing except "the formalities of Scotus and the connotations of Occam" (*SA* 1:148).

[20] Melanchthon identifies these three topics, sin, Law, and grace, as "most relevant to us" in his *Theological Introduction* of 1519: "For in these three topics the entirety (*summa*) of our justification is embraced" (*CR* 21:49).

know the shapes, colors, and features of herbs, no matter that he does not know their inherent power? Just so, we must come to know Christ, who has been given to us as our remedy, and to use a scriptural word, our salvific remedy,[21] in some way other than that which the Scholastics urge.

This, finally, is Christian knowledge—to know what the Law demands, where to find the power to fulfill the Law, where to claim grace for sins, how to strengthen a wavering soul against the devil, the flesh, and the world, and how to console the afflicted conscience. Do the Scholastics teach these things? Does Paul, in his Epistle to the Romans, which he wrote as a summary of Christian doctrine, philosophize about the mysteries of the Trinity, the mode of the incarnation, active and passive creation?[22] Certainly not! But what does he treat? Of course he treats the Law, sin, and grace, the sole foundations for knowledge of Christ. How many times does Paul testify that he desires that the faithful have a rich knowledge of Christ![23] For he foresaw that we would rid ourselves of salutary doctrinal topics and turn our attention to useless arguments that have nothing to do with Christ.

Therefore, I will lay out these topics in such a way that they present Christ to you, strengthen your conscience, and uphold your soul against Satan. Too many seek nothing from Scripture but topics about virtues and vices. But this is a philosophical, not a Christian, exegesis.[24] Why I say so, you will soon understand.

---

[21] E.g., Luke 2:30.

[22] Thomas Aquinas (*Summa* I, q. 45, art. 2) makes a distinction between active and passive creation, arguing that since creation cannot be considered apart from its relationship with the creator, creation should be viewed first of all as God's action in creating, which is the very essence of the thing that has been created (active creation), and secondly as the creation which has been received passively by the thing that has been created (passive creation).

[23] Cf. 2 Corinthians 4:6; 10:5; Ephesians 1:17; 3:4; 4:13; Philippians 3:8; Colossians 2:2.

[24] This criticism is directed primarily against Erasmus, whose list of potential common topics in his *Manner or Method* (1519) contains nothing but subjects of morality (*AS* 3:170–4). Melanchthon is arguing for a theology of Christ against Erasmus's famous "philosophy of Christ" (*philosophia Christi*). In his address to the University of Wittenberg on the doctrine of Paul (1520), Melanchthon issued a similar, thinly veiled criticism of Erasmus and his *philosophia Christi* (*SA* 1:36).

HUMAN POWERS, ESPECIALLY FREE WILL[25]

Augustine and Bernard have written on free will.[26] It should be noted that in his later writings against the Pelagians Augustine retracted many of his former ideas.[27] Bernard is inconsistent. Some of the Greeks also wrote on free will, but sporadically. As I will not be relying on the opinions of men, I will explain the matter very simply and clearly. Generally speaking, authors both old and new have obscured this article because they have so interpreted the Scriptures that they might at the same time satisfy the judgment of human reason. It did not seem humane to teach that man sins of necessity. It seemed downright cruel to blame the will for not having the power to turn itself from vice to virtue. And so they attributed more to human powers than was proper and then oscillated curiously when they saw that the Scriptures opposed the judgment of reason at every turn.

And though Christian doctrine is, especially in this article, thoroughly at odds with philosophy and human reason, still philosophy has, little by little, crept into Christianity. A godless teaching concerning free will has been accepted and the benefits of Christ have been obscured through that impious and carnal wisdom of our reason. This term "free will" has been used, though it is completely foreign to divine Scripture and to the sense and judgment of the Spirit. And by it, as we shall see, saints have often been offended. In addition, the word "reason" has been adopted, taken

---

[25] Latin: *liberum arbitrium*. The term *liberum arbitrium* is always translated "free will" in this translation, while the term *voluntas* is always translated "will."

[26] Augustine (354–430) wrote *On Free Will* (*MPL* 32:1221–1310) in 388 and 391 before the Pelagian controversy. It was written in response to the determinism of Manichaeism. In it he grants some freedom to the will. Bernard of Clairvaux (1090–1153), in his tract *On Grace and Free Will* (*MPL* 182:1001–30), grants the will the power to consent to grace.

[27] The controversy with Pelagius led Augustine to stress man's inability to work righteousness or believe without the Spirit, most famously articulated in *On the Spirit and the Letter* (*MPL* 44:199–246), which Melanchthon cites favorably later in this work. Augustine writes, "But we must oppose very fiercely and strongly those who think that the power of the human will itself can by itself, without God's help, either attain righteousness or make progress in turning to it" (*On the Spirit and the Letter*, 4; *MPL* 44:202). In the *Heidelberg Disputation* (1518) and again in his *Assertion* against the bull of Pope Leo X (1520), Luther cites Augustine as proof that he is teaching nothing new on the bondage of the will: "Free will can do nothing but sin" (*On the Spirit and the Letter*, 5; WA 1:59–60; 7:142; AE 31:49; 32:92).

from Plato's philosophy, and is equally pernicious. For just as we, in these latter times of the Church, have embraced Aristotle instead of Christ, so also immediately after the Church's founding Christian doctrine was undermined by Platonic philosophy.[28] So it has come about that no untainted literature exists in the Church outside of canonical Scriptures. Everything taught in the commentaries reeks of philosophy.

Now first off, we have no use for the philosophers' numerous divisions in their treatment of human nature.[29] We simply divide man into two parts. For there is in him, first, the faculty of knowing, and then there is the faculty of pursuing or resisting what he knows. The faculty of knowing is that by which we sense or understand, reason, compare, and deduce. The faculty from which our affections arise is that by which we either eschew or embrace what we know. This faculty is sometimes called "will," sometimes "affection," and sometimes "appetite." I do not think that there is any need here to make distinctions between the senses and the so-called intellect, or between the appetite of the senses and the higher appetite.[30] For we are treating the higher appetite, that is, not merely the appetite in which exist hunger, thirst, and other affections common with animals, but also the appetite where love, hate, hope, fear, sadness, anger, and the other affections that arise from these are present. They call this appetite the will.

Knowledge serves the will, and so they invent a new term, "free will," to designate the will as it is joined with knowledge or with

---

[28] This adoption of Platonic terms and concepts was especially prevalent among the early Christian apologists, who were attempting to give a defense for the Christian doctrine of God to pagan philosophers. Platonic terms and ideas were particularly popular in Alexandria. Already in the second century, Clement of Alexandria (c. 150–215) used Platonic terminology and concepts to explain and inform Christian doctrine.

[29] Melanchthon has Aristotle in mind, whose philosophical divisions were adopted by Peter Lombard, Thomas Aquinas, and other Scholastics (Lombard *Sentences* II, dist. 24, chs. 3–4; cf. Aquinas *Summa* I, q. 64, art. 2; q. 80, arts. 1–2; q. 83, arts. 1–4; II, q. 82, arts. 1–5).

[30] These Aristotelian divisions distinguished between the baser sensitive appetite, which is subject to the bodily organs, and the higher intellectual appetite, which is subject to the intellect (Aristotle *De Anima* 3.10–1; Lombard *Sentences* II, dist. 24, chs. 3–4; Aquinas *Summa* I, q. 80, art. 2).

intellectual judgment.[31] For the will in man is like a tyrant in a republic: just as the senate is subject to the tyrant, so is knowledge to the will, so that even if one's knowledge offers good advice, the will nevertheless rejects it and runs wild in its passion, as I will soon explain more clearly. Again, they call the intellect, as it is joined with the will, "reason." We will use neither the term "free will" nor "reason," but will call the parts of man the faculty of knowing and the faculty that is subject to the affections, that is, to love, hate, hope, fear, and the like.[32]

It was necessary to point all this out so that it might be easier later on to specify the distinction between Law and grace, or, more to the point, so that it might be known with more certainty whether or not man possesses any freedom at all. It is amazing how much effort both ancients and moderns have exerted on this subject. As for me, if anyone wishes to criticize what I say here, I will happily put up a staunch defense. For I only wanted to give a very rough definition of

---

[31] So Lombard *Sentences* II, dist. 24, ch. 3: "Free will (*liberum arbitrium*) is a faculty of reason and the will (*voluntas*). . . . And it is called free as concerns the will (*voluntas*), which can be turned to some object, but a judgment (*arbitrium*) as concerns the power of reasoning."

[32] Melanchthon adopts the terminology of John Gerson, who wrote in his *On Mystic Theology* that man consists of "intellect" (*intellectus*) and "affection" (*affectus*) or a "cognitive power" (*vis cognitiva*) and an "affectionate power" (*vis affectiva*), though Gerson himself complicates this simple distinction with several Scholastic divisions (*G* 3:250; 258–61; cf. Pöhlmann, 26, n. 36). Melanchthon's use of the term *affectus*, here translated with the technical term "affections," has precedent in Luther, especially in his commentary on the Psalms (see esp. WA 5:176–225), and in the humanist tradition from which Melanchthon came (Maurer 2:257). The word is versatile and denotes both the inner disposition (i.e., the will itself) and the affections or emotions associated with it. Melanchthon's division of man into the intellect and the affections plays a major role in this work and stands as a serious attempt to articulate Lutheran anthropology over against the anthropology of the Scholastics. Melanchthon wants to dislodge the term "free will" from the discussion of man altogether, both—as he says—because it is not a scriptural term, and because by replacing treatment of the "free will" with treatment of the "affections" he is able to articulate the human condition by using biblical, and specifically, Pauline language, which speaks of "the heart," "affections," "the mind," and "knowledge." Thus the Scholastic treatment of the relationship between the will and reason in man (the concept of "free will") is replaced with the Reformation emphasis that man's affections are turned in on himself in clear violation of God's Law. This translation uses primarily the technical term "affection," but in certain contexts uses the terms "desire," "passion," "inner disposition," or "emotion."

man, and I believe I have spoken about the parts of man as much as was necessary.

Now the Law, that is, the knowledge of what we are obligated to do, pertains to the faculty of knowing, while virtue and sin pertain to the faculty of the affections. Freedom cannot properly be said to belong to the cognitive part of man, since it is taken to and fro as it obeys the will.[33] But there is freedom in the ability to act or not to act, in the ability to do something in this way or that way. And so the question arises whether or not the will is free and to what extent.

I respond that since everything that comes about happens necessarily according to divine predestination, our will has no freedom. Paul writes in Romans 11:[36], "Since from him and in him," and so on; and in Ephesians 1:[11], "Who works all things according the judgment of his will"; Matthew 10:[29], "Are not two sparrows bought with a penny, and not one of them will fall to the earth without your Father?" What, I ask, could be clearer than the following sentence? Proverbs 16:[4], "The Lord has worked all for his own sake, even the godless for the evil day." And again, chapter 20:[24], "A man's steps are directed by the Lord, but who can understand his own path?" Again, chapter 16:[9], "The heart of man chooses its own path, but the Lord directs his steps." Jeremiah 10:[23], "I know, O Lord, that man's path is not in his own power, nor is it in man's power to direct his steps." The divine histories also teach the same thing. Genesis 15:[16], "Not yet have the iniquities of the Amorites been completed." And in 1 Samuel 2:[25], "They did not listen to their father's voice, because the Lord wanted to kill them." What is more fortuitous than that Saul goes out to search for donkeys and is anointed by Samuel and made king? Again, in 1 Samuel 10:[26], "Part of the army, whose hearts God had touched, departed with Saul." In 1 Kings 12:[15], "The king did not assent to the people, because the Lord had rejected him, so that he might

---

[33] Melanchthon is here in agreement with the Scholastic theologian Duns Scotus (c. 1265–1308), who held that as a natural power the intellect does not have the freedom to choose or not to choose. It cannot choose not to understand, but naturally either understands or fails to understand (*In metaph.* 9.15, n. 6). Scotus, however, gave extreme freedom to the will and held that it possessed the power to choose or not to choose. The view that the will is the highest part of man and that knowledge therefore serves the will (voluntarism) is also found, among others, in John Gerson (1363–1429), whose works Melanchthon had studied (*SA* 1:96, 142–4; cf. Maurer 2:245–6; Pöhlmann, 28, n. 37).

undertake the word that he had spoken by Ahijah the Shilonite to Jeroboam the son of Nebat."

And what else is Paul doing in Romans 9 and 11 except consigning everything that happens to divine predestination? Though the judgment of the flesh or of human reason abhors this decree, the judgment of the Spirit embraces it. For you will never learn with more certainty what fear of God or trust in God means than when you take this decree concerning predestination to heart. Or does Solomon not stress this point everywhere in Proverbs in order sometimes to teach fear of God, sometimes trust in God?[34] Does he not also stress it in his little book, Ecclesiastes?[35] For believing firmly that all things happen by God's will does much to suppress and condemn the wisdom and judgment of human reason. Or is it not with great effect that Christ in one place comforts his disciples saying, "All the hairs of your head are numbered" [Luke 12:7]?

"What then," you will say, "is there no contingency (to use their word) in things, no chance, no luck?" Scriptures teach that everything happens of necessity.[36] Although there may seem to you to be some contingency in human affairs, human reason must here be repressed. So Solomon, in deep thought about predestination, says, "And I understood that man cannot discover any reason for all the works of God that happen under the sun" [Ecclesiastes 8:17].

But I must seem a fool to begin a work with predestination, the most disagreeable of subjects. What does it matter, after all, whether I place at the beginning or the end of my compendium a subject that has bearing on every part of the discussion?[37] But since it is an absolute necessity that I begin with the article on free will, how can I cover up the judgment of Scripture on predestination? For Scripture denies any freedom to our will through the necessity of predestination. Besides, I do not think it is wholly unproductive for young minds to meditate on this judgment, that all things come about

---

[34] E.g., Proverbs 14:12, 27; 16:4, 11–12, 33; 20:24.

[35] E.g., Ecclesiastes 9:1.

[36] So Luther in his *Assertion* against the bull of Pope Leo X (1520): "All things . . . happen by absolute necessity," and again "[I]n regard to spiritual things, all things are necessary" (WA 7:146). This statement had already been condemned as heresy at the Council of Constance (1414–18).

[37] Melanchthon uses irony to underscore the necessity of beginning his work with a discussion of predestination.

not because of human plans or efforts, but according to the will of God. Or does not Solomon in his Proverbs, which he wrote for the youth, teach predestination from the very beginning?[38]

It is due to that godless theology of the sophists[39] that this judgment concerning predestination is commonly thought to be somewhat too harsh. For their theology so stressed upon us the contingency of things and the freedom of our will that our tender ears now recoil from the truth of Scripture. So that we may give further attention to those who have taken some offense at what we have spoken about predestination, we will consider more closely the very nature of the human will. The studious reader will thus be able to understand that the sophists are mistaken not only in regard to theology, but also in regard to natural judgment. But we will speak about predestination soon in its own place, and we will show as briefly as possible what godless things the sophists have said about it in their commentaries.

Eck[40] says that Valla[41] desired to know more than he had learned because he confuted the opinion of the schools on free will, which means, of course, that he was a marvelously jocular babbler. But if those sorcerers[42] want to make the same objection against me, that I

---

[38] Cf. Proverbs 1:28–33; 2:6–9.

[39] That is, the Scholastic theologians. The pejorative term "sophist" derives from the name given to teachers of rhetoric in Athens during the fifth century BC. From the fourth century BC on, the term was used as an insult to discredit those who developed clever or intricate arguments (cf. Plato *Symp.* 203d; Dem. 18.276; 19.246; Aeschin. 1.125, 175; 3.202).

[40] John Eck (1486–1543) was a German Scholastic theologian who championed the cause of Rome against Luther and Melanchthon. In his work *Chrysopassus* (1514), he had condemned Valla's position on the bondage of the will and insinuated that Valla was not competent to write on such a topic. Erasmus, in his *Diatribe on Free Will* (1524), also dismisses Valla: "Laurentius Valla's authority does not hold much weight among theologians" (*AS* 4:24).

[41] Laurentius Valla (1407–57) was an Italian humanist whose dialogue *On Free Will* denied the freedom of the human will based on divine predestination. Although he here approves of Valla's conclusions, in later editions of his *Loci* Melanchthon censures Valla by name as a determinist (*SA* 2:236).

[42] The accusation of sorcery originated in classical Athens as a common anti-rhetorical device meant to stress the danger of an opponent's reliance on words instead of substance (cf. Plato *Symp.* 203d; Dem. 18.108, 119, 132; Aeschin. 2.124, 153). Melanchthon himself wrote paraphrases of speeches by Demosthenes, Aeschines, and other Greek orators, in which such accusations abound (*CR* 17:683–938).

am a grammarian dealing with theology, what can I respond, except to say that they should evaluate the substance, not the speaker?[43] What matters at present is not my occupation, but whether or not I have taught the truth. But neither should the business of theology be thought too far above me. I am, after all, a Christian, and Christian doctrine ought to belong to all.

I. But if you consider the power of the human will as a natural capability, it cannot be denied that there is in it, according to human reason, some freedom in external works. One experiences for himself that it is within his own power, for example, to say hello or not, to get dressed or not, to eat meat or not.[44] And the pseudo-philosophers, who attribute freedom to the will, have locked their eyes on this contingency of external works.[45] But because God is no respecter of external works but considers the inner motions of the heart, Scripture is silent concerning this freedom. Those philosophers and modern theologians who teach this kind of freedom imagine a morality based on some external and affected civility.

II. Our inner affections, on the other hand, are not in our power. For practical experience shows us that our will cannot of its own power push aside love, hatred, or similar affections, but one overrules another, so that, for example, you stop loving someone because he hurts you. Nor will I listen to the sophists if they deny that love, hate, happiness, sadness, envy, ambition, and similar human affections pertain to the will. For hunger and thirst are not now under

---

[43] Eck wrote a tract in 1519 entitled: *Eck's Response to those things which Philip Melanchthon, the grammarian from Wittenberg, falsely ascribed to him concerning the Theological disputation at Leipzig* (CR 1:97–103). In this little work, Eck repeatedly belittles Melanchthon as a teacher of Greek and Latin and a grammarian (*grammaticus, grammatista*), unfit to engage in theological disputes. Melanchthon, in his *Defense against Eck* (1519), writes that he is content to be thought foolish in Scripture and unable to grasp the "sublime questions of the theologians" (*SA* 1:12–22).

[44] Melanchthon grants the same limited power to free will in AC XVIII: "Concerning free will they teach that the human will has some freedom to produce civil righteousness and to choose things subject to reason. But it does not have the power to produce the righteousness of God or spiritual righteousness without the Holy Spirit."

[45] Cf. Luther *Assertion* (1520): "The inconsistency or (as they call it) the contingency of human affairs deceives these pathetic men, and they turn their foolish eyes to the affairs themselves and the works involved in them, never looking at God to see in him the things that are above human affairs" (WA 7:146).

discussion. But what is the will except the source of affections? And why do we not just use the word *heart* instead of *will*? For Scripture calls the highest faculty of man the heart, that is, that part of man from which affections arise. But the schools deceive themselves when they imagine that the will naturally opposes its affections or can push aside an affection, so long as the intellect advises and recommends it.

III. How then does it happen that we humans often choose something different from what we desire? First of all, since sometimes we do choose something in our external action different from what our heart or will desires, it can happen that one emotion is overruled by another. For example, it cannot be denied that Alexander of Macedon was a lover of sensual pleasures. Yet because he yearned for glory more, he chose labor and spurned sensual pleasures—not because he did not love them, but because he loved glory more.[46] For we see that different kinds of affections rule in different kinds of people, that everyone is led by his own peculiar desire. In base natures the desire for possessions dominates and in more liberal dispositions—according to human judgment—pursuit of fame or popular favor.

IV. Then again, it can perhaps happen that something is chosen completely contrary to all affections. But when this happens, it is a pretense, as when someone treats a man whom he deeply despises and against whom he wishes evil with kindness, tenderness, and friendliness, and this for no apparent reason. Even if this person does not realize that he has been overcome by some other affection (for there do exist dispositions so nice that they flatter even those whom they hate), I maintain that he is pretending friendship in the external act, in which there seems to be some liberty according to nature. And this is the will that our stupid Scholastics conjure up, namely, such a power which, no matter that you are under the influence of the affections, can still moderate and temper affection. Thinking along these lines they teach their fake repentance.[47]

---

[46] So Plutarch: "The heat of Alexander's body seems to have made him fond of drinking and heated in temperament. But even when he was young, his self-control was manifest in the way he was unmoved by bodily pleasures and only moderately embraced them, and this in spite of his violent and intense disposition; but his love for glory made his mind both serious and high-minded beyond his years" (*Alexander* 4.4–5).

[47] Melanchthon treats the Scholastic doctrine of repentance below, pp. 175–82.

Although you are under the influence of the affections, they think
that your will has the power to elicit (to use their terminology) good
acts.[48] They think that if you hate someone, your will can decide no
longer to will this hatred. So, although we are by nature godless and
so far from loving God as to hate him virulently, they teach that the
will can elicit the act of loving God. I ask you, dear reader, whether
you do not think him insane who has imagined that we possess such a
will. Would that a sophist would attack me on this issue, so that I
could confute that godless, stupid, and wickedly philosophical
opinion about the will with a formal work and a full discussion![49] For
when he who hates decides to push aside his hatred, unless he has
actually been overcome by a stronger affection, it is obviously a
feigned mental exercise, not a work of the will. If Paris should decide
to push aside his love for Oenone, unless he was actually overcome
by a stronger affection, it is a feigned and faked mental exercise.[50]
Since we are by nature liars, it can happen that our heart together with
our intellect controls our external members, our tongue, hands, and
eyes, contrary to our soul's desire. Thus Joab controlled his tongue
and eyes so that he might appear to address Amasa as politely as
possible, but he could not make his heart push aside the affection that

---

[48] Latin: *vim ... eliciendi ... actus bonos*. Melanchthon has Duns Scotus in mind,
whose works became the standard for a new school of thought, Scotism, which
stressed the superiority of the will over the intellect (voluntarism). Scotus taught that
the human will had the native power to dispose itself toward or elicit acts that meet
the bare requirements of the Law (*In sent.* II, d. 29, q. 1). Thus the naturally good act
of the will which can merit grace was called an "elicited act" (*actus elicitus*). Gabriel
Biel (c. 1420–95), another late and influential Scholastic theologian who wrote a
commentary on the *Sentences*, follows Scotus in teaching the power of the human
will to elicit good acts, going so far as to say that the will can "elicit the act of loving
God above all things of its own natural powers" (*In sent.* II, d. 28, art. 1, dub. 1). In
1519, at the Leipzig Disputation, John Eck had argued the case for this freedom of
the will to elicit good acts against Luther (cf. *SA* 2:14).

[49] Erasmus would later attack the Lutheran position on free will, but directed his
Diatribe on Free Will (1524) (*AS* 4:1–195) against Luther, whose reply entitled *The
Bondage of the Will* (1525) (WA 18:600–787; AE 33:15–295) is the most fully
articulated presentation of the Lutheran doctrine on the power of the human will (cf.
SD II 44).

[50] Paris of Troy was married to the nymph Oenone. When Aphrodite rewarded him
with the hand of Helen of Sparta, Paris was overcome by a stronger emotion,
abandoned his wife, stole Helen from Menelaus, king of Sparta, and thus began the
Trojan War (cf. Ovid *Heroides* 5).

it produced. Rather, he put this affection aside when it was overcome by a stronger affection, which overwhelmed him [2 Samuel 20:7–10].

V. The schools do not deny that the affections exist, but they call them an infirmity of nature and think it is enough if the will possesses the ability to elicit various acts. But I deny that there is any power in man that can seriously oppose his affections, and I think that these elicited acts are nothing but a fictitious mental exercise. For since God judges hearts, the heart along with its affections must be the highest and most powerful part of man. Otherwise, why would God consider man according to his weaker part and not rather according to his better part, if the will is somehow different from the heart and better and stronger than the part that contains the affections? What will the sophists respond to this? But if we had preferred to use the word "heart," as Scripture does, rather than the Aristotelian term "will," we would have easily avoided such foolish and crass errors. Indeed, Aristotle is hardly incorrect when he defines the will as the selection of things in external works. But what do external works have to do with Christian discipline, if meanwhile the heart is corrupt? Besides, Aristotle himself did not even teach these "elicited acts" that have been invented by Scotus.[51] However, my intention here is not to confute those sophists but to teach you, Christian reader, what you should pursue. I confess that in the external selection of things there is a certain freedom, but I completely reject the idea that our inner affections are under our power. Nor do I grant that any will possesses the genuine power of opposing its affections. Of course, I am speaking about natural man. For in those who have been justified by the Spirit, good affections fight evil affections, as we will teach below.

VI. Moreover, what is the point of boasting about our freedom in external works when God requires purity of heart? Everything that godless fools have written about free will and the righteousness of works comprises nothing but a thoroughly pharisaical tradition. As soon as our affections grow a little stronger, they necessarily burst forth, as the saying goes: "You can drive nature out with a fork, but it will always return."[52] How often do we convince ourselves that we have done a good work when we do something that has the outward

---

[51] See p. 34, n. 48.

[52] Horace *Epistle* 1.10.24.

appearance of a good work, and this because we fail to look at the base affection from which the work proceeds? "For there is a way," says Solomon, "which looks good to man, but whose end leads to death" [Proverbs 14:12]. And the prophet Jeremiah declares that "man's heart is corrupt and inscrutable" [Jeremiah 17:9]. Also, David, "Who understands his errors?" and, "Do not remember my ignorance" [Psalm 19:12; 25:7]. Therefore, man's affection forces him to many things that he cannot even properly understand because he is blind. Furthermore the Christian mind should consider not the outward appearance of a work, but the nature of the affection in his soul, not the nature of freedom in external works, but whether any freedom exists in the affections. Let the pharisaical Scholastics preach the power of free will. The Christian will acknowledge that nothing is less in his power than his own heart. If only the stupid Scholastics realized how many thousands of souls they have killed by their pharisaical nonsense about free will![53] But we will soon have more to say about man's inner affections when we treat original sin.

SUMMARY

If you consider the human will according to predestination, there is no freedom in external or internal works, but everything happens according to divine design.

If you consider the will according to external works, natural judgment concludes that some freedom exists.

If you consider the will according to the affections, it is obvious that no freedom exists, as even natural judgment attests.

As soon as the affections have begun to rage and boil, they cannot be controlled and they burst forth.

You see, my reader, how much more straightforward and reliable my writing about free will has been in comparison to either Bernard or any of the Scholastics. Moreover, what I have discussed up to this point will become clearer as I treat the remaining topics of my compendium.

---

[53] Latin: *pharisaica sua deuterosi*. Deuterosis is the class of laws abrogated by the coming of Christ. The use of the word here is meant to accentuate the pharisaical nature of a theology based on free will.

SIN

The sophists have done a wonderful job obscuring this article, too, arguing about the relations of reason[1] in sin, making distinctions about actual and original sin, and much else that I need not recount here. A compendium is not, after all, the best place to list all their musings. We will treat the matter briefly and use the normal, scriptural term "sin."

WHAT IS SIN?

I. Original sin is an inborn propensity and a natural impulse that actively compels us to sin, originating from Adam and extending to all his posterity.[2] Just as fire rises because of the power innate to it and just as in a magnet there is an innate power by which it attracts iron to itself, so in man there is an inborn power to sin. Scripture does not distinguish between actual and original sin, since original sin is also clearly an actual corrupt desire. Rather, Scripture simply calls both original vice and actual vice sin, though sometimes it calls what we consider actual sins "the fruits of sin" as Paul likes to do in Romans.[3] And what we call original sin, David sometimes names "crookedness" and sometimes "iniquity." But there is no reason to discuss here those stupid distinctions concerning sin. Sin is a corrupt

---

[1] "Relation of reason" (*relatio rationis*) or "being of reason" (*ens rationis*) is a term derived from Aristotle (*Categories* 6a37–8b24; *Metaphysics* 1003a–b) denominating a relation or concept that properly exists only in the mind. Aquinas calls sin a being of reason (*ens rationis*) insofar as it truly exists (*prout verum*), since it exists only as a deprivation of being and so is correctly called a being (*ens*) only as an intellectual object (*In sent.* dist. 37, art. 2).

[2] What is translated here as the adverb "actively" is the noun *energia*. Despite Melanchthon's attacks on Aristotelian terminology in this treatise, he is well aware of Aristotle's distinctions between potentiality (*dynamis*) and actuality (*energeia*). By referring to the *energia* of sin, Melanchthon is stressing the fact that sin is not a latent possibility in man, but an ever active force. He treats this matter more thoroughly below under "The Power and Fruits of Sin."

[3] Cf. Romans 6:21.

inner disposition (*affectus*) and a depraved agitation of the heart against the Law of God.

THE SOURCE OF ORIGINAL SIN

II. After creating man without sin, almighty God was present with him through his Spirit, who aroused him to pursue righteousness. Had Adam not fallen, the same Spirit would be guiding all his descendants. But now after the sin of Adam, God is at enmity with man, so that his Spirit is not present with him as his guide. So it is that the soul, blind and lacking the light and life of heaven, esteems itself with all eagerness, seeks its own advantage, has nothing but carnal desires, and hates God. No words can describe the corruption of the human heart. The creature who is not filled with love of God necessarily loves himself most. The flesh cannot love spiritual things.

So we read in Genesis [6:3], "My Spirit will not remain in man, because he is flesh." And Paul writes in Romans 8: "Those who are of the flesh," that is, those who lack the Spirit of God (for even from the passage just quoted from Genesis it follows that "flesh" designates human powers lacking the Spirit of God), "desire the things of the flesh" [v. 5]. And again, "The affection of the flesh is enmity against God" [v. 7]. Therefore when the sophists teach that original sin is a lack of original righteousness (for so they speak), they speak correctly. But why do they not add that where there is no original righteousness or Spirit, there is really only flesh, godlessness, and contempt of spiritual things?

Human nature's primary and highest affection is love of self. Man is driven by this love to will and desire only those things that seem good, agreeable, pleasant, and glorious to his nature. This love of self also drives him to hate and fear those things opposed to his nature and to oppose whoever keeps him from what he wants or commands him to obey or seek what he does not want. How unfathomable is the misery of humanity! So arises in man hatred of God and his Law. Therefore, God is to man a consuming fire, as we will soon explain in more detail.[4]

III. Now the Pelagians are said to have denied the existence of original sin. Augustine has refuted this teaching of theirs in several

---

[4] Cf. Exodus 24:17; Deuteronomy 4:24; 9:3; Hebrews 12:29.

learned works.⁵ In fact, Augustine's argument against the Pelagians is so supremely excellent that almost all his other works seem rather dull in comparison. We will cite some passages from Scripture that testify to the existence of original sin. Nothing could be more clearly articulated than Ephesians 2:[3], "We were by nature children of wrath, as also were the rest." Now if we are children of wrath by nature, we are certainly born children of wrath. For what else is Paul saying here except that we are born with all our powers subject to sin and that no good ever exists in human powers? In Romans 5, he begins a discussion about sin, grace, and the Law where he teaches that sin has been passed down to all men. But how is one man's sin passed down unless all are born sinners because of the one? Nor can it be denied that Paul is discussing original sin in this passage. For if he were speaking of his own and others' personal sins, he could not say that the many have died because of one man's transgression. Unless one wants to do damage to the text, it cannot be denied that Paul is not talking about so-called actual sin.

In fact, if Adam is not the author of sin, then Christ is not the sole author of righteousness, but Adam has to be co-author with him. Also if Paul only means to speak of his own and others' personal sins, why do children, who have committed no so-called actual sins, die? Since sin is the only reason for death, children must be guilty of sin and have sin. But what kind of sin? Obviously, original sin. Now Paul speaks of that sin through which all have been condemned to death. Of course, we are here inspecting a typically Pauline figure of speech. For just as he does here in Romans, so also in 1 Corinthians [15:22] he writes, "Just as all die in Adam, so in Christ all will be made alive." The prophet's exclamation is relevant here: "Behold, I was conceived in iniquities and in sins my mother conceived me!" [Psalm 51:5]. David clearly means that he was born a sinner. Besides, if "every desire of the thoughts of the human heart is always vain and corrupt," as Genesis 6:[5] claims, it follows necessarily that we are born with sin. Now if we are all blessed in Christ, it follows necessarily that we are cursed in Adam. But what does it mean to be cursed, except that we are damned for our sin? This condemnation of sin is signified in the various kinds of uncleanness in the types of the

---

⁵ E.g., *On the Spirit and the Letter* (*MPL* 44:199–246); *Against Two Letters of the Pelagians* (*MPL* 44:549–641); *Against Julian* (*MPL* 44:641–874).

Law as well as in the slaughter of the Egyptians' firstborn sons. Nor is there any reason to treat this matter further, since Christ's words in John [3:6] are sufficiently straightforward: "What is born of the flesh is flesh." As we demonstrated above, what is flesh seeks its own benefit and loves itself. And what need do we have of rebirth if our first birth is not subject to sin? More to the point, if the birth of the flesh is good, what need do we have of rebirth from the Spirit?

THE POWER AND FRUITS OF SIN

IV. It is easier to refute the old Pelagians than the neo-Pelagians of our day, who do not deny the existence of original sin but do deny that the power of original sin is such that all human works and all human endeavors are sins. Accordingly we will treat the active power of sin a bit more thoroughly. Original sin is a living, active force, bearing fruit in the form of vices in every part of us and at every moment. For when does the human soul not burn with evil desires? And we do not even notice the most despicable and shameful of these desires. Everyone sometimes feels greed, ambition, hatred, envy, jealousy, sensual passions, and anger, but few recognize their arrogance, pride, pharisaical deceit, contempt of God, disbelief in God, and blasphemy, even though these are our primary affections.

There are those who lead very honest lives in outward appearance. Paul, in fact, testifies that he had led an irreproachable life before coming to the knowledge of Christ.[6] But these people have no reason to boast, since their souls, even without their knowing it, are subject to the vilest and lowest affections. Indeed, what if God should, at some time, perhaps at their death, open the eyes of these so-called saints so that they recognize their vices and diseases? Would they not understand what Isaiah decreed—that all the glory of the flesh is as the glory of grass [Isaiah 40:6–8]? You see how deep, or rather how inscrutable, the wickedness of the human heart is. And yet our sophists are still shameless enough to teach the righteousness of works, satisfactions, and philosophical virtues.[7]

---

[6] E.g., Philippians 3:4–6.

[7] Following the Greek and Roman philosophical tradition, Peter Lombard, Thomas Aquinas, and other Scholastics recognized four philosophical virtues, which they called cardinal or principal virtues: prudence, fortitude, temperance, and justice (Lombard *Sentences* III, dist. 33; Aquinas *Summa* I–II, q. 61). These philosophical

Granted that there was constancy in Socrates, integrity in Xenocrates,[8] self-control in Zeno.[9] But since these resided in impure souls they should not be considered true virtues but vices. Or, to put it more precisely, the shadows of these virtues arose in them because of their esteem and love of themselves. Socrates was patient, but he loved fame or at least was self-satisfied with his virtue.[10] Cato was brave but due to his love of praise.[11] In fact, God has poured out these shadows of virtues upon the nations, upon the godless, and upon whomever else he pleases, just as he gives beauty, riches, and similar gifts. Since human reason is completely enraptured by this facade parading itself as virtue, our pseudo-theologians are deceived by their blind natural judgment and urge us to study philosophical virtues and the merits of external works. But what do philosophers generally teach? The best of them teach nothing but trust and love of self. Marcus Cicero, in his *The Ends of Good and Evil*, derives all manner of virtues from love and esteem of self.[12] How much arrogance and conceit can be found in Plato![13] It seems to me that if someone with a

---

virtues are distinguished from the theological virtues of faith, hope, and love (Aquinas *Summa* I–II, q. 62), derived from 1 Corinthians 13.

[8] Xenocrates of Chalcedon (c. 395–313) was a philosopher of the fourth century BC, a student of Plato, and eventually the leader of the Academy founded by Plato. Among other things, he stressed that virtue was the key to happiness.

[9] Zeno of Citium (c. 334–262) was the founder of Stoicism. Self-control was a primary Stoic virtue, since emotion was thought to be evil and to cloud the purity of human nature, which should be directed by logic (*logos*).

[10] There is here an implicit criticism of Erasmus, who in the most famous section of his *Adages* (III.iii.1) treats the saying *The Sileni of Alcibiades*. Sileni were statues with grotesque outward appearances but when opened up revealed the beautiful image of a god. Erasmus gives Socrates (along with Jesus!) as an example of a Silenus, arguing that he looked like nothing on the outside but was pure on the inside. Melanchthon turns this assessment on its head by showing that Socrates and other philosophers looked beautiful in view of their external actions but were inwardly vicious.

[11] Cato was a statesman of the late Republican period famous for his bravery, immortalized in the epic poem of Lucan, the "Civil War." Cato took over the republican cause in the West following the death of Pompey after the Battle of Pharsalus (48 BC). He committed suicide rather than receive pardon from Julius Caesar.

[12] In Book I of this work, Cicero has an interlocutor argue for Epicurean self-interest.

[13] In his *Oration* of 1521, Melanchthon explains that Plato's definition of philosophy is knowledge of self, but since only Scripture can show us how miserable we truly

high-minded and forceful disposition reads Plato, it will be hard for him to avoid being adversely affected by Plato's ambition. And Aristotle's teachings amount to little more than a love of arguing. In fact, he should not be considered among the hortatory philosophers at all, not even last among them. But we will speak about philosophy later when we treat the nature of laws.

V. And to sum the whole matter up, all men through their own natural powers are truly sinners and do nothing but sin. Genesis 6:[5], "Every desire of the thoughts of the human heart is always vain and corrupt." And the same judgment is repeated in chapter 8:[21], "The perception and thought of the human heart is corrupt from childhood." In the Vulgate we read, "prone to evil," and although this is not far from the sense, I would still prefer to use the original reading, which is clearer and simply affirms that man is corrupt.[14] But I am not going to let any Thomist elude Moses and say that because a proclivity or inclination is not an act, it cannot be sin.[15] For so these senseless sophists philosophize.[16]

Isaiah 9:[17], "All are hypocrites and worthless; every mouth has spoken foolishness." Again, Isaiah 41:[29], "Behold all are vain; and their works are vain; wind and useless are their counsels." Once again, Isaiah 53:[6], "We all like sheep have gone astray, each one has turned aside to his own way. And the Lord has put on him the iniquity of us all." In this last passage the prophet explains with a clear prophecy both the history of the passion and its fruit. For he predicted that Christ would suffer so that he could appear the most dejected of all men; then also that he would suffer to justify many, since we are all, of course, sinners, and we are justified in no other way than through faith in Christ. And concerning those who would be justified by their own strength and works and not through faith in Christ, he says, "He will give the godless for his grave and the rich

---

are, Plato's encouragement to know ourselves can only lead to hypocrisy (*SA* 1:81–82).

[14] Genesis 8:21 in the Vulgate reads, *sensus enim et cogitatio humani cordis in malum prona sunt ab adolescentia sua*, ("for the perception and thought of the human heart are prone to evil from youth"). See also the Vulgate translation of Genesis 6:5: *cuncta cogitatio intenta esset ad malum* ("every thought was intent on evil").

[15] Thomas Aquinas defines sin as a bad human act (*Summa* I–II, q. 71, art. 1–6).

[16] Melanchthon uses alliteration (*sic philosophantur stolidi sophistae*) to stress the slippery maneuverings of Scholastic logic.

for his death" [v. 9] and, "He will divide the spoils of the strong" [v. 12]. For the godless, the rich, and the strong are obviously those who are ignorant of Christ and champion the human righteousness of the free will, philosophical virtues, and human strength. You see how Isaiah describes the Gospel in all its power with his brief sermon. But you, O Christ, grant your Spirit to open up and explain these mysteries to us.

Now let us also hear David, who makes this same observation in many passages, as when he says that every man is a liar [Psalm 116:11]. But he also devotes the entirety of Psalm 14 to this point, where he declares, "The fool has said in his heart, 'There is no God'; they have become corrupt and abominable in their pursuits. There is no one who does good. The Lord looks down from heaven on the sons of Adam to see whether there is any who understands or seeks after God. All have failed and have together become useless. There is no one who does good; no, not even one," etc. [vv. 1–3]. Here he does not accuse man of simple vices but of the most appalling crimes: impiety, unbelief, foolishness, hatred, and contempt of God. And no one can comprehend these vices except through the Spirit. What will you say here, you sham theologians? What works of the free will, what human powers will you preach to us? You pretend not to deny original sin, but then you teach that man can do something good by his own powers. Can a bad tree bear good fruit? Or do you not realize that here the prophet describes the tree along with its fruits, since he speaks not only of the fool's heart, but also of all man's pursuits, plans, desires, works, and endeavors?

Now as regards the topic of man, you see how great the difference is between the teachings of philosophy or human reason and Holy Scripture. Philosophy looks at nothing but the facades that men exhibit. Holy Scripture perceives the innermost affections. These affections, though incomprehensible to man, rule him, and so Holy Scripture judges works with regard to the affections. And since in all our works we seek after our own advantage, these works must really be sins. Since I do not wish to mention the crassest desires, I will speak of those who lead ostensibly good lives. Are not some drawn to this kind of morality by an aversion to human interaction, some by a fear of what may happen, some by ambition, some by a love of tranquility? (For these are the reasons given for leading an ostensibly more moral life both by ancient philosophers and by very many of our contemporaries.)[17] Still others are drawn by a feigned fear of divine punishment. And the list of reasons could go on. For who can unravel the labyrinth of the human heart? Especially since the diversity of personal temperaments corresponds to the diversity of affections. Now who is there among all humanity who by nature would not prefer to indulge his personal inclinations; who would not resent the compulsion of the Law? It is irrelevant whether or not you feel it right now or not. For the time will most certainly come when you will feel how offended your soul is that its desires are restrained by the Law.

Besides the passages already cited, there is John 1:[12–13], "As many as received him, he gave power to become sons of God, to those who believe in his name, who have been born not from blood, nor from the will of the flesh, nor from the will of man, but from God." You see what is condemned: blood, the will of man, the will of the flesh, that is, everything whatsoever that belongs to the powers of human nature. But sons are reborn of God. And I add this last passage, passing over many others that the studious reader will examine for himself: "As the branch cannot bear fruit by itself unless it remain in the vine, so neither can you, unless you remain in me" (John 15:[4]).

While we are speaking about this subject, we should refute what those godless sophists growl in opposition. For they explain away these abundantly clear passages, saying that it is true that man according to nature cannot do good meritoriously. For so they speak. And so they invent two kinds of good work, meritorious and non-meritorious.[18] They only do this so that they do not have to condemn as vice the philosophical virtues of the free will, which are merely the

---

[17] Erasmus, who continually stressed tranquility of life as the result of virtuous action, is no doubt meant to be included among these contemporaries. Erasmus's love of tranquility led him to advise Melanchthon, in a letter of 1519, to stay out of theological discussions and concentrate exclusively on the liberal arts. Erasmus also advised Melanchthon not to engage in argument with the "enemies" of liberal arts, so that "by modesty and mildness of behavior we may appear superior to them" (CR 1:78).

[18] Melanchthon directs this criticism especially against Occam and the nominalists, who distinguished between a good work that is meritorious by God's grace and a good moral work, which can be done according to the powers of nature. So Occam writes, "Natural powers incline toward a good, moral action after [the fall into] sin just as before" (In sent. lib. 2, q. 19; cf. Pöhlmann, 64–65). This distinction is closely related to the more common distinction between congruent and condign merit, for which see p. 52, n. 34 below.

outward shadows of virtues. What godlessness! Or is it not playing with words to render the term "good" ambiguous so that some good works merit eternal life but others do not?

But you should certainly not think that man can do anything good or meritorious through the powers of his nature. For Scripture declares that every desire of the thoughts of the human heart is vain and corrupt [Genesis 6:5]. Certainly that which is vain and corrupt is not only not meritorious of eternal life (allow me to use their terminology), but not good at all. Thus David, "Every man is a liar" [Psalm 116:11]. And Isaiah, "All are hypocrites and evil; every mouth has spoken foolishness" [Isaiah 9:17]. Isaiah is not just making a point about what is and what is not meritorious. He is speaking of plain evil! Moreover, from the passages that I have treated up to this point and from those that I will soon add, anyone can easily refute by himself this sort of nonsense promoted by the Scholastics. These godless sophists did not evaluate works according to the heart's inner disposition but considered them philosophically. And this is the reason for their senselessness.

What is the general theme dominating nearly all of Paul's epistles, especially Romans and Galatians? Is it not the teaching that all the works and endeavors of human powers are sin? Consider the third chapter of Romans, where he says that all men are under sin and draws this teaching admirably and beautifully from the testimonies of the prophets. Then in the eighth chapter, after arguing that we cannot fulfill the Law, he contrasts the flesh with the Spirit, teaching that the flesh is thoroughly subject to sin, but that the Spirit is life and peace. Here the sophists call the flesh the sensual appetite,[19] but they are forgetting the phraseology and manner of speaking in Scripture. For when Scripture uses the word "flesh," it is not speaking of the body as a part of man. It is rather speaking of the entire man, body and soul. And as many times as Scripture contrasts the flesh with the Spirit, it means to designate the flesh as the highest and most excellent powers of human nature apart from the Holy Spirit. In contrast, Spirit designates the Holy Spirit himself and his activity and work in us. So John 3:[6], "What is born of the flesh is flesh; what is born of the Spirit is spirit." And John 8:[15], "You judge according to the flesh."

---

[19] The sensual (or sensitive) appetite consists of the desires that are subject to bodily organs (eating, drinking, sexual lust, etc.). See p. 27, n. 30 above.

And Genesis 6:[3], "My Spirit will not remain in man, because he is flesh." Therefore, we should understand the word "flesh" as embracing all the powers of human nature. Otherwise all of Paul's arguments in Romans will make no sense. For he likes to argue in the following way: "Since the flesh cannot keep the Law, the Spirit is needed to keep it." If here we should take flesh as signifying only a part of man, how will Paul's enthymeme make sense?[20] For one could challenge his conclusion in the following way: "Although the flesh could not fulfill the Law, still some better part of man could, and so the Spirit is not needed to fulfill the Law."

But in allowing the philosophers to be our teachers we have forgotten not only the meaning of Scripture but also its manner of speech. As we read in Ezra [10:2], "We have married foreign women" and made their language our own. Instead, we should use the term "flesh" to designate the highest powers of human nature and its noblest endeavors. The fruit of the flesh includes both the impressive virtue of Socrates or Cato and the assassination of Caesar. The fruits of the flesh include both the most impressive virtues of Paul with which he was blessed before he came to know Christ and the adulteries of the Clodians.[21]

Now what we here call "flesh," we usually name the "old man," which also signifies all the powers belonging to human nature. And the term itself clearly encourages this meaning. For only someone who lacks common sense would argue that merely a part of man is indicated by the term "old man." Seriously, who thinks only of the body when he hears the term "man"? Moreover, Paul uses the terms "old man," "flesh," and "body of sin" interchangeably. In fact, the term "outer man"[22] means exactly the same thing as "old man" or

---

[20] An enthymeme is a loose syllogism that assumes and thus omits a major or minor premise. In this case, the full syllogism would be this: (a) no flesh can keep the Law without the Spirit (major); (b) our flesh does not have the Spirit (minor); (c) our flesh cannot keep the Law (conclusion).

[21] The reference is to Clodius Pulcher and his sister Clodia. Clodius was rumored to have dressed up as a woman in order to break into Julius Caesar's house and carry on an affair with Caesar's wife. Caesar would later divorce her because of this scandal (Plutarch *Caesar* 9–10). Cicero's masterpiece of invective, the *Pro Caelio*, is directed in large part against Clodius's sister, Clodia, an infamous femme fatale. Many of Catullus's poems are devoted to his love affair with Clodia, to whom he gives the moniker Lesbia.

[22] 2 Corinthians 4:16.

"flesh," that is, not merely the outer parts of man but all man's natural powers. But I will speak more about the parts of man below when I deal with grace. It should be enough for now to have taught what the term "flesh" means. It is simply untrue that there is something in unregenerate man, in a man not washed clean by the Spirit, that cannot be called flesh and therefore vicious.

Since we are looking into Paul's judgment concerning the natural powers of man, I add his words: "What was impossible for the law because it was weak through the flesh, God did by sending his Son in the likeness of sinful flesh, and because of sin condemned sin in the flesh, so that the righteousness of the law might be fulfilled in us, who walk not according to the flesh but according to the Spirit" [Romans 8:3–4]. Up to this point Paul has set forth the chief point of his argument, namely, that since it is impossible for us to fulfill the Law because we are flesh, God sent his Son to satisfy the Law for us who, though dead because of the flesh, live by the Spirit. I ask now, what is it that he calls "flesh" in this passage? Since it is obvious that the Holy Spirit and his motions and impulses are called "Spirit," it necessarily follows that "flesh" includes everything in us foreign to the Holy Spirit. Moreover, the apostle gives a reason for his judgment: "Those who are of the flesh desire (*affectant*) the things of the flesh, but those who are of the Spirit desire (*affectant*) the things of the Spirit. For the affection of the flesh is death, but the affection of the Spirit is life and peace" [Romans 8:5–6]. It is clear why the Law cannot be satisfied by the flesh: because those who are of the flesh desire the things of the flesh. It is as if Paul were saying, "You Pharisees and hypocrites think that you can keep the Law by your own powers. You seem to do good works outwardly. You seem to be blessed with the noblest virtues. But all this is a facade. For since you are flesh, you seek your own advantage, ostensibly doing good works, but only because of fear of punishment or love of gain or some other fleshly affection. Nor can any feeling for God exist in you since you are flesh. And so you cannot will or seek after the things of God." In fact no matter how good someone seems to be outwardly, nobody loves God so much that he willingly consents to death and hell, if God so wills.[23]

---

[23] So Luther, *Heidelberg Disputation* (1518): "Therefore, whoever glories in the law as if he were a wise and just man, let him glory in that he has been confounded, that

It cannot be expressed how many important things the apostle includes in one short little verse, "Those who are of the flesh desire the things of the flesh." And on the other hand, "Those who are of the Spirit desire the things of the Spirit." That is, in those whom the Spirit fills there is an understanding of God, trust in God, love of God, just as on the other hand there is nothing in the flesh except contempt for and hatred of God. This is what the apostle means when he says, "The desire of the flesh is death, but the desire of the Spirit is life and peace." And he continues, "The desire of the flesh is enmity against God, for it is not subject to the law of God, nor indeed can it be" [Romans 8:7]. Look, please, at Paul's conclusion, which determines that all the power of the flesh is at enmity with God and cannot be subject to the Law of God. But if it cannot be subject to the Law of God, how can we have any doubts about the fruits it bears? Moreover, he does not merely say that it *is not* subject to the Law, but that it *cannot be* subject to the Law. And so it follows that all the works of men, no matter how praiseworthy they seem in outward appearance, are utterly vicious sins, deserving of death. If they so desire, let the sophists here usher in their frivolous distinctions about the flesh and the Spirit, about the good and the meritorious, and all the similar nonsense that they have manufactured to tear Paul's meaning from us. For what is clearer than Paul's statement that the righteousness of the Law is not fulfilled except in those who are of the Spirit? Therefore, those who have not been filled with the Holy Spirit do not satisfy the Law. But what is failure to keep the Law except sin? For every motion and impulse of the soul against the Law is sin.

Therefore when the sophists teach that original sin is the loss of the favor of God and the lack of original righteousness, they ought to add that since we lack the Spirit and blessing of God, we are cursed; since we lack light, there is nothing in us except darkness, blindness, and error; since we lack truth, there is nothing in us except mendacity; since we lack life, there is nothing in us except sin and death. So Paul explains what he means by the term "children of wrath" in Ephesians 2:[3], "And we all formerly conducted ourselves in the desires of our flesh, doing the will of the flesh and its thoughts, and we were by nature children of wrath." When we treat the powers of the Law below it will be possible to speak to this topic much more, so I do not

---

he has been cursed, that God is angry with him, and that he must die, as Romans 2 puts it: 'Why do you glory in the law?' " (WA 1:363; AE 31:69). Cf. Ap IV 7.

want to dwell any longer on it here. For when the Law, which convicts all men of sin, is revealed, then it finally becomes clear what the power of sin is, as the apostle writes to the Galatians: "For Scripture has confined all under sin so that the promise of faith in Jesus Christ may be given to all believers" [Galatians 3:22]. You can gather from what we have discussed in this section what should be thought about human powers and whether free will really possesses any liberty, as the theologians boast, since they consider everything according to their own judgment without reference to Scripture. For what liberty can exist without the Spirit, since the sin in our flesh, a veritable tyrant over us, even troubles men who are overflowing with the Spirit? For what saint has not deplored this servitude, or rather, this captivity? And Paul says in Romans 7 that he sees a law in his members, fighting against him and bringing him into captivity. This law of the members or tyranny of sin is the strength and power of sin, which is born in us. But we will speak below about those who are righteous because of the Spirit but sinners because of the flesh.

From the foregoing it also follows that the demands of the Law are impossible, as we will discuss more thoroughly below. What we cited above from Romans 8, that the flesh cannot be subject to the Law of God, is clear enough. So also is the passage in the same chapter, which says that "it was impossible for the law" to justify,[24] that is, it was not enough for the Law to show us what we should do, but the Spirit also had to be given through Christ to kindle in us a love for the Law. And here collapses that godless and inane opinion of moral philosophy and free will maintained by the theologians, which the loudmouthed Scotists constantly stress, that the will can conform itself to every command of right reason, that is, that the will can will whatever right reason and the right counsel of the intellect command.[25] In opposition to this opinion, Paul says that it was impossible for the Law to justify. That is, because the flesh is weak and opposed to the Law, it was not enough for the Law to prescribe what we should do. But here they have launched a counterargument based on the fabrication of a new will that can elicit acts no matter the

---

[24] Romans 8:7; cf. v. 3.

[25] Although Scotus was a voluntarist (that is, he believed that the will is superior to the intellect), he and the school that followed him (the Scotists) were insistent that the will needed to consult the intellect and right reason in order to make the appropriate decisions (e.g., *Quodlibet* q. 18).

direction the affection draws it. But if they had observed the expression and usage of Scripture, they would have easily seen that their fabrications about elicited acts are the lies and idle thoughts of the intellect. For our bodily members can sometimes be forced in a direction different from the affection's attraction, but when this happens it is a simulated and deceitful action.

Though I will shortly give a full explanation of the Law's power, as long as I am on the topic I cannot restrain myself from showing the Christian reader the fatuous, absurd, and godless contrivances of the sophists with which they prove that we can love God by means of our natural powers. For they blather that since a lesser good can be loved, namely, a creature, therefore a greater good can be loved.[26] Is this, then, the way Christians express things, seasoned with salt according to Paul's wishes?[27] No, this is a laughable way of speaking, purely Aristotelian and worthy of Aristotelian theologians. First of all, it is the nature of love that we love nothing except what seems good, pleasant, and advantageous to us, so that we love everything with an eye to our own advantage. You love wealth and money not because it is a good thing in itself, but because it seems to be of service to your life's enjoyment. So no matter how good God is, you do not love him unless you think that he is useful to you and your plans. Consequently, if you loved God in this way—with an eye to your own advantage—you would be affecting a servile love, and in your perverse and corrupt natural affection you would clearly be sinning. But never do you love even to this extent. For we never sense the benefits of God unless our heart has already been purified through the Holy Spirit and God's kindness has been imprinted on a pure and pious heart.

Moreover, what happens when your conscience displays an angry God to you, threatening you with everlasting death and with that terrifying hour of his countenance as David recounts?[28] When plagued by experience not of good things but only of evil, of

---

[26] So Gabriel Biel, whose thought was greatly influenced by Scotus, contends: "Man ascends from a knowledge and love of himself to knowledge and love of God. Now since man naturally loves himself with the love of friendship, he also loves everything that is good for him with the love of desire, and so he loves God, who is his highest good" (*In sent.* III, d. 26, q. unica, art. 3, d. 2).

[27] See Colossians 4:6.

[28] See Psalm 139:7–12.

punishments inflicted by God, tell me, can human nature look to God with love and happily bear even the punishment of hell? But when the conscience has terrified the mind, there arises such opposition to and terror of God that he is viewed as an executioner, cruel, vengeful, and, what is most terrible, unjust. Tell me, you sophists, what will those elicited acts of yours or your fictitious "noble will" accomplish in this situation? Or will that day of wrath and fire not declare that those righteous works of man's free will are nothing but a lie and a facade, and that all glory of the flesh is like the glory of the grass? Was not Israel terrified of the fire and smoke, no, even the face of Moses itself, when the Law was given? Was the earth not moved and made to quake and the foundations of the mountains shaken and moved when God became angry with them? But I hope to speak a good deal about this matter later when the power of the Law is under discussion.

First of all, then, the reader should understand that we love nothing except what is advantageous to us. But God wants to be loved freely, not in view of what is advantageous. After all, he who loves advantage loves himself, not God. And how many times and in how many places do the Scriptures warn against this corrupt love. But we must address another piece of sophistry, not so dissimilar to the first. It should not be considered absurd, they maintain, to teach that even without the Holy Spirit we can love God more fervently than we love ourselves, since after all we often lay down our lives for perishable things, for people, for loved ones, for children, and for wives.[29] In responding to this we must take into account our affections. First of all, no one is happy to die by nature. Even those who put their lives at risk for their country or family would themselves obviously prefer to live. So Curtius would have preferred to live.[30] Lucretia would have

---

[29] See p. 50, n. 26. Gabriel Biel goes so far as to say that the free will "could elicit the act of loving God above all things of its own natural powers, even if grace were not poured out on it" (*In sent.* II, d. 28, q. 1, d. 1).

[30] Marcus Curtius was a legendary Roman soldier. According to the historian Livy, a large chasm appeared in the middle of the Roman forum, probably due to an earthquake (7.6). The Romans immediately assumed that the gods demanded a sacrifice, and one of their soothsayers recommended that they throw what was most valuable to the Romans into the chasm. Curtius insisted that military valor was Rome's most valuable asset and rode on a horse into the chasm. The Romans threw offerings in after him.

preferred to live.[31] But because our human nature so disdains adversity, we prefer not to exist rather than to have a miserable existence. For example, we would rather die than freeze. Pyramus would have preferred to live, but because he judged that life without Thisbe would be unhappy for him, he wanted to end his misery and get rid of it, as it were, along with his own life.[32] Saul would have preferred to live but committed suicide because of anger, desperation, and fear of dishonor, as if to put an end to all adversities at the same time as his life. But why am I attempting to give such an exact account of the affections when rare deaths such as those of Lucretia, Saul, and the like are marvelous examples of divine majesty?[33]

Now the sophists have promoted a doctrine of congruent merit, maintaining that we merit grace by moral works, that is, by working in congruence (to use their language) with the powers of human nature.[34] You yourself, reader, should understand that this teaching is

---

[31] According to legend, Lucretia was raped by the son of the Roman tyrant Tarquin the Proud. Having been so disgraced, she called her father and husband to her side and told them what had happened. After securing their promise that they would avenge her, she took her own life (Livy, 1.57–58). These events led to the overthrow of the last king of Rome and to the establishment of the Roman Republic (509 BC).

[32] Pyramus and Thisbe are the archetypes for Shakespeare's Romeo and Juliet. Their families despised each other and would not allow them to marry. When they arranged to meet, Pyramus saw Thisbe's veil torn apart by a lion and assumed that she had been killed. He therefore fell on his own sword. Thisbe then found Pyramus dead and killed herself (Ovid *Metamorphoses* 4.55–166).

[33] Melanchthon again proves the incapacity of man to make any progress toward spiritual righteousness by (1) experiential and biblical anecdotes dealing with human affections and (2) the doctrine of divine predestination. See pp. 26–36 above.

[34] According to Aquinas, the merit of congruence (*de congruo*) is measured according to the capacity of the human will, "for it seems congruous that God should reward the man who works according to his ability" (*Summa* I–II q. 114, art. 3). The merit of condignity (*de condigno*), on the other hand, is measured according to God's promise to reward those who do good in Christ and so "the value of the work depends on the dignity of the grace" (*Summa* I–II q. 114, art. 3). The nominalists stressed that congruent merit could be earned by the one who does what is in himself (*facere quod in se est*), who would thus be rewarded by God's mercy with first grace. According to Gabriel Biel: "The soul, by the removal of its hindrance and by a good movement toward God elicited by the free will, can merit first grace *de congruo*. . . . God accepts the act of the one who does what is in himself in order to grant him first grace" (*In sent.* II, dist. 27, q. unic., concl. 4). John Eck also insisted on the ability of the free will to merit grace by doing what is in oneself: "By doing what is in himself a man prepares himself *de congruo* for grace. . . . Man therefore has the ability to

an immeasurable blasphemy and insult to the grace of God. Indeed, since outside of the inspiration of the Holy Spirit the powers of human nature can do nothing but sin, what will we merit by our endeavors except wrath? Those elicited acts are facades and lies, and those misnamed "good" intentions prescribed by the sophists are false pretexts. Nothing is so opposed to grace as those pharisaical preparations, so far are we from gaining grace through them. The tireless persistence of Paul in attacking this godlessness can be seen in several places, but especially throughout his Epistle to the Romans, where he does nothing except insist that grace is not grace if it is given in exchange for works. For what place is there for mercy if there is regard for our works? What is the glory of grace (to use Paul's terminology),[35] if it is owed to our works? Paul plainly teaches in Romans 3 that all are under sin's dominion and that those who believe are justified freely. And what about his statement in Romans 9:[31] that Israel by pursuing the Law did not arrive at the righteousness of the Law? He is saying that those who try to keep the Law by the powers of their free will never keep the Law but only simulate it in outward appearance.

In Isaiah 55:[1–3], the prophet Isaiah invites us to Christ as if we were shoppers who could buy without paying: "Come, buy wine and milk without money and without trading. Why do you spend money on what is not bread and your labor on what does not satisfy?" Isaiah is saying that we should not trust our works because they will only frustrate us. He continues, "Come and listen. Eat what is good, and your soul will delight in its fullness. Incline your ear [that is, believe] and your soul will live and I will make an eternal pact with you, the sure mercies of David" (that is, I will promise the mercy that was guaranteed and assured to David). Jeremiah writes, "Cursed is the man who trusts in man, making flesh his strength and removing his heart from the Lord. For he will be like a myrtle tree in the desert and will not see good come his way, but will dwell in drought, in desert, in an uninhabitable and bitter land. Blessed is the man who trusts in the Lord. His confidence will be the Lord, and he will be like a tree that is transplanted over water and that sends its roots to moisture, so that it will not fear when the heat comes," etc. (Jeremiah 17:[5–8]).

---

make it so that he has eternal life through congruent (*de congruo*) merit" (*Chrysopassus* 3.60; cf. *CR* 1:98).

[35] Ephesians 1:6.

You can look up the rest of the passage yourself. In fact, this one chapter of Jeremiah is clear enough proof that moral works are nothing but the simulations and lies of our flesh.

So also, Scholastic theology has invented distinctions concerning the beginning of repentance and attrition.[36] But in reality, human nature is sorry for what it has done only because it loves itself and fears punishment. And this love of self and fear of punishment is obviously sin. Moreover, it is impossible not to hate the one who inflicts the punishment, that is, God. But when we acknowledge our sin and despise it, this is God's special work in us. So Hannah sings in 1 Samuel 2:[6–7], "For the Lord leads down to hell and brings back up; the Lord kills and makes alive; the Lord humbles and uplifts." And the prophet Jeremiah, "After you converted me, I repented" [Jeremiah 31:19]. More passages could be added. But why keep going on about this point when Christ said it so clearly in John 6:[44], "No one comes to me unless my Father draws him." Yet the sophists are ignorant of the tropes and figures used in Holy Scripture, and so they throw the passage from Zechariah in our faces, where the Lord says, "Turn to me and I will turn to you" [Zechariah 1:3]. But this does not mean that the beginning of repentance resides in us. Moreover, Augustine has explained the meaning of this passage in more than one place.[37] Nor is this passage hard to understand, except for the sophists

---

[36] Aquinas defines attrition as "a certain but not a perfect displeasure over sins that have been committed," whereas contrition denotes "perfect displeasure" (*Summa* Suppl. III, q. 1 art. 2). Attrition is motivated not by pure love of God but by fear of God or love of self. Unlike contrition, it cannot take sin away (*Summa* Suppl. III, q. 1 art. 1). The Scholastics usually conceived of attrition as a step toward contrition, which was one part of repentance (see below, pp. 175–80). But according to some Scholastics (e.g., Scotus, Biel), if one approaches the sacrament of penance with attrition, he can receive the grace to turn his attrition into contrition and thus receive forgiveness of sins. Luther in *The Babylonian Captivity of the Church* explains this doctrine: "Even more audacious and wicked are those who have invented a so-called 'attrition,' which is supposed to become contrition by the power of the keys, which they do not understand. This attrition they attribute to the godless and unbelievers, and thus contrition is completely abolished" (WA 6:544; AE 36:84). See also Heiko Oberman, *The Harvest of Medieval Theology: Gabriel Biel and Late Medieval Nominalism* (Cambridge, MA: Harvard University Press, 1963), 146–60.

[37] In accord with the famous prayer in his *Confessions*, "Give what you command and command what you will" (10.29), Augustine explains that the Christian response to God's command, "Turn to me," is to pray with the Psalms, "Turn us, O God" (Psalm 80:3; 85:4). See, e.g., *On Grace and Free Will*, 5.10 (*MPL* 44:887–88); *On the Merits and Forgiveness of Sins*, 2.5.5 (*MPL* 44:153–54).

who have studied nothing but their logical handbook (*parva logicalia*).[38]

God turns to us in two ways, that is, both before and after we repent. God first turns to us when he leads us to repent by the inspiration of the Holy Spirit, when he terrifies us and confounds us by showing us our sin. But he turns to us again after repentance, when he puts a limit and end to our punishment, when he comforts us, and when he openly declares that he is on our side. Zechariah is talking about this second manner of God's turning to us when he says, "Turn to me and I will turn to you," that is, "Repent, and I will put an end to your punishment." For the prophet is exhorting those who had returned to Judea from exile in Assyria to learn from the example of their fathers and to repent, unless they wish to experience God's wrath again and suffer the same punishments as they had previously. Therefore, we cannot conclude from this passage that the beginning of our repentance is in our own hands. It is God who invites and draws us to himself, and after he has drawn us, he removes our punishments from us and declares that he has been appeased and is reconciled to us. And just because he commands us to turn to him does not mean that it is in our power to repent or turn to him. God also commands us to love him above all things. But it does not follow that we have it in our power to do it simply because he commands it. On the contrary, it is precisely because he commands it that it is not in our own power. For he commands the impossible to commend his mercy to us, as we will discuss below when we treat the Law.

Furthermore, why have the sophists not taken notice of the following passage also found in the prophet Zechariah, "And I will convert them, because I will have mercy on them. And they will be as they were before I drove them out" (10:[6]). Note that God himself says that he will convert Judah, and this not because of their good

---

[38] The *Parva logicalia* were tracts written by Peter of Spain (c. 1210–77), a logician and physician usually identified with Pope John XXI (1276–77). Building on Aristotelian logic, the *Parva logicalia* introduced logical categories concentrating especially on the properties of terms (semantics). The work contributed greatly to further Scholasticism after Thomas Aquinas. A large part of medieval university education was devoted to the study of the *Parva logicalia* and countless commentaries were devoted to it. In his *Defense against the Parisian Theologians* (1521), Melanchthon repeatedly mocks the Scholastics for relying on this work instead of Scripture (*SA* 1:141–62). Melanchthon's condemnation of the *Parva logicalia* reflects his humanist roots and echoes, among others, Erasmus.

deeds but because of the mercy he has for them. I commend similar passages to your diligent study, Christian reader. For when you become more familiar with Scripture, you will have no problem dismissing the subtleties of the sophists.

You have here, dear reader, as much as I thought should be said about the power of our inborn corruption. Those who want to be formed by reading and meditating on divine Scriptures instead of human commentaries will need nothing more. But no amount of commenting can satisfy those who think nothing but carnal thoughts, whose minds have been confused by dubious arguments and the various judgments and opinions of men. The Holy Spirit, who expresses himself so intimately and simply in Holy Scripture, is at one and the same time the most simple and reliable teacher. And when your mind has, as it were, been formed according to Scripture, then you will understand the nature of this article perfectly, simply, and precisely, just as you will other points of theology.

Those who depend on men's judgment and assessment instead of the Spirit's do not discern things as they really are but see only fleeting shadows of reality, just like those in Plato's cave.[39] For who of the philosophers and Scholastic theologians has understood the true nature of virtue or vice? The so-called theologians measured original sin by external works alone, and meanwhile failed to see the wickedness of the soul and its inner disease. They should have concentrated on the depravity of certain affections, but reason does not notice all affections, nor does it perceive those affections against which God's Spirit especially wages war: blasphemy, hatred of God, love of self, lack of faith in God, and countless other sins of this kind. These affections are so ingrained in man that they occupy his entire nature and hold it captive. They are not confined to some one part of man, to the sensitive appetite alone, as the Scholastics teach. They call the affections an infirmity, but an infirmity that can be overcome by human powers. Scripture, on the other hand, states that carnal affections cannot be overcome except by the Spirit of God, since only those whom the Son has freed are truly free (John 8:[36]). So their fictions about external works, acts elicited by the will, and similar

---

[39] In Book VII of *The Republic* (ca. 514a–520a), Plato tells an allegory about people who had lived their entire lives in a cave. They were chained and facing a wall. As people walked between a fire and them, they saw the shadows on the cave wall. Since all they knew were these shadows, they came to consider them to be reality.

inventions should not impress you at all. God judges according to the heart, not the external work. For, as we read in 1 Samuel [16:7], God does not see as men see.

Since it was by pursuing philosophy that our so-called theologians came up with their good works and their facade of external works, we can see even here how much damage philosophy has inflicted on Christianity. Yet that single parable about the foolish virgins in the Gospel is sufficient to show how good works merit nothing [Matthew 25:1–13]. For the virgins represent nothing but pharisaical righteousness, that is, the shadows of external works. Yet what else do the philosophers teach when they discuss virtues besides external works? Do they not restrict everything to external works and their fictitious elicited acts? But they are "blind and leaders of the blind" [Matthew 15:14]. And so our hope must be that God turn our minds from the judgment of human reason and philosophy to a spiritual judgment. For such is the blindness of human reason that we cannot understand the full nature of sin and righteousness without the light of the Spirit. All the capabilities of human reason are but darkness. The Spirit of Christ is light. He alone teaches all truth. Flesh, or human reason, cannot fix its eyes on the shining face of Moses, and so it puts a veil over the Law and judges only concerning external works or so-called "propositions" or "intentions," which the Scholastics simply made up.[40] That is, to use Paul's terminology, they judge according to the letter, "but the Spirit searches and penetrates the deepest parts" [1 Corinthians 2:10].

Now to give a summary of what I have written about original sin, I will add some theses as an inventory (ἔλεγχον) of the preceding discussion.

1. Sin is a desire (*affectus*) against the Law of God.

2. Since we are born children of wrath, we are also born without the Spirit of God.

3. Since the Spirit of God is not in man, he understands, loves, and seeks nothing but the things of the flesh.

4. Therefore, there is in man contempt for and ignorance of God, along with all the vices that Psalm 14 describes, "The fool has said in his heart, 'There is no God' " [v. 1].

---

[40] Intentions, as defined by the Scholastics, are acts by which the mind tends toward its intellectual objects, whether that object be real or primal (primary intention) or a mental abstraction or *ens rationis* (secondary intention).

5. So it is that man by his own natural powers can do nothing but sin.

6. For it is not merely a part of man, the so-called sensitive appetite, that is subject to sinful affections.

7. Since Scripture testifies that the human heart is unclean, it follows that all human powers are impure.

8. For the heart signifies not merely the sensitive appetite, as the Scholastics call it, but the seat of all affections, including love, hatred, blasphemy, and unbelief.

9. Just as the heart signifies the seat of all human affections, so also flesh designates all the natural powers of man.

10. Everything that is done through the powers of nature belongs to the flesh. Whether the constancy of Socrates or the self-control of Zeno, they are nothing but carnal affections.

11. In one place in 1 Corinthians, Paul called the work of reason "natural," (ψυχικὸν) and this includes the philosophical virtues.[41]

12. And in the same place, what is "natural" (τὸ ψυχικόν) is openly condemned as sin.

13. Elsewhere he sometimes designates with the word "flesh" everything that is worked in us outside of the Holy Spirit's work, no matter how good it may appear outwardly. This is obviously the meaning of the word in Romans 8:[3], where Paul says that the righteousness of the Law could not be fulfilled by the flesh. Who does not recognize that here the term "flesh" designates the best powers of man, the powers that seem according to men's judgment to have the ability to obey the Law? The third chapter of 2 Corinthians teaches the same thing.

14. I wanted to point this out, so that the Scholastics do not trick anyone when they distinguish between an intellectual and sensitive appetite, and then attribute corrupt affections to the senses but free the intellectual appetite from vice.[42]

15. Those passages of Scripture that I cited above sufficiently refute this opinion of the Scholastics. Nor can they run to Origen, pretending that his talk about the soul, the flesh, and the spirit

---

[41] 1 Corinthians 2:14.

[42] See, e.g., Aquinas *Summa* I, q. 80, art. 2.

supports them.[43] What do we care what Origen thinks anyway? We are discussing the judgment of Scripture, not of Origen.

16. The Scholastics deny that every work of man is a sin because they have fixed their eyes only on external works and so stare upon the veiled face of Moses. They were not judging concerning the affections. But God judges hearts and affections.

17. This is also why they invented the concept of free will. For they recognized that there is sometimes some freedom in external works. Thus the flesh judges concerning external works. The Spirit, on the other hand, teaches that all things happen necessarily according to predestination.

18. Experience teaches that there is no freedom in the affections.

19. When once everything in the Scriptures began to be restricted to external works, all Scripture was obscured, and lost was the understanding of what sin is, what grace is, what the Law is, what the Gospel is, what Moses is, and what Christ is. And this darkness, worse than that imposed on Egypt,[44] we owe to the godless and cursed philosophy of the Scholastic pseudo-theologians.

20. It will become obvious that reason does not understand this inborn impurity, corruption, and wickedness of the heart that we call original sin and that all saints deplore, when the Law is revealed, that is, when God opens the eyes of your conscience, as we will explain below when we discuss the Law.

While we are treating this topic, we should also discuss the fruits of sin, that is, the different kinds of vices. This is what the apostle does when he recounts the fruits of the flesh in Galatians [5:19–21]. But everyone will recognize these fruits by himself. It is enough for

---

[43] The minority opinion in theological anthropology, held by early Platonists such as Clement of Alexandria and Origen, is that man consists of three parts: body, soul, and spirit. Though no major Scholastics held to this opinion, favoring instead the dualist partition of man into body and soul, the humanist Erasmus gravitated toward the Platonist Origen and adopted his tripartite view of man. In his *Diatribe on Free Will* of 1524, Erasmus does run to this tripartite scheme to prove that good affections exist in man outside of the Holy Spirit: "Yet not every affection of man is flesh, but there is the affection which is called soul, which is called spirit. By this affection we progress to honorable things. And they call this part of the soul 'reason' or ἡγεμονικόν, that is, principal. Unless, perchance, there was no progression toward honorable things in the philosophers, who taught that death should be sought a thousand times before baseness should be committed . . ." (*AS* 4:126).

[44] Cf. Exodus 10:21–23.

the Christian to know that all the works of nature, all the affections and endeavors of human powers, are sins. If we consider the different kinds of vices from the different kinds of affections, as we should, no one could number all his affections. Besides, those who have judged the types of virtues and vices from the external appearance of works have too often handed down vices for virtues and virtues for vices. Therefore, we will leave the judgment of these things to each individual's own spirit.

LAW

Since the Law is called the knowledge of sin [Romans 3:20; 7:7], the topic on laws will explain the power and nature of sin much more clearly. So if the preceding section seemed to be lacking anything, the following topic should make up for it. But we are not trying to collect everything that can be said about every possible chief point. We are merely making a catalogue of the most common topics so that you can see the foundation on which a summary of Christian doctrine rests and so that you can understand what you should especially have in view when interpreting Scripture. And I want you to learn these topics not from my commentary but from Scripture, so that I function not as a teacher but as a prompter. For believe me, it makes a big difference whether you seek the material for things of such import from the sources or from the ponds. The waters are not only sweeter when they are drawn from the source, as the poet has said, but also purer.[1] How much more certain are the precepts of the Scriptures than what is gleaned from the commentaries!

Now the Law is the judgment that demands good and forbids evil. "Right" is the authority to act according to the Law. The ancients have said much both in favor of laws and against laws, and before long we will show from what source their judgments have sprung. Some laws are natural, some divine, and some human.

[NATURAL LAW]

I have not yet seen anything of merit written about natural laws, neither by the theologians nor by the lawyers. For since they are called "natural," the principles that govern them should be collected by way of human reason through natural syllogism. But I have not yet seen anyone do this, nor do I know whether this can even be done given that human reason is so bound and blind. But Paul does teach that there is a law of nature in us. He does so with a marvelously elegant and well-argued enthymeme in Romans 2, reasoning in the

---

[1] See Ovid, *Letters from Pontus*, 3.5: "For although water that is brought to us tastes sweet, the waters that are drunk from the source itself are more pleasing."

following way: the gentiles have a conscience that either defends or accuses their actions. It is therefore a law. For what else is the conscience except a judgment over our actions that is derived from some law or common principle? And so natural law is a judgment common to all and suited to the formation of morals. To it, all men assent together. Thus God has engraved it upon everyone's mind. For as there are in the theoretical disciplines, like mathematics, certain common principles or κοιναὶ ἔννοιαι ἢ προλήψεις[2] (such as that the whole is greater than the parts), so are there in ethics certain common principles and a priori conclusions (for the sake of instruction, we need to use their terms), which serve as rules over all human actions. These you should properly call natural laws.

Marcus Cicero, in his books *On Laws*, copies Plato and derives the foundations of laws from human nature.[3] And although I do not condemn this reasoning, I see it as more urbane than precise. Moreover, there are very many godless notions in Cicero's argument, as is generally the case when we follow the methods and devices of our reason rather than the precepts of Holy Scripture. For judgment based on human comprehension is generally deceptive because of our inborn blindness. As a result, although a certain moral blueprint has been engraved upon our minds, we still can hardly grasp it. And when I say that God has imprinted the laws of nature on human minds, I mean that the understanding of these laws is a certain concreated condition[4] (to use their language). This knowledge is not a discovery made by our genius. Rather, it is a standard that God has placed in us for judging what is moral. I am not concerned to make this agree with Aristotle's philosophy.[5] For what do I care what that wrangler thought?

---

[2] "Common understandings or preconceptions."

[3] Cicero, *De legibus*, 1.15–18, esp. 18: "The law is the height of reason, which is inborn in our nature and which commands what should be done and forbids the opposite."

[4] Latin: *habitus*. Thomas Aquinas allows that natural law is a *habitus* only in the sense that the human condition possesses and (to a certain degree) understands natural law. Natural law itself, of course, cannot be a *habitus* since it is not the means by which we act but the object of our action (*Summa* II, q. 94, art. 1).

[5] This is just as much a slight against Aquinas and the Scholastic tradition as it is an indictment of Aristotle. Aquinas used (or misused) Aristotle to formulate an extensive treatment of natural law (*Summa* I–II, qq. 90–108, esp. 94). Other Scholastics followed suit.

But I will pass over what we have in common with the animals, such as the birth and care of life and procreation. These things the lawyers classify under the law of nature, but I identify them as natural affections inborn in all living creatures. But the following seem to be the foundations of the laws that properly pertain to man.[6]

I. God must be worshiped.

II. Because we are born into a certain society in life, nobody should be harmed.

III. Human society requires that we possess all things in common.[7]

We have taken the first law about worshiping God from Romans 1, where Paul unmistakably counts it among natural laws. For he says that God has declared his majesty to all men by the creation and governance of the whole universe [Romans 1:19–20]. But arguing how God's existence can be deduced with a human syllogism is characteristic more of curiosity than piety, especially since it is not safe for human reason to blather about such things, as I warned at the beginning of this compendium.[8]

The second law, which warns against harming anyone, is unmistakably derived from common necessity, since we are all born connected with one another and obligated to each other, as Scripture indicates when it says that it is not appropriate for a man to live alone, but that help must be given to him for the betterment of his life [Genesis 2:18]. And so this law commands us not to harm anyone,

---

[6] In *The Chief Points* of 1520, the precursor to this first edition of the *Loci*, Melanchthon lists 9 common principles: (1) God must be worshiped. (2) Life must be protected and propagated. (3) Life must be born. (4) Marriages must take place. (5) Offspring must be preserved. (6) Nobody should be harmed. (7) Property and income should be enjoyed in common. (8) To preserve life, things need to be bought and sold. (9) To preserve the life of the general populous, evil people must be detained and restrained (*CR* 21:25).

[7] The concept of an ideal utopian society in which everyone shared everything was popular among the humanists of northern Europe and was influenced by their study of the classics and in particular by their adoration of Plato and his works, especially the *Republic*. So Thomas More wrote his *Utopia* in 1516, and Erasmus dreamed of a paradise built on ethical reform (cf. *Adages* I.i.1, *AS* 7:358–62). Melanchthon's understanding of sin and human nature, however, requires him to acknowledge that this natural law is not absolute and must give way to a capitalistic exchange of goods (see p. 65, n. 11).

[8] This is another swipe against Aquinas, whose five proofs for the existence of God rely on the syllogistic argumentation of human reason (*Summa* I, q. 2, art. 3).

that is, that we should all eagerly love each other so that by zealously doing our duty all may experience our kindness. Therefore, this law embraces the divine laws that we not kill anyone, steal others' property, and the like.

Perhaps you will ask: "Why then do magistrates kill criminals?" My response is that after the fall of Adam imprinted the mark of sin on us all, it is the condition of human affairs that evil people often harm good people. And so the human race very often must depend on the protection of the law against harming others. Therefore, those who disturb the public peace and hurt innocent people must be coerced, restrained, and removed from the public so that by their removal more people can be protected. The law remains: harm no one. But if someone has been harmed already, the one who did the harming has to be removed so that more people are not harmed. It is more important to preserve the entire population than one individual or another. Therefore, he is removed who threatens harm to the entire population by the commission of one crime or another that shows his harmfulness. For this reason the state has magistrates, punishes criminals, and wages wars, all of which the lawyers assign to the right of nations.

The third law, which concerns sharing things, evidently arises from the nature of society among the human race. For if among a few friends the common adage should be valid, τὰ τῶν φίλων κοινὰ, that is, that all things should be shared among friends, why should the same proverb not be valid among all men?[9] For all people should be in harmony with one another, just as brothers are in harmony with brothers, children with parents, and parents with children. The law against harming others demands this.

But because human greed does not permit us to enjoy all things in common, this law must be governed by a higher law, namely, the law against harming others. Things should be held in common only insofar as public peace and the safety of the populace allow. For, generally speaking, lower laws must be governed by higher laws and public sharing has to be kept within certain bounds. Therefore, the third law needs to be replaced with another law, namely, that property should be divided, seeing that the common safety of the people

---

[9]Cf. Erasmus *Adages* I.i.1, who begins his work with this same adage: τὰ τῶν φίλων κοινὰ.

demands it. Further, because it is the condition of human affairs that we at least need to share some things since by nature things should be held in common, it has been decided that they be shared in their use, namely, by contracts, purchases, sales, renting, leasing, etc. Plato recognized this when he said in the fifth book of his *Laws* that a state was best governed which approximated this common adage as closely as possible: all things are common among friends.[10] In this state not only would things be held in common among citizens, but also everyone's own members, eyes, hands, feet, and mouth would serve the public good. Nor could we ask for a better example of a well-governed state than that in which this dictum could be observed: τὰ φίλων κοινά. Therefore, contracts have been invented through which one may share his possessions with many others, so that there can be at least some sharing of things.[11]

So much concerning the general outline of natural laws, which you can summarize in the following way:

I. Worship God.

II. Since we are born into a common society in life, harm no one but be helpful and kind to everyone.

III. If it cannot happen that absolutely no one is harmed, then it should be so arranged that the fewest are harmed. Those should be removed who disturb public tranquility, and for this reason magistracies and punishments should be instituted to deal with criminals.

IV. Property must be divided for the sake of public peace. But let some alleviate the lack of others through contracts.

Whoever wishes may add the individual opinions of the poets, orators, and historians that are usually applied to the law of nations (*ius gentium*), such as are read here and there concerning marriage and adultery, gratitude and ingratitude, hospitality, the exchange of property, and other matters of this kind. But to me it seemed sufficient to note the most common examples. Moreover, we should not rashly regard any opinions of pagan writers as if they were laws,

---

[10] *Laws* 739b–c; Erasmus cites and comments on the same passage in *Adages* I.i.1.

[11] While Melanchthon agrees with other humanists that all things should be held in common, he rejects the humanist anthropology of Erasmus that would hope for the actual practice of communism. Since men are sinners, it is impossible to share all things in common except in their use, that is, through private ownership and exchange of goods.

for too many popular opinions reflect the corrupt affections of our nature rather than genuine laws. Take, for example, this passage from Hesiod, "Love the one who loves you and approach the one who approaches you. We give to the one who gives to us, and do not give to the one who does not give to us."[12] In these verses, Hesiod measures friendship according to utility alone. That popular expression, "Give and take," does the same thing.[13] Related to this opinion is the sentiment that force should be fought off with force, as Euripides' *Ion* illustrates, "It is good for those who are doing well to honor piety. But when someone wishes to harm his enemies, no law stands in his way."[14]

Also in civil law, as they call it, there are many things that reflect human affections instead of natural laws. For what is more foreign to the law of nature than slavery? And in some contracts the details that matter most are unjustly concealed. But more on this elsewhere. A good man will fashion civil constitutions according to a just and good rule, that is, with both divine and natural laws. And whatever is instituted against these laws can be nothing but unjust. So much for the laws of nature, but I invite you, if you can, to organize them with more precision and refinement.

DIVINE LAWS

Divine laws are those laws that God has decreed through the canonical Scriptures. They have been arranged under three categories: some are moral, some judicial, and some ceremonial.[15] Moral laws are those laws that have been commanded in the Decalogue. The student should refer all the moral laws that are taught in the whole of Scripture to these laws contained in the Decalogue. For how many times is the same law repeated in the Scriptures? But right now we have to make sure that we do not explain the Decalogue as if it concerned external works alone and then divide it into counsels and

---

[12] Hesiod, *Works and Days*, 353–54.

[13] Greek: δός τι καὶ λάβε τι. Cf. Erasmus, who deals with the same proverb and points out that Aristotle finds fault with friendship based purely on utility or pleasure (*Adages* II.viii.8; cf. *Nicomachean Ethics*, 1156a–b).

[14] Euripides *Ion* 1045–47.

[15] This was a widely recognized division, also made by the Scholastics. Cf. Aquinas *Summa* I–II, qq. 100–105.

commandments like the Scholastics.[16] Therefore, I will run through the types of laws briefly.

The first three commandments are these: "You shall have no other gods," "You shall not take the name of your God in vain," and "Remember to sanctify the Sabbath day." It is obvious that Christ was explaining these commandments when he gave this Law: "You shall love the Lord your God with all your heart and with all your soul and with all your mind" [Mark 12:30]. But the distinction between these three laws seems to be as follows. Although all three pertain to the same thing, namely, to the true worship of God, the first, "You shall have no other gods," properly refers to the affections. It forbids us to love or fear anything besides God or to trust in our wealth, virtue, intelligence, righteousness, or any other creature whatever, but commands us to trust only in the goodness of God. Yet these affections are not in our power. In fact, they are so far removed from us that no one but the most spiritual can understand what trust, fear, and love of God are. To this Law pertain the many things written in the prophets about fearing God, trusting in God, and the like. Moreover, it is amazing how the words of this Law commend both faith and fear to us. For when God says, "I, the Lord your God, am steadfastly jealous, visiting the iniquity of the fathers upon the children," etc. [Exodus 20:5], he terrifies with his threats and declares that the power of his anger must be feared. But when he adds that he has mercy on thousands of those who love him [Exodus 20:6], he is clearly offering his goodness and commanding that we love him, trust in his goodness, etc. But much greater things are commanded than I can explain with human words.

---

[16] The common Scholastic distinction between evangelical counsels and commandments was already well established when Lombard wrote his *Sentences* (III, dist. 36, ch. 3). Aquinas gives a detailed definition: "This is the distinction between counsel and commandment, that the commandment entails necessity, while the counsel is left to the choice of the one to whom it is given. Therefore in the new law, which is the law of liberty, counsels have been added over and above the commandments, but this is not the case with the old law, which was the law of slavery. Therefore, it should be understood that the commandments of the new law have been given concerning those things that are necessary for obtaining the goal of eternal bliss, into which the new law brings them immediately. But counsels should be understood as governing those things through which a person can better and more easily obtain the goal just mentioned" (*Summa* I–II, q. 108, art. 4).

The Scholastics taught that love of God was the same as willing his existence, wanting him to listen, not envying him his kingdom, and many things of this kind. They taught these things with words so obscure that not even the students in their schools could understand them. For it cannot be known what it means to love God unless the Spirit teaches it, that is, unless you are animated by the Spirit and so experience this very love. This is the work of the First Commandment: to trust in God, to love and fear God. This is the worship concerning which Christ says, "The true worshipers will worship the Father in Spirit and truth" [John 4:23]. Appropriate outer worship will naturally follow such affection as this.

The Second Commandment forbids us to use the name of God carelessly. It clearly teaches that when we use God's name we should bear witness to our faith in God as well as to our fear and love of God. And just as the First Commandment is positive, commanding faith and love, so also is this commandment positive. For it commands us to celebrate the name and glory of God, to call on the name of God, to flee for refuge to the name of God as to a well-fortified sanctuary. "Let us swear by the name of God" (Deuteronomy 6:[13]). And as David encourages us, "Let us sing psalms to his name" [Psalm 68:4]. We should confess with Solomon, "The name of the Lord is a well-fortified tower" [Proverbs 18:10]. We should praise and celebrate God's kindness toward us, we should give thanks to him, and as the apostle says, we should do absolutely everything to the praise of the Lord [Colossians 3:23]. You see that the Second Commandment flows from the First.

The Third Commandment commands us to sanctify the Sabbath Day and so rest from all our work. Accordingly, it commands us to bear and endure the work of God, which is our mortification. The First Commandment demands faith, the Second demands praise of God's name, the Third demands submission to the work of God in us. Those who preach moral works and the power of the free will violate this commandment in particular. For it demands that the free will be put to death. Since the people of the New Testament hold a perpetual Sabbath, their flesh is continually put to death and their spirit made alive. Those champions of free will are ignorant both of the Sabbath and of Christianity. They are enemies of the cross of Christ, who attempt to justify themselves by their own works and endeavors. Thus they follow the example of the man who collected wood on the Sabbath (Numbers 15:[32–36]).

You see then that the three commandments—that we should trust in God, praise God, and submit to his work in us—are all included in this sentence: "Love God with all your heart," etc. For anyone who loves in this way clearly also trusts, fears, praises, and submits with great eagerness. I have not undertaken to give a full explanation of the Law, since that would be impossible in a compendium. But I wanted to make you aware of these things so that you would know that they err who think that nothing is commanded of us beyond human capabilities. If anyone would like a broader explanation of the commandments, he should above all consult Luther's little German book *On Good Works*.[17]

When it comes to this topic, the sophists err in two different ways. First, they suppose that the highest love of God is not required or commanded in this life.[18] And they think the same thing about the other affections. But again, the following text is a clear and sufficient refutation of their opinion: "You should love the Lord your God with all your heart, with all your soul, and with all your mind" [Mark 12:30]. Now if God requires our whole heart for himself, he never allows a part of it to be directed to the creature. If only some Elijah would arise and teach these men what a pathetic error it is to think that a part of the heart must be given to the creature and a part to God![19] This commandment cannot be kept as long as we are in the flesh, but it is not therefore void. Rather, we are all guilty as long as we do not pay what we owe. And this is what we already said—all

---

[17] WA 6:196–276; AE 44:21–114. Melanchthon was very fond of this work, writing to his friend John Hess in 1520, "I'm also sending along an excellent little work by Martin on faith and good works, which you will enjoy reading, as you do all his works" (*CR* 1:201). Melanchthon takes much of his treatment of the commandments up to this point from this tract written by Luther in 1520.

[18] Aquinas makes a threefold distinction concerning man's obligation and ability to love God completely, maintaining that if "completely" refers to God, it is true that God should be loved completely, and likewise if "completely" refers to man, then man should love God with his whole heart, mind, etc. But if "completely" refers to the relationship between God and man, that is, to the actual love itself, it is impossible for man, a finite creature, to love the infinite God completely, and such love is not expected of him (*Summa* I–II, q. 27, dist. 5; cf. q. 184, dist. 2).

[19] Melanchthon had already been calling Luther "our Elijah" for some time (cf. *CR* 1:451, 453–54).

men really are constant sinners and constantly sinning. When we discuss grace below, we will need to examine again to what extent we are justified and to what extent we are sinners.[20]

Then again, the sophists are dreaming when they suppose that we can fulfill these and the other commandments by our own powers. They think that the commandments are dealing only with external works, as if we are being commanded not to worship other gods or idols with external ceremonies and rites and such. But the very words of the Law require us to explain the Law as governing our affections: "You should love the Lord your God with all your heart." Now the flesh loves itself above all and trusts in its own good works, wisdom, and righteousness. For this is what the apostle says in Romans 8, that the flesh seeks its own advantage and cannot be subject to the Law of God. Therefore, it cannot love God, trust in God's goodness, etc. To love God is a great and incomprehensible thing. For love of God entails embracing his will in all things with a happy and grateful heart, even when he condemns and kills. And so, sophist, I ask you whether nature can will hell and eternal punishment.[21] But if you admit that it cannot, admit also that the flesh cannot willingly love God.

Christ explains the rest of the commandments, those called the Second Table, in this way: "You should love your neighbor as yourself" [Matthew 22:39]. He explains them more extensively with his long sermon in Matthew 5. And the apostle lists the almost countless laws of love in Romans 12. But the sophists have also explained these laws as if they concerned only external works, as if the Law were satisfied if you refrain from the act of murder, from openly committing adultery, etc. In contrast, Christ explains the Law as governing the affections and this with definite examples. In regard to the law "You shall not murder," he commands that we be helpful, honest, generous, and ready to do our duty to anyone who may need it, that we should not repay evil with evil, that we should not go to court for our possessions, and in short, that we should not resist evil but love even our enemies happily and purely. So also, with the law "You shall not commit adultery," they think that it has been satisfied

---

[20] A variation of Luther's famous *simul iustus et peccator* ("at the same time righteous and sinner"), first articulated in his commentary on Galatians of 1519 (WA 2:497; AE 27:231).

[21] See p. 47, n. 23.

if we do not shamefully engage in the external action. But when Christ explains it, he teaches that God demands chastity and purity of heart so that we may not even have base desires. The diligent reader will examine the other commandments in the Gospel by himself.

COUNSELS

The sophists commit a horribly godless error when they make "counsels" out of Divine Law. They teach that God does not command certain things as a necessity but merely urges us to do them, so that if anyone wants to obey them, he may. But they free whoever does not obey these counsels from any danger. Moreover, they generally include among these counsels those commandments that are found in Matthew 5, namely, loving your enemies, not resisting misfortune, shunning lawsuits and courtroom contentions, helping those who harm you, forgiving, lending to anyone who has need with no hope of return. We say that all these things are required, and we number them among the commandments. For Christ openly condemns those who love nobody but their friends, equating them with Gentiles and publicans. So also he threatens blame and judgment on anyone who gets angry with his neighbor or shows contempt for him by saying, "Racha" [Matthew 5:22]. But if he were merely giving us advice not to get angry, why did he threaten judgment? If we are free either to get angry or not to get angry against someone who does us wrong, why does he warn of punishments? If someone warns of punishments, he is not advising; he is requiring. Besides, since it is a commandment to love your neighbor, does love not embrace all that they count among the counsels? And in Romans 13:[8–10], Paul refers all these things to the Law: "You should love your neighbor as yourself." And 1 John 3:[18], "Little children, do not love in word or in tongue, but in deed and in truth," that is, love from the heart and purely, and bear witness to your love with zealous and dutiful actions. Now if they count among the laws the dictum, "You shall not covet," etc. (*non concupisces*),[22] why do they not categorize as laws all that this commandment embraces? Or is it not a work of concupiscence to be angry with an enemy, to seek vengeance, or to be unwilling to risk

---

[22] In line with Augustine and drawing from Romans 7, Melanchthon includes all sinful desire under the word *concupiscere*. The commandment "You shall not covet" means, "You shall not be concupiscent," and so forbids any sinful desire.

money on the poor? They should confess, then, that these are required, since we are clearly forbidden to covet anything.

In fact, as long as they are annulling a part of the Law, why do they not interpret the entire Law as a counsel? But you will say, "My personal property is in jeopardy if I have to give charity indiscriminately." I answer that this is your excuse for greed, arising from the wisdom of the flesh. For it will be easy for the Spirit to judge how much should be given, and a spiritual man will suffer lack willingly if by so doing he allays the need of his brother. Or do you not know that you owe to your brother what you want done to yourself? "But won't we be exposed to harm from everyone if we cannot defend ourselves?" Yes. And this is the life of the cross, that you be exposed to harm. "Won't evil men take our possessions if we can't take them to court?" The magistrate will be there to make sure no citizen harms another. It is your job to bear this kind of situation with grace. But why am I trying to refute the arguments of carnal wisdom, when it is impossible for anyone but the spiritual to approve of God's Law? You will not understand what Christ commands or why he commands it unless you want to do what he commands.

Carnal subtleties of this kind have also infected the sophists. To them it did not seem humane that everyone should share everyone else's possessions with the result that nobody could lay claim to his own property. It was also considered barbarous for the lazy to enjoy leisure and benefit from the wealth of others in security. And so the commandments were changed into counsels, and the most destructive idea, that states cannot be governed according to the Gospel, has become common. As if Christ had taught something that pertains only to insignificant little monks and not rather to the entire human race! Now what could be more universal than the Gospel, which Christ commanded to be preached to the whole world? Moreover, in his epistle to Marcellinus, which is the fifth of the Augustinian epistles, Augustine also refutes this kind of carnal slander against the law forbidding vengeance.[23] But he does not prohibit magistrates from punishing crimes. Rather, these bear the sword for the purpose of terrifying evildoers, as the apostle says (Romans 13). And yet he does forbid us to return like for like in our private lives and in our desire

---

[23] *Ep.* 138.9–15. In medieval publications, a set of five letters written from or to Marcellinus was regularly placed at the beginning of the volumes of Augustine's epistles.

for vengeance. The magistrate is there to make sure the state suffers no harm. It is your job to endure and ignore private injuries. But perhaps this point will be discussed more thoroughly below.[24]

But there *is* a counsel found in the Gospels, and this is the only one as far as I know—celibacy. Concerning it, Christ says, "Whoever can receive it, let him receive it" (Matthew 19:[12]). And in his First Letter to the Corinthians, Paul says, "Concerning virgins, I do not have a commandment from the Lord, but I do give counsel, as one who has obtained mercy from the Lord so that I might be faithful. Therefore, I think that this is good because of the present necessity, that it is good for a man to be as he is. Are you bound to a wife? Do not seek to be loosed. Are you loosed from a wife? Do not seek a wife," etc. (7:[25–27]). But is it not because of celibacy that you argue about whether counsels are superior to commandments? These are the absurdities of the Scholastics, who do not understand what a commandment is or what a counsel is. For no matter how celibate a man is, he cannot fulfill the law against adultery since it cannot happen that concupiscence does not inflame him, no matter how chaste he is. But concupiscence is forbidden by the commandment. It can happen sometimes that married men are closer to keeping this commandment than virgins.

MONASTIC VOWS

But what about monastic vows? First of all, as concerns the very nature of a vow, Scripture neither commands nor advises us to vow anything. And God approves of nothing except what he commands or advises. And so I do not see how one becomes godly through a vow. Mosaic Law did not command anyone to make vows, but it did allow it. Since the Gospel is a complete liberty of the Spirit, it knows nothing at all of the slavery of vows. It certainly appears to me that the custom of vows has been approved because of a singular ignorance of faith and of the liberty of the Gospel. The practice of making vows sometimes conflicts with faith and the liberty of the Spirit. The Scholastics even teach that a work done according to a vow is better than a work that is done without a vow.[25] Godless men,

---

[24] See pp. 187–89.

[25] See Aquinas *Summa* I–II, q. 88, art. 6, who lists three reasons why a work done to fulfill a vow is better than a work done without a vow: (1) because an act done to

who determine godliness from works rather than from the Spirit and faith! And why do they say a work is better because of the vow attached to it when vows are neither commanded nor advised?

Further, please consider what is being vowed. Celibacy, poverty, and obedience are promised with vows. I do not deny that celibacy has been recommended. But since the weakness of our flesh is such that even Christ denies that all can accept his speech about celibacy, what good does it do to make so precarious and dangerous a lifestyle common to so many thousands of men? Of the ancient hermits, as far as we can tell from the historical accounts, there were few who succeeded in their struggle with the flesh, even though they were constantly disciplining their bodies with fasting from food and drink and were greatly fortified against the snares of the devil by their knowledge of divine Scripture. How will we succeed when we live in such luxury, in the highest leisure, so helpless, so ignorant of Holy Scripture and the Gospel? Indeed, unless you are thoroughly instructed in the Gospel, your struggle with Satan will be futile. And the outcome teaches us how wisely we make our vows.

Moreover, poverty is required of all Christians by divine right,[26] and so it does not pertain only to monks. But the poverty of the Gospel is not common beggary. Rather, it consists in holding one's possessions in common with all, being generous, giving to all who are needy, and conducting one's affairs so as to relieve the poverty of others. The poverty of the Gospel does not consist in a lack of possessions, but in treating your possessions as if you consider yourself the manager of another's property and not your own. This is what Paul teaches in Ephesians 4:[28], "But let him rather labor, working with his hands, which is good, so that he may have the resources to provide for the need of him who is suffering." The words of the Gospel can also be applied here: "Go and sell all that you have, and give to the poor" [Matthew 19:21]. For Christ wanted this man to be poor in the sense that he should give. In our day, however, we define poverty simply as receiving things from others. You see how

---

fulfill a vow is an act of religion, (2) because the one who does something to fulfill a vow subjects himself to God, and (3) because the vow fixes the will steadfastly on good.

[26] The term "by divine right" (*iure divino*) means that God orders or ordains something. This term is opposed to "by human right" (*iure humano*), which designates something ordered or instituted by humans.

far from the Gospel the institution of begging is? Just as poverty is required, so also is the labor of obtaining things, not for our own sake but for the sake of our brothers. So far is beggary from being an acceptable institution.

Finally they promise obedience. But we all owe this obedience individually to our parents, teachers, and magistrates by divine right. Therefore, there is no special perfection in the monastic way of life. But I do not want to argue about monks now. Let them consider how Christian it was for them to think that monasticism is preferable to every other kind of life lived by men. They consider Christianity not according to the Spirit but according to the appearance of external works. Formerly, monasteries were simply schools where students lived in celibacy of their own will and only so long as they wished, where they shared all things with their fellow students, and willingly obeyed and respected their teachers. At the same time, they chanted psalms, prayed, and conversed. And this entire way of life was not carried on to achieve some special Christianity or a state of perfection, as they say now, but to give basic training and education to imperfect people. How I wish that this were the state of monasteries today! Then we would have more pious schools and less superstition and godlessness. For in what part of Christianity does the Antichrist reign more powerfully than in monastic servitude?

JUDICIAL AND CEREMONIAL LAWS

Judicial and ceremonial laws remain to be discussed, but there is no point in saying much about them in a compendium. Judicial laws about legal judgments, penalties, and public trials were given to the Jewish people in divine Scripture. The New Testament knows nothing of laws of this kind since litigation is forbidden to Christian people, poverty and the sharing of possessions are commanded, and the courtroom is prohibited, as Paul teaches in 1 Corinthians 6:[7], "Now it is entirely wrong that you have lawsuits among yourselves."[27]

Ceremonial laws have been given for sacrificial rites, the distinction of days, vestments, victims, and other things of this sort. It is clear that in these ceremonies the mysteries of the Gospel are adumbrated, as the epistle to the Hebrews and some passages in the epistles to the Corinthians teach. So also the writings of the prophets

---

[27] See p. 158, n. 12.

COMMONPLACES: LOCI COMMUNES 1521

testify to the same thing. They generally accommodated the types of the Law to the mysteries of the Gospel allegorically (ἀλληγορικῶς). There are very many examples of this in the Psalms. Accordingly, we should seek allegories in laws of this kind, but prudently. For here even great authors often play the fool worse than children. Only rites and actions that are given for the purpose of signifying other things allow for allegorical interpretation.[28] For example, the sacrifices of the Levitical priesthood were given as signs of the priesthood of Christ. Now, only someone who is thoroughly versed in all of Scripture will succeed in treating allegories. But it will be easy for the Spirit, or rather common sense, to judge to what extent and to what end allegories should be employed. Provided that they are treated properly, these allegories are conducive to understanding the power of both the Law and the Gospel. The epistle addressed to the Hebrews demonstrates this. When it compares Aaron with Christ, it is amazing how clearly it sets Christ before our eyes and how appropriately it teaches what benefits the world has received through Christ and what the priesthood of Christ has conferred on the human race, with the result that we are not justified in any other way except through the priesthood of Christ.[29]

It remains to discuss the power of the Law and its abrogation. These topics should properly be considered here, but since their treatment cannot be understood without comparing the Law with the Gospel, we will discuss both the power of the Law and its abrogation later, after I have spoken about the Gospel. Right now, we will add to this section a discussion concerning what we should think about human laws.

---

[28] Melanchthon's distrust of allegorizing springs from his conviction that Scripture is clear and allows for an obvious interpretation according to common sense. When signs or events are given for the purpose of foreshadowing future events or signifying spiritual truths, allegorizing is necessary and proper, and Melanchthon himself does not shy from allegorizing in these cases. But as he goes on to show, the clarity of Scripture is not the only hermeneutical principle at stake. While proper allegorizing is "conducive to understanding the power of both the Law and the Gospel," improper or excessive allegorizing draws the reader away from the text and therefore away from the teaching of Law, sin, and grace. See pp. 21 and 108.

[29] See Hebrews 5:1–11.

HUMAN LAWS

Humans laws are all the laws that men have established. And as
human affairs stand right now, some human laws are civil and some
pontifical. Civil laws are those laws that magistrates, princes, kings,
and cities institute in their state. In Romans 13:[1–3], Paul teaches
what should be thought concerning the authority of this sort of law,
when he says, "Let every soul be subject to the higher powers. For
there is no power except from God. But what powers exist have been
instituted by God, so that whoever resists the power, resists the
institution of God. But those who resist acquire for themselves
condemnation. For princes are not a terror to good works, but to evil."
Indeed, the purpose of magistrates and civil laws is none other than to
punish and prevent injustices. Thus laws are enacted for the division
of property, the forms of contracts, and the punishment of
wrongdoers. For the magistrate is the minister of God, a wrathful
avenger against him who does wrong. But it is not acceptable for a
magistrate to legislate against divine law, nor should we obey
anything contrary to divine law, as it is written in Acts [5:29], "We
ought to obey God rather than men." And from this passage the
prudent reader will easily be able to judge to what extent we are
subject to human laws. But maybe we will speak more about
magistrates later when we treat the condition of mankind.[30]

But what about pontifical laws? Insofar as the priests legislate
concerning legal disputes and judgments, they are clearly worldly
princes. Otherwise, as far as legal disputes and judgments are
concerned, divine law subjects the priests themselves to the civil
magistrates, kings, and princes. Now while the princes close their
eyes the priests themselves have founded godless and terribly
tyrannical laws to benefit themselves, concerning the exemption of
churches from taxes, their own revenues, etc. Here the kindness of
love demanded that those who are the richest should relieve the public
need by sharing their money and income. But instead they outlaw and
curse with horrible threats anyone who asks a priest for a tribute, a
tax, or other things of this kind, which are collected from everybody
for the public welfare. But I will speak to this at some other time. Let
it be enough to have pointed out that the laws of priests concerning

---

[30] Melanchthon includes a section entitled "Magistrates" at the end of this work, pp.
187–89, and discusses the class divisions of laity and clergy on pp. 87–88.

civil affairs have been established contrary to love and by means of sheer tyranny.[31]

When it comes to faith, neither the priests nor the councils nor the Church catholic have the right to change or legislate anything. Rather, articles of faith should be examined simply, according to the rule of Holy Scripture. Nor should anything be considered an article of faith that is handed down outside of Scripture. First of all, Paul orders the Galatians that nothing should be changed when he says, "If anyone preaches to you something other than what you have received, let him be anathema" [Galatians 1:9]. Besides, how can a spirit be prophetic if it disagrees with Scripture? On the contrary, the spirit that prophesies against the truth is a liar. And Paul writes to Timothy, "If anyone teaches differently and does not submit to the sound words of Jesus Christ, he is arrogant" [1 Timothy 6:3]. And yet many godless things have been decreed contrary to Scripture. But we will speak of this shortly.

Furthermore, Paul testifies to Timothy that whatever men— whether the Church or a priest—legislate outside of Scripture should not be considered an article of faith: "As for you, remain steadfast in what you have learned, knowing from whom you have learned it" [2 Timothy 3:14]. He thinks it is important that we know the source of what we have learned. Now how will we know the origin of human opinions unless we can test them against Scripture? For it is quite obvious that whatever the Scriptures confirm has its origin in the Holy Spirit. But whatever is promoted outside of the Scriptures, it is uncertain whether it has its origin in the Spirit of God or from a lying spirit.[32] Paul commands the Thessalonians to test all things and to

---

[31] In his *To the Christian Nobility of the German Nation* of 1520, Luther discusses the same subject at length (AE 44:116–217).

[32] During the publication of this work, Melanchthon was dealing with just such a circumstance, as the Zwickau Prophets came preaching against infant Baptism and promoting a new government based on the rule of the Gospel. Melanchthon wrote to the Elector concerning these self-proclaimed prophets: "I have heard them. The things they preach about themselves are astounding, namely, that they have been sent by the audible voice of God to teach, that they have intimate conversations with God, that they see the future, in short, that they are prophets and apostles. I really can't say what I should think of them. For sure and for important reasons I don't want them to be despised, because many proofs make it obvious that there are in them certain spirits. But no one but Martin could easily cast judgment on them" (*CR* 1:513–14). Appalled at the violence and disturbance aroused by the preaching of these prophets, Melanchthon was soon convinced that these spirits had nothing but contempt for the

hold on to what is good [1 Thessalonians 5:21]. And elsewhere he commands that the spirits be tested, whether they are from God.[33] How, I ask, will we test the spirits unless we examine them according to a certain rule? And surely this rule is Scripture, since it is clear that Scripture alone has the certainty of having been established by the Spirit of God. It is irresponsible to give councils the authority to establish articles of faith, since—to name just one reason—it is possible that there is nobody in the entire council who has the Spirit of God.

In Samaria the priests of Baal prophesied, and the kings of Israel governed everything according to their oracles. Why should it be surprising if godless men bereft of the Spirit of God also prophesy in our day? The priests in Judah assumed the same prerogative in opposition to Jeremiah and the Spirit of God when they said, "Come, let us conspire against Jeremiah. For the law will not depart from a priest, nor counsel from a wise man, nor speech from a prophet" [Jeremiah 18:18]. Yet how is this different from what the church of the papists says today: "The authority to legislate is ours; a council is ruled directly by the Holy Spirit and cannot err; Holy Scripture is unclear and ambiguous; the right and ability to interpret Scripture is ours," and many other things of this kind.

Now there is also a clear prophecy in Ezekiel 7:[26] that the heads of the church will fall into error: "The law will depart from the priest and counsel from the elders." And in Matthew 24:[24], "False christs and false prophets will arise and will perform great signs," etc. Moreover, even if the gathering of councils should abound with the Spirit of God, Scripture teaches that it can still make mistakes: "When a prophet has made a mistake and has spoken a word, it is I the Lord who have deceived that prophet" (Ezekiel 14:[9]). And in 1 Kings 22:[22], "I will go out and I will be a lying spirit in the mouth of all the prophets." But there is no need to spill much ink on this point. Paul says that he did not assent to flesh and blood [Galatians 1:16]. Should we then trust in flesh and blood?

Gospel of Christ, since "they confuse matters divine and human, sacred and secular, using Christ's name as a pretext" (*CR* 1:547).

[33] Melanchthon has 1 John 4:1 in mind.

Tell me, why do you trust the Synod of Nicaea instead of that of Rimini?[34] Surely not because the authority of the Roman pope confirmed it? But you do just this and in fact prefer the authority of the pope to both council and Scripture.[35] This is not only godless, but plain foolish. For why do you approve the Synod of Antioch, which condemned Paul of Samosata because he denied the divinity of Christ?[36] The whole thing, after all, was conducted without the authority of the Roman pope. At the Council of Alexandria, where decrees were issued concerning the three persons of the Godhead against Sabellius, there was no mention of the Roman pope.[37] Nowhere can it be read that the Roman popes attended the Council of Nicaea.[38] The Greek writers for the synods of Constantinople and Ephesus have made no mention of the Roman pope, so that it is probable that he was not present at these synods and certain that he did not preside over them.[39] Moreover, those synods over which the

---

[34] The Council of Rimini (or Ariminum) refers to councils called by the Arian sympathizer, Emperor Constantius II, one held in the West in modern day Rimini, Italy, the other in the East in Seleucia in 359. At Rimini the adoption of a new creed drafted at the fourth Council of Sirmium in 358 was proposed, which was sympathetic to Arianism and eschewed the use of the terms *homoousios* (consubstantial [with the Father]) or *homoiousios* (of like substance [with the Father]), opting instead for the vague *homoios* (like [the Father]). It therefore departed from the creed approved at Nicaea in 325 and was a short-lived victory for the Arians.

[35] Melanchthon is again drawing from Luther's *To the Christian Nobility of the German Nation* of 1520, in which Luther attacks papal claims to authority over the interpretation of Scripture and the calling of a church council (see AE 44:132–38).

[36] Between 264 and 269 several synods were held in Antioch to address the teachings of Paul of Samosata, who was bishop of Antioch. Paul of Samosata stressed the unity of God to the point of denying the three persons (Monarchianism) and held that Christ was a human person blessed with the divine power of the Logos (Adoptionism). He was condemned and deposed at the last of these councils.

[37] Sabellius was a modalistic Monarchian of the early third century who denied the doctrine of the Trinity. At the Council of Alexandria in 362, Sabellianism and other theological heresies were condemned.

[38] The Council of Nicaea was held in 325 to address the Arian heresy. Arius denied that the Son was of the same substance as the Father.

[39] The first Council of Constantinople was held in 381. Pope Damasus I was not in attendance. The Council of Ephesus was held in 431. The Nicene Creed was affirmed, and Nestorius, archbishop of Constantinople, was condemned as a heretic for his denial that Mary was the mother of God (*theotokos*). Cyril of Alexandria led the charges against Nestorius. Pope Celestine I was not a major protagonist at the council and did not himself attend, though he did send letters through his legates.

Roman popes have presided have often erred. Stephen VI rescinded the acts of Pope Formosus by the authority of a council.[40] John X then condemned Stephen's judgment during the assemblies in Ravenna.[41] Since the synods disagree with each other in this instance, one of them is necessarily wrong. The Council of Lyons should be considered godless because it sanctioned the books of decretals, in which so many cruel and godless decrees have been arranged.[42] In addition, we see that almost nothing is done in the popes' gatherings outside of promoting Roman tyranny, whether subjugating emperors, protecting the inheritance of Peter, increasing the wealth of the priests, or oppressing the Greek Church. The decree *Ad abolendam*, which concerns heretics, is clearly heresy itself as it curses all who think or teach anything about the sacraments different from the Roman Church's teaching and observance.[43] Yet the Greeks, who have many rites and traditions different from the Roman Church, are not heretics. The decrees of many councils about indulgences are godless. Among other things, the Council of Constance condemned the most evangelical of statements. For it condemned the simple distinction between good and evil works, that is, that every work is either good or evil, not neutral. Yet this is what the Gospel states, "Either make the tree good," etc. [Matthew 12:33].[44]

But there is no point in recounting so many examples when the abominable codices of pontifical laws are extant, from which you can read what you want. We have recorded these things to warn against

---

[40] In 897, during the so-called Cadaver Synod, Pope Stephen VI (according to some sources, he is Stephen VII) had the body of the previous pope, Formosus, exhumed, placed on a throne, tried, and condemned. Formosus' papacy and all of his acts were declared void. Stephen was acting under the influence of a powerful Roman family that had propelled him to the papacy and had contested the previous election of Formosus.

[41] Both Pope Theodore II (897) and Pope John IX (898–900) convened synods to overturn the acts of the Cadaver Synod and reinstate Formosus' papacy and acts. The last of these synods was at Ravenna (898).

[42] The First Council of Lyon was held in 1245.

[43] The decretal *Ad abolendam* ("To abolish") is a bull of 1184 by Pope Lucius III. It condemned everything taught outside the authority of the papacy as heresy.

[44] The Council of Constance was held from 1414 to 1418 to decide the problem of the three popes, who were all claiming legitimacy at the same time. It also condemned as heretical the teachings of John Wycliffe and John Hus, the latter of whom it tried, condemned, and executed after guaranteeing him immunity.

rashly accepting the common opinion bandied about that the councils cannot make mistakes. Now since it is common knowledge and crystal clear both that councils have erred and that they can err, tell me, reader, why we should consider a decree that has no scriptural support an article of faith, simply because it was decreed by a council. Since it is more than obvious that councils can make mistakes, why are their decrees not measured against Scripture? It should be far from the Christian mind to think that someone can establish an article of faith, when it is uncertain whether that person is capable of deceiving or being deceived.

Peter says that the interpretation of Scripture is not of private, that is, of human exposition. Will we then allow men to establish articles of faith? No. We follow Scripture because it leads our way, and as Peter says, is "a light shining in a dark place,"[45] especially since the prophet says that the morning light will not dawn for those who do not have their foundation in the judgment of "the Law and the testimony" (thus the well-known passage in Isaiah 8:[20]). The passage in Paul's First Letter to the Corinthians also applies here, where Paul asserts concerning Christian doctrine that no other foundation can be laid except what has been laid [1 Corinthians 3:11]. That is, there is no doctrine, there are no articles necessary for salvation outside of Scripture. The Day of the Lord will test, he says, whatever has been added to the foundation of Scripture. But if they must be tested on the Day of the Lord, why are they accepted as if they were well-established doctrine necessary for salvation?

There is a decree about the transubstantiation of the bread into the body of Christ in the Sacrament.[46] There is a decree about the primacy of the pope, and this contrary to the decisions of the ancient synods.[47] Since these have been promoted outside of the certain approval of Scripture, why should they be accepted as sure teachings?

---

[45] Greek: λύχνον φαίνοντα ἐν αὐχμηρῷ τοπῷ. 2 Peter 1:19.

[46] In 1215 the Fourth Lateran Council stated that the bread and wine of the Lord's Supper are transubstantiated into the body and blood of Christ. Thomas Aquinas would later give philosophical justification to this doctrine, which teaches that the bread and wine no longer exist substantially in the Supper but that only their accidents (shape, color, size, etc.) remain (*Summa* III, q. 75, arts. 1–8).

[47] Melanchthon is probably referring to the bull *Etsi non dubitemus*, issued in conjunction with the Council of Florence in 1441, which set the pope above the councils.

The apostles in Acts confirm their doctrine with the authority of Scripture. And this is Paul's constant practice. Christ invites faith in himself through the Scriptures when he commands that we search the Scriptures that witness of him, when he says that the Father supports him, and when he says that the testimony of two people should be accepted, just to name a few examples out of many.[48] In Deuteronomy [12:32], the Lord commanded that nothing be added or subtracted to his word. This passage clearly teaches that no one should teach anything as an article of faith when he is not certain whether it is God's Word. The prophets, Christ, and the apostles certainly knew that what they were teaching was God's Word. This is why they wanted people to believe them, or rather, their message.

What has just been said thoroughly convinces me that we should consider nothing an article of faith unless Scripture clearly teaches it. The Parisians will burst at this, since in their inept and godless condemnation of Luther they call the teachings of the councils and the schools the grounds of faith.[49] I believe the Council of Nicaea concerning the divinity of the Son because I believe Scripture, which so clearly proves to us the divinity of Christ that not even the Jews can decline, as blind as they are, to attribute divinity to the Messiah. In addition to others, the passage in Jeremiah 23:[6] is clear: "And this is the name that they will call him—our righteous God." I think that the other synods should likewise be judged according to Scripture.

But will the Church make decisions about morals and ceremonies too? I don't know that the popes or synods have made any decisions about morals, unless perhaps the papistic laws about wars, litigation, and celibacy have to do with morals. Yet if you examine these according to the rule of the Gospel, nothing less godly or more Scythian could be established.[50] But we will speak about ceremonies

---

[48] See John 5:39 and 8:17–18, respectively.

[49] In a nominal response to Luther's arguments against Eck at Leipzig in 1519, the theological faculty of the University of Paris issued a condemnation of Luther's doctrine in April 1521. Melanchthon responded with his *Philip Melanchthon's Defense of Luther against the Mad Decree of the Parisian Theologians* in October of the same year. The work is a biting critique of Scholastic doctrine and the stale adherence to it by the theological faculty at the University of Paris (see p. 21, n. 6 above).

[50] A classical allusion, but one that also has precedent in Colossians 3:11. The Scythians, who lived north of the Black Sea, were known in ancient Greece for their

since the papists consider them their kingdom. First off, so that I may include both morality and ceremonies under the same restriction, bishops may not mandate anything outside of the teachings of Holy Scripture. For Christ sent his apostles to teach what he himself had handed down to them: "Teaching them to observe everything that I have commanded you" (Matthew 28:[20]). Therefore, he has taken away the power to establish new laws and new rites. Christ does not command his apostles to teach anything except the Gospel. How then will the bishops prove that they have the right to establish laws? Maybe from the passage where Christ says, "He who hears you, hears me" [Luke 10:16]? But in Matthew 10:[41], he says that he wants a prophet to be received in the name of a prophet. Therefore, he does not want a false prophet to be received, that is, a man who teaches human inventions and the traditions of men.

Scripture calls these men "dreamers" [Jeremiah 27:9]. But please, you papists, you Solons, you lawgivers (νομοθέται), produce one syllable from the Scriptures that gives you the authority to establish laws.[51] Yet Scripture withholds the authority to establish laws when it commands that nothing be added or subtracted from the Law of God. Paul also forbids this power when he calls ministers of the Spirit overseers of the new testament [2 Corinthians 3:6]. For a minister of the Spirit is one who condemns the hearts of all through the Law of God and consoles them again through the Gospel, which is efficacious because of the Spirit of God. Tell me, what do human traditions have to do with this? Do not human traditions deal only with external works? Scripture's judgment concerning traditions can be nothing but clear since it condemns them so often. Jeremiah 23:[28] calls them chaff: "What does the chaff have to do with the wheat?" He also calls them lies and dreams. Isaiah [28:8] calls them filthy vomit and dross. Ezekiel [23:1–20] calls them fornications, donkey flesh, and horse secretions. Other prophets call them various other names. Paul calls them elegant speech or golden words

---

brutish and barbarian ways. Herodotus records that they drank the blood of their enemies (*Histories* 4.64). Along with the Thracians, they were the constant object of the Greeks' derision as the quintessential unsophisticated barbarians.

[51] Solon was an Athenian lawgiver of the early sixth century BC whose name was constantly cited as an authority to be respected in Athenian law courts. Litigants in Athenian lawsuits would frequently call upon the authority of Solon to give greater authority to the laws according to which they were prosecuting or defending.

(χρηστολογίας).[52] And passing over many other examples, I appeal to Paul, who asserts the origin of human traditions: "In the last times some will fall from the faith, giving heed to false spirits and the doctrines of demons, who speak the lie in hypocrisy and whose conscience has been burned, forbidding marriage, ordering fasting from foods that God has created," etc. (1 Timothy [4:1–3]). Note that this lying spirit is the author of traditions about celibacy, the distinction of foods, etc. But what else are the pontifical canons except traditions about celibacy, the distinction of foods, and similar trifles? In Matthew 15:[9], Christ cites Isaiah [29:13], "In vain they worship me with the commandments of men."

What then? How do human traditions bind consciences? Do they sin who violate human decrees? I answer that papal laws should be borne just as we bear any injury or tyranny, according to the passage in Matthew 5:[41], "Whoever compels you to go a mile, walk with him also another two." But they can be tolerated only insofar as the conscience remains untroubled by them: "We ought to obey God rather than men" (Acts 5:[29]). Therefore when traditions obscure faith, when they are an occasion for sin, they should be violated. Nor does he sin who violates them outside of scandal while following the judgment of the Spirit. But we will speak about scandal later.[53] Besides, you have clear passages of Scripture teaching that consciences should not be bound by human traditions: "All are yours, whether Paul or Apollos" (1 Corinthians 3:[21–22]). That is, neither Paul nor Cephas has the authority to bind your consciences. And in the same epistle we have the clear words, "You were bought at a price, do not become slaves of men" (1 Corinthians 7:[23]). But those who have had the freedom of their consciences stolen from them through traditions do become slaves of men. For just as Christian freedom is freedom of the conscience, so also the slavery of Christians is the slavery of their conscience. The passage clearest on this point is in the Epistle to the Colossians [2:20–23], "If you have indeed died together with Christ, why are you still troubled by traditions as if living in the world?" And he adds, repeating their traditions in mimetic fashion (μιμητικῶς), " 'Don't touch,' 'don't taste,' 'don't handle,' (which are all things that are destroyed by use)

---

[52] See Romans 16:18.
[53] See pp. 191–93 below.

according to the commandments and doctrines of men. And these indeed have an appearance of wisdom in devotion and humility and severity to the body, but they are not of any use against the compulsion of the flesh." In Jeremiah 23, the Lord warns that false prophets are not to be heard. Without a doubt, this should be applied to circumstances where consciences are put in danger. This is how he puts it: "Do not listen to the words of prophets who prophesy to you and deceive you: they speak the vision of their own heart, not from the Lord" (Jeremiah 23:[16]). In this case I have somewhat contemporary supporters, especially Gerson, who agrees with us that consciences should not be bound by human traditions and that he who violates human tradition does not sin so long as a scandal does not arise from it.[54] I could wish that Bernard had spoken his opinion a little more freely on this matter in his *On Dispensation*.[55] But the Spirit will render the surest judgment, as it is written, "Where the Spirit of the Lord is, there is freedom" [2 Corinthians 3:17]. And, "The Spirit judges all things, and he himself is judged by nobody" [1 Corinthians 2:15].[56]

I would not be able to enumerate the different kinds of decisions that have been made by the councils and popes without recounting all of canon law and the entire history of the Church. But we will report a few examples of such traditions from which we can see the importance of Scripture's constant warning that nothing is so adverse to piety as the teachings of men. The Synod of Nicaea decided upon certain forms of penance (*poenitentia*).[57] I do not presume to judge with what spirit the fathers decreed it, but I do see that a good part of the Gospel, or rather the very power of the Gospel, has been obscured by this tradition. For from this synod the practice of satisfactions first arose. Maybe they were tolerable in the beginning when the Church's understanding of the Gospel was still rather pure, but this did not last

---

[54] Gerson was quite critical of the host of ecclesiastical traditions that seemed to him at times to be strangling the church. See, e.g., *On the Unity of the Church*, 3 (cf. Pöhlmann, 152).

[55] *De praecepto et dispensatione* (*MPL* 182:859–94).

[56] Here Melanchthon replaces "spiritual man" (*pneumatikos*) with "Spirit." According to Melanchthon, the spirit in the Christian is the Holy Spirit himself and the motions of the Holy Spirit in him. See p. 164 below.

[57] The word *poenitentia* can be used to refer both to repentance and to the Roman Catholic sacrament of penance.

for long. What slaughter of consciences has come about from satisfactions! Grace has been obscured, and what the Gospel attributes to faith has begun to be attributed to satisfactions. What could be more godless or more dangerous than this? And the Synod of Nicaea certainly set the stage for these evils. How much better it would have been to follow Paul's example in observing repentance. Paul welcomed back that memorable adulterer after he had repented without requiring any satisfaction, and in his Second Epistle to the Corinthians, he advised that a rebuke is sufficient (2 Corinthians 2:[4–7]. But the pseudo-theologians of our time, following the ancient tradition of the Nicene Synod, have made satisfactions a part of repentance. Clearly there is no error worse than this.

What trouble that papistic confession has given even to pious consciences! How many thousands of souls it has destroyed! And this, even though Paul wanted the Corinthians to make sure that this adulterer not be overwhelmed with too much grief! But tell me, what are the Roman pontiffs who invented confession doing, except grieving terrified and truly pious consciences as miserably and cruelly as possible?

Now that Christianity has been divided into so many kinds of stations in life, what is the point of Christian love and simplicity? Some are laymen, others monks, others clerics, and among these there are countless divisions, which could perhaps be tolerated if it were not for their contentious and ambitious competitions. And then to some of these stations in life the unbearable burden of celibacy has been added. It was the Synod of Nicaea again that acted on celibacy.[58] But there is no need to relate what this tradition has brought about, since in no other way could sinful desires be so freely indulged than by this tradition. When Paul is discussing virginity in 1 Corinthians 7, he does not dare to prescribe anything because he does not want to throw a noose around anyone. Instead, he wants people to choose the kind of life in which they can constantly serve God without any

---

[58] Melanchthon is referring to Canon 3 of the Council of Nicaea (325), which forbids a member of the clergy to live with a woman disciple unless the woman is his mother, sister, aunt, or a woman "beyond suspicion." Most scholars agree that this canon does not demand clerical celibacy but condemns the practice of clerics housing women who bear no relation to them. According to tradition, the Council of Nicaea was persuaded by a certain Paphnutius not to take up the issue of clerical celibacy, and so avoided the issue so as not to cause unnecessary hardship for married clergy.

distraction, εὐπρόσεδρον τῷ κυρίῳ καὶ ἀπερισπάστως.[59] For so the apostle speaks [1 Corinthians 7:35]. But who are less constant or εὐπρόσεδροι, who are more violently torn from God, than those burning with the flames of the flesh? Paul provides for this and does not command celibacy. In fact, when he writes to Timothy he even calls the tradition of celibacy a "doctrine of demons" [1 Timothy 4:1]. Satan has conquered and this law has been accepted and promulgated among so many thousands of men and this to the great detriment of Christianity.

And now the Eucharist has been restricted to a special class of men, to the priests. Christ, who wishes to be the common possession of all the pious, is now stolen and used by the priests alone. And so the benefit of the mass and the power of the Eucharist have been completely obscured. The Eucharist has become nothing else than a chance for the priests to do business. For Satan has come up with the lie that priests ought to sacrifice on behalf of the people, that masses can be sold to the people, and other things of this kind. The proper use of the mass would not have been lost had the people not been divided into the different classes of priests and laity. O the horrible and abominable godlessness that reigns today in the papistic masses![60]

But why keep listing examples? You have the foregoing examples as proof that no tradition has ever been so godly in outward appearance that it did not cause great harm to Christianity. For what seems more agreeable than that there be satisfactions for public crimes in the Church? But these satisfactions obscured grace. What could be more decorous than that bishops live celibate lives? But through this celibacy the road was opened to sinful pleasures. What could be more reverent (according to human, not spiritual judgment) than that the use of the Eucharist not be commonly distributed to all? But by this practice the benefit of the mass has been destroyed. So it

---

[59] English: "constant and without distraction to the Lord."

[60] So Luther in *The Babylonian Captivity*: "The third captivity of this sacrament is by far the most godless abuse, because of which there is almost nothing more accepted and more believed in the Church today than that the Mass is a good work and a sacrifice. Moreover, this abuse has opened the floodgates to infinite other abuses up to the point that now faith in the sacrament has been completely destroyed, and they have made God's sacrament into mere merchandise, a market, and a sort of business transaction" (WA 6:512; AE 36:35).

is that traditions have an appearance of wisdom, but it is this very appearance that is so harmful—the very facade and mask of the godless and depraved Jezebel.[61]

---

[61] Cf. Revelation 2:20; 1 Kings 16–21; 2 Kings 9.

THE GOSPEL

Up to this point we have treated the nature of sin and of laws perhaps more briefly than the subject deserved. For we are not writing a commentary but tracing a general outline of topics that you should follow when studying Holy Scripture. Now we will discuss the Gospel and grace. And from these subjects more light will also be shed on the preceding topics. For the discussion of the abrogation and power of the Law has been reserved for this topic. Further, just as the nature of sin cannot be understood except from an examination of various laws, so also the power of grace cannot be known except from a description of the Gospel. And just as we have discussed the condemnation of men and their curse up to this point, so now we will discuss the restoration of men and their blessing.

Generally speaking, there are two parts of Scripture: Law and Gospel. The Law displays sin, the Gospel grace. The Law shows the disease, the Gospel the cure. To use the words of Paul, the Law is the minister of death, the Gospel the minister of life and peace [2 Corinthians 3:7–10]. "The power of sin is the law" [1 Corinthians 15:56], whereas, "The Gospel is the power of salvation for everyone who believes" [Romans 1:16]. But Scripture has not handed down Law and Gospel in such a way that you should think the Gospel is only what Matthew, Mark, Luke, and John wrote, or that the books of Moses are nothing but Law. Rather, the message of the Gospel is spread throughout all the books of the Old and New Testament. And so, too, are promises. Likewise, laws are also spread throughout all the books of the Old and New Testament. Nor is the common opinion correct that holds that the distinction between the Law and the Gospel depends on the times of their revelation,[1] though it is true that sometimes the Law is presented and sometimes the Gospel, at various times and in differing order. But as far as human comprehension is concerned, all time is a time of Law and Gospel, just as in all times all

---

[1] For a brief exposition of this "common opinion," see Lombard *Sentences* III, dist. 40. Implicit in this opinion is the belief that the Gospel is, at least in part, a fuller, more spiritual exposition of the Law: "As far as morals are concerned they [Law and Gospel] are the same, but they are revealed more fully in the Gospel" (ibid.).

men have been justified in the same way—their sin has been revealed by the Law, and grace has been revealed through the promise or through the Gospel.

The times of revelation vary, for sometimes the Law is revealed and sometimes the Gospel, and in different order. The Scriptures clearly attest to this. For you see that besides natural law, which in my opinion has been imprinted upon human minds, specific laws have also been given by God. For example, a law was given to Adam not to taste of the tree of the knowledge of good and evil, and to Cain that he should not be angry with his brother, and again that whoever killed Cain would be sinning. In this way, God was constantly renewing the knowledge of natural law by his Spirit's preaching, since it was now darkened in human minds blinded by sin. And so I almost want to say that natural law is not an inborn or infused judgment, but rather the laws received by one's fathers and continuously handed down, as it were, through their hands to posterity. Just as Adam taught his descendants about the creation of the universe and the worship of God, so he warned Cain not to kill his brother, etc. But let us return to the Gospel.

WHAT IS THE GOSPEL?

Just as the Law is that by which correct living is commanded and sin is revealed, so the Gospel is the promise of God's grace or mercy, that is, the forgiveness of sin and the testimony of God's kindness toward us. By this testimony our souls are assured of God's kindness. By it, we believe that all our guilt has been pardoned, we are strengthened to love and praise God, to be happy and to rejoice in him, as we will explain below in discussing the power of the Gospel. Moreover, Christ is the guarantee of all these promises, and for this reason we should refer all the promises of Scripture to him. For Christ was revealed obscurely at first, but afterwards he was made known more and more clearly.

After Adam had fallen and had been sentenced to everlasting death, he would no doubt have perished if the Lord had not comforted him with the promise of grace. God describes the tyranny of sin when he says to the serpent: "I will put enmity between you and the woman and your seed and her seed," and immediately victory is promised: "The very seed of the woman will crush your head" [Genesis 3:15]. In my judgment, it is better to refer the pronoun in this passage to the seed instead of referring it to the woman as our texts do.[2] This is the first promise, the first Gospel. By it Adam was consoled, and by it he conceived a sure hope of his salvation. Therefore, he was also justified. And then the promise was made to Abraham that in his seed all the nations would be blessed. Surely this promise could not be understood except concerning Christ. This, then, is Abraham's bosom,[3] and all who have been received into it have been saved. That is, those have been saved who believed the promise that was made to Abraham. This is the promise that the Scripture of the New Testament constantly proclaims.

The diligent reader will be able to gather all the promises about Christ under this topic, since these promises are clearly nothing other than the Gospel itself. Deuteronomy 18:[18–19], "I will raise up a prophet for them similar to you in the midst of their brothers, and I will put my words into his mouth, and he will speak to them all that I have commanded him. But whoever does not want to listen to his words, which he will speak in my name, I will be an avenger against him." Christ is promised to David in 2 Samuel 7:[12–13], "I will raise up your seed after you, which will come out of your loins, and I will make his kingdom strong. He himself will build a house for my name, and I will secure the throne of his kingdom forever and ever." And because of these promises Christ is called the Son of David by the prophets. Ezekiel even calls Christ David.[4] Generally the prophets recount both the Law and the promise of Christ. It will be beneficial for the pious mind to mark these divine promises and to have them readily available, because they are wonderfully effective in strengthening and encouraging consciences.

So in this way God revealed the Gospel immediately after Adam's fall and gradually made it clearer and clearer until he sent Christ, as Paul writes in Romans 1:[1–2], "The Gospel of his Son, which he promised concerning his Son beforehand through the prophets in the Holy Scriptures." And the writings of our Evangelists do nothing but testify that the promises have been fulfilled. This is also why Matthew begins his Gospel the way he does: "The book of

---

[2] The Vulgate reads: *ipsa conteret caput tuum* ("She will crush your head").

[3] Melanchthon is working from the imagery of Luke 16:22, where Lazarus rests in Abraham's "bosom."

[4] Ezekiel 34:23–24; 37:24–25.

the generation of Jesus Christ, the son of David, the son of Abraham"
[Matthew 1:1]. And I call the Gospel the promise of God's grace,
blessing, and kindness through Christ. But there are also promises of
temporal things in the Scriptures in addition to this promise of eternal
blessing. Examples of this kind of promise are the promise made to
Noah and the many promises in the Law concerning land, wealth, etc.
These are not only figures of spiritual promises, but of themselves are
testimonies of God's grace and mercy. Therefore, they should
comfort our consciences and encourage us to glorify God. We will
treat these very promises below when we discuss faith, what faith is,
and how it justifies.[5]

You see the plan of the Holy Spirit in the Scriptures, how he
teaches the pious so sweetly and persuasively and acts for no other
reason than to save us. All of Scripture is either Law or Gospel. The
Books of Moses sometimes teach the Law and sometimes the Gospel.
In fact, the Gospel is sometimes even hidden in the Law itself. For
what can you find more evangelical than the promise that the Spirit of
God adds as an explanation (αἰτιολογίᾳ) to the First Commandment:
"Having mercy on thousands of those who love me and keep my
commandments" [Deuteronomy 5:10]? And look how Moses the
lawgiver suddenly becomes an evangelist, that is, a herald of grace
and mercy, when he says in Exodus 34:[6–7], "Lord God, you who
are merciful and gracious, patient and full of much compassion and
true, you who guard your mercy for thousands, you who forgive
iniquity and crimes and sins, although there is nobody who is
innocent of himself before you." Try to provide a more evangelical
pronouncement in all the writings of the New Testament! In this way,
the Books of Moses sometimes teach the Law and sometimes the
Gospel.

I am not now discussing figures, but only those passages that are
clearly to be taken literally. For these are the passages that should be
sought first and foremost. The sacred histories are examples
sometimes of laws and sometimes of the Gospel. For clearly the
terrible case of Saul pertains to the laws. But the case of David
pertains to the Gospel, since although he had forced himself on
another man's wife, yet he obtained grace. The pronouncement of the
prophet was clearly the voice of the Gospel: "The Lord has taken

---

[5] See pp. 115–40 below.

your sin away. You will not die" (2 Samuel 12:[13]). One should evaluate similar examples in the same way. The prophets are teaching the Law when they condemn hypocrisy, godlessness, false security, and other such vices. For they denounce hidden vices and hypocrisy above all. They also proclaim the Gospel as often as they comfort, uplift, and assure weak consciences with their promises about Christ, which are so full of life that the apostle's question can ring out clearly: "Who will separate us from the love of God?" [Romans 8:35].

In the same way, the apostolic writings of Matthew, Mark, Luke, and John teach sometimes the Law and sometimes the promises, and in them there are examples of both the grace and the wrath of God. The examples of Zacchaeus, the centurion, and the Syrophoenician woman testify to God's mercy. The blindness and madness of the Pharisees are an example of God's wrath. The apostolic histories do differ from those of the Old Testament in that they bear witness to a Christ who has already been sent, whom the Old Testament had only promised. They also explain the promises about grace, righteousness, and eternal life more clearly than either Moses' or the prophets' writings. The apostle Paul instructively (διδακτικῶς) contrasts the Gospel with the Law and sin with grace. He does this especially in his Letter to the Romans, which I consider a kind of index καὶ κάνονα[6] for all of Scripture. The other epistles, since they are generally hortatory (παραινετικαὶ) in nature, pertain to the Law, though every single one of them touches on the message of the Gospel at some point. And this the diligent reader may observe for himself.

We have pointed these things out primarily to overturn the commonly held error about Law and Gospel and the Old and New Testament that the godless, sophistic professors of theology have promulgated. They teach that Christ has replaced Moses and has given a new law called the Gospel, that it is contained in Matthew 5 and 6, and that the difference between the Law of Moses and that of Christ is that Moses' Law requires only external works, whereas Christ's Law also demands the affections.[7] As if the Mosaic Law

---

[6] English: "and guide."

[7] While the Scholastics did not make such a stark distinction between the Old and New Testament, they did maintain that the old law did not forbid inward motions of the heart in all cases, but only in some (e.g., the Sixth, Ninth, and Tenth Commandments). So Aquinas writes that "the precepts of the new law are weightier

teaches some hypocritical and pharisaic righteousness! What, after all, is the false appearance of external works other than pharisaism? Let the prophets also bear witness that Mosaic Law requires the affections, for they continually command people to acknowledge God, fear God, and live justly and righteously. Maybe the sophists will even concede to me that the prophets taught the men of their times these things before the incarnation of Christ. Honestly, what could be more obvious than that passage from Jeremiah that, whether the sophists like it or not, has to refer to the Law of Moses? He says in chapter 7:[22–23], "I did not speak with your fathers and I did not command them a word in the day when I led them out of the land of Egypt about burnt offering and sacrifices. But this word I commanded them, saying: 'Listen to my voice, and I will be your God and you will be my people.' " Tell me, Thomas, what entered into your mind that you would teach that nothing is required in the Mosaic Law except pharisaism, that is, external works, and this when even Moses so often and clearly demands the affections?[8] To pass by many passages, does he not forbid desiring our neighbor's property and such in Exodus 20? He has already condemned the work when he prohibits stealing and adultery. Therefore, you will concede that he is guarding against the affection with these words, "You shall not covet your neighbor's house, nor shall you desire his wife, nor his slave," etc. [Exodus 20:17]. And in Deuteronomy he adds, "And now, Israel, what does the Lord your God seek from you, except that you fear the Lord your God and walk in his ways and love him and serve the Lord your God with your whole heart and your whole mind, and that you keep the commandments of the Lord and his ceremonies, which I today am commanding you, so that it may go well with you" [10:12–13]. And again, "Circumcise the foreskin of your heart and do not be stubborn," etc. [10:16]. You could find six hundred passages of this

---

than those of the old law because in the new law interior motions of the soul are prohibited, which are not expressly prohibited in the old law in all cases, although they are prohibited in some" (*Summa* I–II, q. 107, art. 4). Likewise, Biel, channeling Lombard, writes that when Augustine says that the Old Testament restrains the hand, not the soul, by "Old Testament" he means the ceremonial and judicial laws of the Old Testament. Biel also agrees with Aquinas that the old law demanded inner affections only in some cases (*In sent.* III, dist. 40, q. unic., art. 3, dub. 1).

[8] See preceding note.

kind in Moses.[9] So it is not unclear that Moses commands both affections and works.

Christ explains the Law in the same way (for grace cannot be preached without the Law), and he censures the interpretation of the Pharisees and scribes. For he says from the beginning that we will not enter the kingdom of heaven unless our righteousness exceeds the righteousness of the Pharisees and scribes. The Pharisees' interpretation was that the commandment "You shall not kill" was satisfied if you kept your hand back from murder; that the commandment "You shall not commit adultery" was satisfied if you did not have intercourse with your neighbor's wife. Christ teaches that the Law demands the affections of the heart, not merely the external simulation of works. For the Law forbids concupiscence. The Law also prohibits vengeance, and so it demands that we love our enemies: "You shall not hate your brother in your heart, but charge him in public and do not hold his sin against him. Do not seek revenge nor be mindful of the injury against the sons of your people. You shall love your neighbor as yourself" (Leviticus 19:[17–18]). And I do not understand why Jerome preferred to translate neighbor "friend" (for that is how our texts read), since the Hebrew word signifies a relative rather than a friend, and the Septuagint interpreters translated it πλησίον (neighbor), with Paul following suit in Romans 13:[9] when he cites this exhortation of the law.[10] But the main point of that passage in Moses is that the Jews should love one another, both friends and enemies, doing good even to those who do not deserve it. Isaiah 58:[6–7] gives support to this passage, since it clearly forbids vengeance and requires love even for enemies. And Proverbs 20:[22], "Do not say: 'I will return evil for evil.' Wait for the Lord, and he will liberate you."

Now as far as I know, you cannot find the following words anywhere in the Law: "You shall hate your enemy." So it is clear that Christ meant to condemn the pharisaical tradition, not the judgment of

---

[9] The number 600 was commonly used in classical Latin to designate an innumerable amount. It seems, though, that the number 600 is used deliberately here to correspond to the alleged 613 commands found in the Jewish law. Cf. Gabriel Biel *In sent.* III, dist. 40, q. ult., art. 1; Erasmus, *Diatribe on Free Will* (*AS* 4:116).

[10] The Vulgate translation of Leviticus 19:18 reads, *diliges amicum tuum sicut temet* ("You shall love your friend as yourself"). The Hebrew word in question, *reah*, can be translated either "neighbor" or "friend," depending on the context.

the Law itself. The Jews had received the command to kill the Canaanites (Exodus 23:[20–33]), and some think that Christ was alluding to this when he spoke about the dictum concerning avenging ourselves against our enemies [Matthew 5:43]. But if this is true, what else can we say Christ meant except that, just as the Jews had formerly been commanded to love Jews, whether friend or foe, so now we, both Gentiles and Jews, should love friend and foe alike? For the Gospel has been revealed and the wall of division torn down, as Paul says [Ephesians 2:14], and the distinction between Gentiles and Jews erased and removed. But what about the fact that the command to Israel only concerned the Canaanites? What about the fact that they were also commanded to love foreigners? We should mention here the decree concerning interest—that foreigners should be charged interest but not fellow Jews. Now, since no one is a foreigner anymore and all are brothers and sisters, charging interest is universally forbidden.

But it cannot be denied that Christ changes some things in the Law, as, for example, the law about divorce. So also, the Jews had the commandment to defend their legal rights by force. Christ, on the other hand, does not order that the Gospel be defended with weapons. Rather, he says to Peter, "Put your sword back in its place. He who takes the sword will die by the sword" [Matthew 26:52]. Still, Christ's primary or proper office is not to establish Law, but to bestow grace. Moses is the legislator and judge. Christ is the Savior, as he testifies of himself in John 3:[17], "God did not send his Son into the world to condemn the world, but that the world might be saved through him." The Law damns because we cannot satisfy it by ourselves. But Christ gives to believers grace for their sin. Now Christ also preaches the Law often, but this is because without the Law sin cannot be known, and unless we perceive our sin, we will not understand the power and fullness of grace. Accordingly both Law and Gospel must be preached together, both sin and grace must be declared. Two cherubim were placed on the ark, representing the Law and the Gospel [Exodus 25:18–22]. So the proper and fruitful preaching of the Gospel is impossible without the Law and vice versa. And just as Christ joined the Law with the Gospel, so also the prophets joined the Gospel with the Law. You also have examples of this connection in the apostolic sermons of Acts, but especially in all the letters of Paul, where it is his general rule to preach the message of the Gospel first and then to give moral instruction.

THE POWER OF THE LAW

We have said that the Gospel is not the Law, but the promise of grace. It now remains for us to teach what the power of the Law is and what the power of the Gospel is. It will then be possible to understand the distinction between Law and Gospel to some degree. Now, in the first place, Scripture differs from human reason concerning the power of the Law. Scripture teaches that the Law is the power of wrath and sin, the rod of the exactor, a thunderous lightning bolt. Human reason teaches that it is the correction of vices and a guide for living. In fact, this is what Cicero calls it in his *On the Laws*.[11] And nothing is more frequently and commonly praised than laws. Our flesh, therefore, could even think Paul insane to call the Law "the power of sin." Thus when the Jews profess that they are disciples of Moses, they refuse to acknowledge Christ (John 9:[28]). Accordingly, to give an exact account of the Law's power, we need to compare two types of men.

The first type includes those who understand the Law carnally and do not think that it requires the impossible. They are blind, understanding neither sin nor the Law nor righteousness. And these are the hypocrites and sophists of all ages. Paul calls this kind of righteousness the righteousness of the works of the Law. It belongs to those who, when they hear the Law, set about to accomplish it by their own works and apply their hands, feet, and mouth to the Law, but not their heart. However much they may think themselves holy, they would prefer to live without the Law. Fleshly pleasures, wealth, and honor still delight them. No one can describe what kind of people these men are better than the Spirit of God. In the first place, they lack faith, that is, their heart does not recognize God at all and refuses to seek after God, as Scripture says [Psalm 14:3]. That is, their heart does not praise God. Rather, it despises him. Moreover, they have turned away from God, as Psalm 14 teaches. That is, since they neither fear God nor trust in him, they turn aside to their own counsels in their contempt for God, and through these counsels they seek wealth or honors for themselves. And besides this, they also try

---

[11] *De legibus* 1.58: "[T]he law ought to be an amender of vices and a commender of virtues."

COMMONPLACES: LOCI COMMUNES 1521

to justify themselves by their own works. Scripture often censures such workers of iniquity. In Psalm 5:[9], David calls them hypocrites in so many words: "There is no justice or honesty in their mouth; they are inwardly vacuous; their throat is an open abyss." The Law does not trouble such men at all because they live with a false and carnal understanding of it. And so the Law cannot do what it has to do in these people. Rather, they invent idols out of the Law for themselves—images of men and shadows of carnal virtues. For since they do not understand the sickness of their soul, they are stupidly secure and are drawn to simulating good works by some carnal affection, whether fear of punishment or desire of benefit. This is the incredible arrogance, conceit, obstinacy, and φιλαυτία of these people. They are so far from satisfying the Law that no one could be further from it.

An example of such a person is the Pharisee in Luke 18:[11] who says, "I am not as other men." And Isaiah describes the drunks of Ephraim: "We have struck a pact with death and we have made a deal with hell" [Isaiah 28:15]. Jeremiah writes, "They do not know how to blush" [Jeremiah 6:15]. In Matthew [7:23] they are called "workers of iniquity." Paul testifies that he himself was such a man before he was converted: "I once lived without the law" (Romans 7:[9]), that is, there was once a time when I thought I was eminently successful in fulfilling the Law, when I surpassed all my peers in the hypocrisy of works, for at that time the Law did not censure me, accuse me, or condemn me. And such are all men who try to keep the Law according to the capacity of reason and by their natural powers. For they understand neither the Law nor their own powers. These are they who contemplate only Moses' back, only his veiled face, as Paul says in his Second Letter to the Corinthians, where he declares that the Jews cannot understand the righteousness of the Gospel because they view Moses with a veiled heart. That is, they do not understand through the Law what the Law demands and how we are nothing but sin and a curse [2 Corinthians 3:12–18].

Up to this point we have dealt with those who attempt to keep the Law through their natural powers according to the power of human reason. Each individual will be able to determine from his own heart who such people are. The following statements of Paul do not properly apply to these people: "the Law is the power of wrath," "the power of sin," "the ministry of death," etc. Although the Law does condemn these people, still they make an idol of it and then do everything with an inexpressible arrogance and affectation of the heart.

Now the second type embraces those to whom these expressions do apply: "the Law is the power of sin," "the power of wrath," etc. To these people, God reveals the Law to lay bare their hearts, to terrify and confound them in the recognition of their sins. These are precisely the people in whom God works through the Law. In hypocrites the Law does nothing. Rather, they pay respect to a shadow of the Law with a shadow of hypocritical righteousness. The Law truly and properly acts in those whose sin is laid bare. And the fact that it really does happen means that it comes from God. Accordingly, Scripture calls this work the judgment and wrath of God, the fury of God, the appearance and face of his wrath, etc. Psalm 97:[2–5], "Judgment is correction from his throne. Fire will go before him and will burn up his enemies all around. His lightning bolts have lit up the whole world. The earth sees and is disturbed. Mountains melt like wax from the face of God, all the earth from the face of the Lord." Psalm 76:[8], "From heaven he has made his judgment to be heard. The earth trembled and was still." And Zechariah 2:[13], "Let all flesh be silent before the face of the Lord." Isaiah 11:[4], "He will strike the earth with the rod of his mouth and with the breath of his lips he will kill the godless." Habakkuk 3:[6], "He has looked on the nations and destroyed them, and the eternal mountains have been crushed."

But why quote so many passages when one of the two parts of Scripture consists in the Law and the work of the Law, to kill and condemn, to lay bare the root of our sin and to confound us? It mortifies not only greed or lust, but the chief evil of all, love of ourselves, the judgment of reason, and whatever good our nature sees in itself. Here it will be obvious how vile is the stench of moral virtues, how the righteous works of the saints are dirty menstrual rags [Isaiah 64:6]. Even Moses had to exclaim, "Not even the innocent is innocent before you" [Exodus 34:7].[12] And Nahum [1:3] says, "He

---

[12] Melanchthon is giving a variation of the Vulgate translation of Exodus 34:7, which reads: *nullusque apud te per se innocens est* ("And before You no one is innocent of himself."). The Hebrew is usually translated as "who [i.e., God] will by no means clear the guilty" (ESV) or something similar. The term "guilty" however, is not in the Hebrew, and it is possible to read the Hebrew with "innocent" as the object of

will not make innocent by cleansing." And David prays, "Do not enter into judgment with your servant" [Psalm 143:2], and, "Lord, do not chastise me in your anger" [Psalm 6:1]. In Isaiah 38:[13], Hezekiah says, "Like a lion, he has crushed all my bones." And this is what John says so concisely, as usual, "The law was given through Moses, but grace and truth came through Jesus Christ" [John 1:17]. Truth is opposed to hypocrisy and grace to God's anger. Moreover, since grace, that is, the mercy and favor of God and true righteousness in our hearts, is bestowed through Jesus Christ, it follows necessarily that the Law is only the author of hypocrisy when it coerces those who are unwilling and who rage against God, but it is the author of wrath when it condemns us as guilty sinners.

Accordingly, Paul explains the power of the Law most thoroughly in Romans 7:[7] when he writes, "I did not know sin except through the law; for I did not know concupiscence except the law said: 'You shall not covet.' " Paul says the same thing in Romans 3:[20], "Through the law is the knowledge of sin." It is as if he were saying that hypocrites are falsely convinced that righteousness is obtained by the Law, since the Law only reveals sin to the heart. Then "taking occasion through the commandment, sin worked all manner of concupiscence in me," that is, when I began to feel the weight of the Law, still less did anything come from the Law, so that instead concupiscence was aroused all the more and began to rage against the judgment and will of God. For "without the law sin was dead," that is, unless the Law had shown me the sin in my heart, unless the recognition of my sin had terrified me, sin would have been dead and would not have burst forth. "For once I was alive without the law." There was once a time when I thought I was righteous, when I did not understand the Law and so did not recognize my sin. And at that point sin was quiet, nor did it show open hostility to God. "But when the commandment came, sin came back to life, but I died" [Romans 7:8–9]. That is, after God had shown me my sin through the Law, I was confounded, terrified, and trembling. In short, I died. And then, finally, the power of the Law became clear. The Law was given so that we would live, but since we cannot do it, it is the instrument of death. Why, then, does the Law kill? "The law is spiritual," that is, it demands spiritual things—truth, faith that glorifies God, love of God.

"clear." Thus, while Melanchthon's translation is quite free, it is not far from the sense. The point of the passage is that everyone stands in need of God's forgiveness.

"But I am carnal," unbelieving, ignorant of God, foolish, full of self-love, etc. [Romans 7:14].

Nowhere does the apostle Paul so thoroughly treat the power and nature of the Law than in the passage just cited. I do not see that there is anything lacking in it. There is no obscurity, no impediment. Everything in it is clear and evident, so that its meaning cannot be doubted.[13] But if the studious reader of Scripture wishes, he could add many other passages scattered throughout Paul's other epistles to support this one.

In his First Letter to the Corinthians Paul writes, "The sting of death is sin, but the power of sin is the law" [1 Corinthians 15:56]. For sin would not confound or terrify if it were not revealed to us by the Law, and so sin would have no power if it were not aroused and laid bare by the Law. Nor even would death have any power if it did not terrify us through the power and work of sin. In 2 Corinthians 3:[5–6] the Law is distinguished from the Spirit in this way: "Our sufficiency is from God who also has made us fit as ministers of the new testament, not of the letter, but of the Spirit. For the letter kills, but the Spirit gives life." The next verses clearly show what he means by "letter" and what he means by "Spirit" when he says, "But if the ministry of death, carved with letters on stones, was glorious, so that the children of Israel could not fix their eyes on Moses' face because of the splendor of his appearance, how will the ministry of the Spirit not be even more glorious?" [2 Corinthians 3:7–8]. The Law is the ministry of death, which confounds, terrifies, and kills the conscience by exposing and revealing sin. The Gospel is the ministry of the Spirit (as we will soon discuss), which consoles, strengthens, uplifts, and gives life to minds that were previously made to tremble in terror.

In Galatians 3:[19], after offering an extended explanation of how righteousness cannot be obtained by aid of the Law alone, the apostle appends the following question, the addition of which seems suitable: "What then is the law?" That is, if it was of no use in obtaining

---

[13] This stress on the clarity of Scripture was a key hermeneutical principle for later Lutheran theologians. It was continuously upheld by Luther and incessantly attacked by his opponents. In his *Diatribe on Free Will* Erasmus, for example, mocks the idea of Scripture's clarity on the issue of free will: "Now I hear the objection: 'What need is there of an interpreter when Scripture is clear?' If it is so clear, why have such upstanding men over so many generations been blind in this area [of free will]?" (*AS* 4:26).

righteousness, what then was its use? "The law was given," he says, "because of transgressions," that is, to increase disobedience. For the knowledge of sin increases sin, both because it rages more implacably when it is coerced and because our nature takes the disturbance badly and becomes angry with God's judgment.

Several types in Scripture also teach that this is the power of the Law. In Exodus 19, when God was about to give the Law, the people were extremely terrified by the thunder, smoke, lightning, clouds, the blast of the trumpet, and all kinds of dreadful spectacles, all of which signify the terrors of the tormented conscience. Or is the voice of the people not the voice of the terrified conscience, saying, "Let the Lord not speak to us, lest we should die" [Exodus 20:19]? And Moses does well in comforting the people, overwhelmed as they are with terror. He is no longer a minister of the Law but an evangelist when he says, "Do not fear. For God has come to test you, to put his fear in you so that you may not sin" [Exodus 20:20]. Oh, what a clear expression of the Gospel Moses gives! Unless the conscience hears it, how will it endure that terrible countenance of the Judge? But we will speak about the comfort of the Gospel later.

Now the light shone from Moses' face so as to blind the people's eyes. And this is why he no longer appeared before the people without veiling his face. For human eyes and minds cannot endure the splendor of God's light.

In summary, the lightning, the torches on the mountain, the splendor radiating from Moses' face—these all clearly show, to borrow a phrase from Paul, the glory of God by which God confounds the human heart.[14] The judgment of God is this very knowledge of sin. Let the attritions of the sophists and their affected contritions together with the scarred consciences of the hypocrites depart from this discussion. Here God examines the depths of the heart. For human reason is so far from recognizing its own sin that even saints and people full of the Spirit need to confess their ignorance. David exclaims, "Who understands his errors?" [Psalm 19:12] and "Do not remember my ignorance" [Psalm 25:7], and there are many other similar examples. Jeremiah 17:[10] says that man's heart is corrupt and inscrutable: "I am the Lord who examines the heart and tests the

---

[14] Cf. Romans 1:23; 3:23; 5:2; 15:7; 1 Corinthians 10:31; 11:7; 2 Corinthians 1:20; 4:6.

soul." And again in Jeremiah 31:[18–19], "You have chastised me, Lord, and I have been taught like an untamed calf. Convert me, and I will be converted, because you, Lord, are my God. For after you converted me, I repented, and after you showed me my sin, I struck my thigh. I was confounded and blushed because I bore the disgrace of my youth." And who is there who imagines that he has kept the Law when it includes the command to deny ourselves (Matthew 16:[24])? In summary, the proper work of the Law is the revelation of sin, or to put it more clearly, it is the consciousness of sin, what Paul calls "the obligation that is opposed to us in its teachings" [Colossians 2:14]. With this phrase Paul defines the conscience far more elegantly and with much more certainty that the sophistic commentators on the *Sentences*, who have invented so many practical syllogisms to define the word "conscience."[15] For what else is the consciousness of sin than the judgment of the Law, showing us the sin in our heart? When Paul in Colossians [2:14] writes of "the obligation that is opposed to us in its teachings,"[16] he means that the conscience is an obligation and that it consists in commandments, that is, the obligation is opposed to us through the commandments, through the Law.

You see that the work of the Law is the revelation of sin. Moreover, under the word "sin" I include all kinds of sin, not only external sin, but internal also—hypocrisy, unbelief, love of ourselves, hatred or ignorance of God, which are the very roots of all human works. God's first work in justifying sinners is the revelation of our sin to us, that is, confounding our conscience, terrifying us, and making us tremble, in short, condemning us. The example of Jeremiah that we just cited illustrates this work of God. Moreover, Paul says, "Through the law I have died to the law" [Galatians 2:19]. And David, stunned by the rebuke of the prophet, exclaims, "I have sinned against the Lord" (2 Samuel 12:[13]). And 1 Kings 21:[27] records for us: "Ahab ripped his clothes," etc. and, as Scripture puts

---

[15] In later editions of his *Loci*, Melanchthon himself would define the conscience in terms of a practical syllogism: "The conscience is a practical syllogism in the intellect in which the major premise is the law of God or the word of God. But the minor premise and the conclusion are the application, approving something that has been done justly or condemning a misdeed ..." (*SA* 2.790). Thus, when the conscience is conceived according to a practical syllogism, a commandment of God should serve as the basis for a person to judge whether or not he has done something wrong.

[16] Greek: χειρόγραφον τοῖς δόγμασιν, ὃ ἦν ὑπεναντίον ἡμῖν.

it, he "walked around with his head down." And in 2 Chronicles 33:[12] it is written of Manasseh that he was "oppressed," to use the scriptural term. In Acts 2:[37] we are told, "When they had heard these things, they were stung in the heart." It is enough to have shown here that the beginning of repentance consists in this work of the Law by which the Spirit of God regularly terrifies and confounds consciences. For human nature cannot by itself recognize the deformity of sin, and so much the less can it despise sin: "For natural man does not understand the things of God" [1 Corinthians 2:14], and, "The flesh desires the things of the flesh" (Romans 8:[5]). The sophists deal with the subject of the beginning of repentance in the fourth book of their *Sentences*, but we treat it here in the opening, as it were, of our work.[17] For the mortification, judgment, and dismay that come about by the Spirit of God through the Law are the beginning of man's justification and of his true Baptism. And just as the Christian life must take its start from here, that is, from the knowledge of sin, so also Christian teaching must begin with the work of the Law.

It is not worth the energy to argue about whether this fear is servile or, as they call it, filial.[18] We will leave discussions of this kind to people with too much time on their hands. Suffice it to say that the arguments of many on this issue make it clear that they have no idea what servile or filial fear are. What is certain is that no one can be blessed with a hatred of sin except through the Holy Spirit. It is equally certain that those who have been terrified in this way will flee the appearance and face of God unless the Spirit of God draws and calls them back, giving them strength to cry out with Paul, "Lord, what do you want me to do?" [cf. Acts 9:6]. The history of Exodus teaches that those who are terrified by the Law flee from the face of God, as when the people addressed Moses, "Let the Lord not speak to us, lest we should die" [Exodus 20:19]. And David says, "Where will

---

[17] Peter Lombard takes up the subject of repentance and the sacrament of penance in the last book of his *Sentences*, distinctions 14–22. Melanchthon is echoing Luther's insistence in the first of his Ninety-five Theses that repentance is not merely the sacrament of confession and satisfaction, but is, in fact, the daily reality of the Christian. The topic of repentance permeates all of Scripture, the entire Christian life, and the whole of Christian theology.

[18] A common Scholastic distinction. According to Thomas Aquinas the proper object of fear is evil, but fear may be directed at different kinds of evil. Servile fear fears the evil of punishment, while filial fear fears the evil of fault (*Summa* II–II, q. 19, art. 5).

I go away from your Spirit and where will I flee away from your face?" (Psalm 139:[7]). The Scriptures are full of many examples dealing with this topic. I believe that I have taught enough about this so as to make the distinction between Law and Gospel more readily understandable. Now you see how great the difference between affected and true repentance is.

THE POWER OF THE GOSPEL

Those who have been thus terrified in their conscience would most certainly be driven to despair, as usually happens to those who have been condemned, if they were not uplifted and strengthened by the promise of God's grace and mercy, which is commonly called the Gospel. If brought to this point, the afflicted conscience trusts in the grace promised in Christ, then it is resurrected and revived, as the following examples will illustrate wonderfully.

In Genesis 3, Adam's sin, his repentance, and his justification are described. After Adam and Eve had transgressed and sought cover and clothing (περιζώματα) for their nakedness (for we hypocrites like to relieve our consciences by our own satisfactions), they were confronted by the Lord. But his voice was intolerable. Before him no covering and no pretext could excuse sin. The conscience lies convicted and guilty when God's voice sets sin before its eyes. They fled. And Adam explains why they fled when he says, "I heard your voice in the garden, Lord, and I was afraid because I was naked" [Genesis 3:10]. Look at this confession and admission (καὶ ἐξομολόγησιν) of the conscience. Meanwhile Adam has a miserable internal struggle until he hears the promise of mercy, the word spoken about his wife: "Her seed will crush the serpent's head" [3:15]. And there was more than a little comfort for their consciences when the Lord dressed them, clearly signifying the incarnation of Christ, for his flesh at last covers our nakedness and relieves the dismay of our anxious consciences upon which the reproaches of the reproachful have fallen (Psalm 69:[9]). We made mention of David a little earlier, how he was confounded by the words of the prophet Nathan. He would certainly have perished, had he not immediately heard the Gospel: "The Lord has taken your sin away. You will not die" [2 Samuel 12:13].

There are some who think that nothing but allegories should be sought in the stories of the Old Testament.[19] But here, if you consider the literal meaning alone, you see how much instruction there is in this one example of David. In fact, we should lock our eyes on this meaning alone, for by it the Spirit of God generously shows us the works of his anger and his mercy.[20] What words could be considered more evangelical than these: "The Lord has taken your sin away"? Is not the forgiveness of sins the chief message of the Gospel and the preaching of the New Testament? You could add to these examples a multitude of stories from the Gospels. So in Luke 7 the sinful woman washes the Lord's feet with her tears, and he consoles her with these words, "Your sins are forgiven you" [v. 48]. And what story is better known than that of the prodigal son who confessed his transgression? Yet how lovingly his father received, embraced, and kissed him, etc. (Luke 15:[17–24])! In Luke 5, Peter is so stupefied by a miracle and so disheartened that he exclaims, "Depart from me, Lord, for I am a sinful man" [v. 8]. But Christ comforts and revives him when he says, "Do not fear," etc. [v. 10]. From these examples I think the distinction between Law and Gospel and their respective powers can be understood. The Law terrifies; the Gospel comforts. The Law is the voice of wrath and death; the Gospel of peace and life, and in short, the voice of the bridegroom to his bride, as the prophet says.[21] And

---

[19] This is directed against Erasmus especially, who writes in his *Sileni of Alcibiades*: "Ancient literature also has its Sileni. If you stay on the surface, sometimes the subject matter is ridiculous, but if you penetrate to the spiritual sense (*anagogen*), you end up adoring God's wisdom. Take the Old Testament, for example. If you look at nothing but the history, and you hear that Adam was formed from the mud, that his little wife was secretly taken from his side as he was sleeping, that a serpent tempted the little woman with an apple as bait, that God walked in the cool air, that a sword guarded the entrance so that the exiles would not return, would you not suppose this was a fable coming from Homer's workshop?" (*Adages* III.iii.1).

[20] This stress on the one, literal sense of Scripture is another hermeneutical principle that became standard for later Lutheran theologians. Melanchthon is departing from medieval tradition (as well as from the exegesis of Erasmus—see previous note), which taught a fourfold method of biblical interpretation: literal, tropological, allegorical, and anagogical. Melanchthon had already stressed the one, literal sense of Scripture in other writings. For example, he writes against Eck in a letter of 1519: "Since there is one, simple sense of Scripture, so also heavenly truth is very simple" (*CR* 1:113–4).

[21] Isaiah 62:5, "For as a young man marries a virgin, so shall your sons marry you; And as the bridegroom's joy is in his bride, so shall your God rejoice in you."

whoever has been so uplifted by the word of the Gospel believes in God and has already been justified, as I will soon explain more thoroughly. It is obvious how much joy and gladness this consolation brings to Christians. Also applicable here are those joyful expressions of the prophets with which they describe Christ and the Church: "And my people will sit in the beauty of peace and in secure tents and in opulent rest" (Isaiah 32:[18]). And again, "Joy and gladness and the voice of praise will be found in her" (Isaiah 51:[3]). "I will reveal to them their prayer for peace and truth. And she will be to me for a name and for joy and praise and exultation to all the nations of the earth" (Jeremiah 33:[6, 9]). "I will give a splendid mouth to the peoples, that they may all call on the name of the Lord" (Zephaniah 3:[9]). "You will make him glad with joy," etc. (Psalm 21:[6]), and, "A light has risen for the just and gladness for the upright in heart" (Psalm 97:[11]).

But why cite so many examples when the giving of the Law on the one hand and the coming of Christ on the other make it sufficiently clear what the power of the Law is and what the power of the Gospel is? For, as we just recounted, Exodus 19 describes how the Law was given with terrifying spectacles. And just as God terrified Israel at that time, so individual consciences are terrified by the demands of the Law and cry out together with Israel, "Let the Lord not speak to us, lest we should die" [Exodus 20:19]. The Law demands the impossible, and by it the conscience is convicted of the guilt of sin. Then terror and confusion so grip the conscience that no remedy would ever be found if he who brought low would not raise up. There are those who seek comfort from their own strength, endeavors, works, and satisfactions, but they accomplish no more than Adam did with his coverings. Likewise there are those who fight sin with the powers of their own free will, but experience teaches that these fail even more miserably: "For there is no safety in the horse; in the abundance of his strength he will not be saved" (Psalm 33:[17]). Again, "Give your help to us, Lord, because the protection of man is futile" (Psalm 108:[12]).

On the other hand, the coming of Christ is described by the prophet Zechariah, "Be glad, daughter of Zion! Rejoice, daughter of Jerusalem! Behold your King comes to you, just and having salvation, although he is poor" (Zechariah 9:[9]). In the first place, when he commands them to be glad, he is teaching them that the word of this

King is different from that of the Law, and so he calls for a joy of conscience that rejoices when it has heard the word of grace. Then there is no tumult, but everything is peaceful, so that you may understand that this is the Author not of wrath, but of peace. This is why Zechariah calls him poor, which the evangelist interprets, as it were, and calls him gentle [Matthew 21:5]. Isaiah refers to the same thing when he says, "He will not break a bruised reed, nor will he extinguish a smoking wick" (Isaiah 42:[3]).

So also the apostle contrasts the face of Moses with the face of Christ in 2 Corinthians [3:12–18]. Moses was terrifying because of the splendor radiating from his face, as we just explained. For who could endure the majesty of God's judgment, since even the prophet begs, "Do not enter into judgment with your servant" [Psalm 143:2]? When the disciples see the glory of Christ on Mount Tabor, they are filled with such a new and wondrous joy that Peter is beside himself and declares, "Lord, it is good that we are here. Let us make three tabernacles" [Matthew 17:4]. For here is the face of God's grace and mercy. Just as the sight of the bronze serpent saved, so are those saved who fix the eyes of faith on Christ (John 3:[14–15]). And this is why the apostles called this happy message εὐαγγέλιον (good news), a most fitting name. For the Greeks also commonly called messages and public announcements of successful accomplishments εὐαγγέλια, as for example Isocrates, "Twice already we have brought good news."[22]

---

[22] Greek: δίς ἤδη τεθείκαμεν εὐαγγέλια. Isocrates *Areopagiticus* 10.5.

GRACE

Just as the Law is the knowledge of sin, so the Gospel is the promise of grace and righteousness. Further, since we have been talking about the word of grace and righteousness, that is, about the Gospel, the topics of grace and justification should be treated next. For in this way a fuller understanding of the nature of the Gospel can be gained.

But when it comes to the term "grace," whoever objects to the Scholastics may do so justly. For they have distorted the holy word "grace" with terrible shamefulness, employing it to designate a quality in the souls of the saints. And the Thomists have been the chief culprits, positing grace as a quality in the nature of the soul, while faith, hope, and love are supposed to be qualities in the powers of the soul.[1] It is amazing to see them contend like foolish old women over the powers of the soul! But let these impious men wallow in their filth, and let these despisers of the Gospel pay the penalty for their nonsense! But you, my reader, pray that the Spirit of God may reveal his Gospel to your hearts. For if it is the Spirit's word, it cannot be taught except by the Spirit. This is what Isaiah means when he says that all will be "taught by God" (θεοδιδάκτους) [Isaiah 54:13].

I. In the writings of the New Testament the term "grace" (*gratia*) is commonly used for the Hebrew חֵן, which the translators of the Septuagint rendered χάριν, as in Exodus 33:[12], "You have found grace (*gratia*) with me," and so on, and many other places. Now this word clearly means the same thing as the Latin word "favor." If only the translators had used the word "favor" instead of the word *gratia*! Then the sophists would have had no opportunity to impose their foolishness when treating this topic. Just as the grammarians say that Julius favors Curio, when they mean that there is favor in Julius by which he has loved Curio, so in Holy Scripture grace means favor, and it is a grace or favor in God by which he has loved the saints. The Aristotelian fictions about qualities should be disregarded. For the most precise definition of grace is nothing other than the kindness of God toward us or the merciful will of God for us. The word "grace"

---

[1] *Summa* I–II, q. 110, arts. 2–4.

does not then signify some quality in us but rather the very will of God or the kindness of God toward us.

II. In Romans 5, Paul distinguishes between gift and grace: "If the many died because of the transgression of one, much more the grace of God and the gift in this grace, which is of the one man Jesus Christ, has abounded to the many" [Romans 5:15]. He calls grace the favor of God by which he has loved Christ and, in Christ and on account of Christ, all the saints. Next, because he is favorable, God cannot but pour out his gifts upon those on whom he has had mercy. So men aid and share their things with those whom they favor. But the gift of God is the Holy Spirit himself, whom God has poured out into the hearts of his people: "He breathed on them and said, 'Receive the Holy Spirit' " (John 20:[22]). And again, "You have received the Spirit of sonship by which we cry out, 'Abba, Father' " (Romans 8:[15]). Moreover, the works of the Holy Spirit in the hearts of the saints are faith, peace, joy, love, etc. (Galatians 5:[22]). It is amazing how superciliously the sophists treat Peter Lombard because he in one place identified grace with the Holy Spirit rather than that fictitious quality of the Parisians.[2] Yet Lombard understood the matter far better than the sophists!

III. But we have explained the meaning of the word "grace" very simply, following the phraseology of Scripture and defining grace as the favor, mercy, and gracious kindness of God toward us. The Holy Spirit himself is a gift whom God gives to those on whom he has mercy. The fruits of the Holy Spirit are faith, hope, love, and other virtues. And this will suffice for the term grace. In summary, grace is nothing else than the pardon or forgiveness of sin. The Holy Spirit is a gift that gives us new life and sanctifies our hearts. As Scripture testifies, "Send out your Spirit, and they will be created, and you will renew the face of the earth" [Psalm 104:30]. Just as the Gospel promises grace, so it promises gifts of grace. The Scriptures are clear on this point, so it seems sufficient to cite just one passage: "After

---

[2] Peter Lombard writes, "The Holy Spirit himself is the love or charity by which we love God and our neighbor" (*Sentences* I, dist. 17, ch. 2). The Scholastics took issue with this statement, teaching instead that the love by which we love the neighbor was a habit or quality inhering in man or an act elicited by man's will. Gabriel Biel writes, for example, "Nor would the Master [Lombard] want to deny that besides the gift of the Holy Spirit we are given another, created gift, which is a habit inclining us to love" (*In sent.* I, dist. 17, q. 3, art. 2, concl. 2).

those days, says the Lord, I will put my law inside them and I will write it on their heart." These words clearly refer to a gift, but the words that follow just as obviously refer to grace: "All will know me, from the least of them to the greatest, says the Lord, because I will forgive their iniquity and remember their sin no more" (Jeremiah 31:[33–34]).

JUSTIFICATION AND FAITH

I. We are justified, therefore, when having been put to death by the Law we are brought back to life by the word of grace that has been promised in Christ, that is, by the Gospel of the forgiveness of sins; when by faith we cling to this Gospel without doubting that Christ's righteousness is our righteousness, that the satisfaction of Christ is our expiation, and that the resurrection of Christ is ours; in short, when we do not doubt at all that our sins are forgiven and that God is now favorably disposed toward us and desires our good. Our righteousness does not, then, consist in our works, no matter how good they are or seem to be. Rather, faith alone in the mercy and grace of God in Jesus Christ is our righteousness. And this is what the prophet says and what Paul asserts so many times: "The just lives by faith."[1] Romans 3:[22] speaks of "the righteousness of God through faith in Jesus Christ," that is, the hypocrisy of works that men consider righteousness is no longer proclaimed, but a different kind of righteousness has been revealed that God reckons as righteousness, namely, the righteousness through faith in Jesus Christ. Romans 4:[5] declares, "Faith is accounted as righteousness to the one who believes." And Genesis 15:[6], "Abraham believed God and it was accounted to him as righteousness." These two verses I especially want to recommend to you so that you may understand that faith is properly called righteousness. For the sophists are offended by this manner of speaking, when we say that faith is righteousness. But in order to examine the nature and power of faith more closely, we will have to inspect its foundation (ὑπογραφὴ) a little more deeply.

II. It is clear enough that the horde of sophists defines faith as assent to those things that the Scriptures teach.[2] Following this definition, they teach that this faith belongs even to the godless. They say that the unrighteous believe and that faith is an idle quality in the soul that is common to godless and godly alike. And in order to dodge the fact that Scripture says that "the just shall live by faith" and that "righteousness is of faith," they invent another faith and call it

---

[1] Habakkuk 2:4; Romans 1:17; Galatians 3:11; cf. Hebrews 10:38.

[2] See e.g., Aquinas *Summa* II–II, q. 2, arts. 1, 9.

"formed," that is, joined with love. And they distinguish this faith from another faith which they call "unformed," that is, the faith that is also in the godless who lack love.[3] So these brilliant men pretend that the apostle falsely attributed to faith what belongs to love so that he could entice as many people as possible to faith by this bait. In addition, they have invented "infused faith" and "acquired faith" and "general" and "special" faith, and many other monstrous words.[4]

But let us pass by this nonsense, for we will shortly refute the sophists with the facts themselves, so that they may concede to us that faith is not what they themselves have called it.

III. The prophet's saying is not unfamiliar: "The fool has said in his heart, 'There is no God' " [Psalm 14:1], and what Paul says in 1 Corinthians 2:[14] is very well known: "Natural man does not perceive the things of the Spirit." And in Ezekiel 29:[9] we read, "The river is mine and I have made myself."[5] Passages of this kind testify that the flesh thinks and understands in nothing but carnal terms. The existence of God, the wrath of God, the mercy of God—these things are spiritual, and therefore they cannot be comprehended by the flesh. Moreover, whatever human nature learns about God outside of the Holy Spirit renewing and enlightening our hearts, no matter what it is, it is not faith but empty speculation. Therefore, it is nothing but affectation and hypocrisy, ignorance and hatred of God. Though

---

[3] The basis of the distinction is found in Lombard *Sentences* III, dist. 23, who distinguishes between faith as a virtue and faith as an "unformed quality." Formed faith is faith formed by love (*caritas*). Later Scholastics consistently distinguished between formed and unformed faith (e.g., Aquinas *Summa* II–II, q. 4, art. 4; Biel *In sent.* III, dist. 23).

[4] So Luther in his *Against Latomus*: "There is no need to recount their nonsense about unformed, acquired, general, and special faith, nor their talk about the principles of faith" (WA 8:54; AE 32:154). "Acquired" faith is faith acquired by human capacity outside of the Spirit, and therefore corresponds to "unformed" faith, whereas "infused" faith is given by the Spirit and therefore corresponds to faith "formed" by love (see e.g., Biel *In sent.* III, dist. 23, especially q. 2, art. 1). While he denigrates distinctions concerning "general" and "special" faith, Melanchthon himself would later speak of a "special" faith (*fides specialis*), "which believes the promise that is presented to it, believing not merely that God exists, but that the forgiveness of sins has been offered" (Ap XIII 21), thus using the Scholastic terms for his own theological purposes.

[5] Melanchthon here follows the Hebrew. The Septuagint and Vulgate texts have "it" instead of "myself." In either case, the statement is Egypt's against God and illustrates the blindness of human nature.

carnal eyes do not recognize this hypocrisy, the Spirit judges all things. We will illustrate the matter with examples.

Saul appears to have had faith in outward appearance, but the end of his life demonstrates his hypocrisy. For he did not believe (I mean from the heart) that the great things that he was doing were directed by God, that they were gifts and works of God's mercy. Instead he thought that they all depended on his own counsels. Now I am speaking here about the affection of his heart when I say that he did not fear the anger of God nor trust in God's kindness. He shows his contempt for God when he makes the sacrifice himself without waiting for Samuel because he does not want the Philistines to outmaneuver him (1 Samuel 13:[8–12]). And he shows contempt for God again when he mimics the Gentiles and erects a trophy for himself (1 Samuel 15:[9]). There was in Saul an opinion that God exists, that he punishes sin, and that he is merciful. Why else would he have offered a sacrifice? But he did not have faith and, to use the admirable terminology of Scripture, he did not seek after God [Psalm 14:2]. He did not honor him.[6] His heart was blind both to the severity and to the goodness of God. What a terrible and wretched sight it is for spiritual eyes to behold this godlessness of the heart! I ask you to examine your own life and, as much as you are able, evaluate the filthiness of your own heart from its fruits. Do you not turn away (to use the terminology of Scripture [Psalm 14:3]) and bend your soul to your own desires? Are you not anxious about food, reputation, livelihood, children, and wife, all because you do not trust in God and fail to consider the fullness of God's mercy? Do you not then rush immediately into some other sins because you despair of God's grace and mercy toward you? No doubt you would do or suffer anything with the utmost gratefulness if only you could attain a certain hope of your salvation! Do you not make money and aspire to riches by whatever means possible because you do not fear God's judgment? But you would most certainly fear him if you believed from your heart, if your mind could conceive of the power of God's wrath. Now when I deny that faith belongs to human nature, I am pointing to this foolishness, ignorance, and blindness of the heart. Faith is something altogether greater and more certain than what the flesh can comprehend.

---

[6] Melanchthon uses German here: *er acht seyn nicht.*

Accordingly, the sophistic faith that they call either "unformed" or "acquired,"[7] and by which the godless assent to the history of the Gospels in the same way as we commonly assent to the histories of Livy or Sallust,[8] is not faith, but opinion. It is the mind's uncertain, irregular, and fickle consideration of God's Word. You now understand what you should think about the faith of the Scholastics, and you now recognize that the sophists teach nothing but mendacity, vanity, and hypocrisy. But if I seem to have spoken too harshly about this teaching of theirs, they should take it up with Paul, not me. Paul calls an affected faith hypocrisy in 1 Timothy 1:[5], "The end of the commandment is love from a pure heart and a pure conscience and unaffected faith." He is saying, then, that faith is sometimes faked. And he talks about hypocrites in Titus 1:[15–16], "To the pure all things are pure, but to the defiled and the unbelievers nothing is pure, but their mind and conscience is polluted. They profess to know God, but they deny him with their actions. For they are abominable, disobedient, and unfit for any good work." But if the faith of the godless people spoken of in this passage were truly faith—for Paul is certainly speaking about people who are godly in outward appearance—he should not call them unbelievers, but should say that they lack love, as the Parisians speak. When writing to Timothy, Paul attributes feigned faith to hypocrites, and he calls them unbelievers when writing to Titus. There is, then, no reason to distinguish between formed faith and unformed faith. For this hypocritical opinion about Christian teachings or divine history, conceived without the Holy Spirit, is clearly not faith. Human nature does not assent to the Word of God, much less is it moved by it. For the sake of teaching I used to call this acquired, unformed faith "historical faith," but now I do not call it faith at all. It is an opinion.

We have said all this so that you might understand that Scripture uses the word "faith" very simply and that this quality of the Parisians, which is also in the impious and despisers of God, cannot be called faith. Rather, the damned "believe" not to give glory to God but because they are forced by circumstance—and this is certainly not faith. The same thing can be said about those who despair, such as

---

[7] See p. 116, nn. 3–4 above.

[8] Livy (59 BC–AD 17) and Sallust (86–c. 35 BC) were Roman historians whose works were held in high regard by the humanists.

Cain and Saul. For what is the difference between them and the damned?

What then is faith? Faith is constant assent to God's every word, and it does not exist outside of God's Spirit renewing and enlightening our hearts. Now the Word of God is both Law and Gospel. Threats have been added to the Law. Scripture calls it fear when we believe these threats, and faith when we trust in the Gospel or God's promises. Fear does not justify without faith. Otherwise the despairing and damned would be justified. But those who fear in this way do not glorify God or believe his every word, since they do not believe in his promises. Therefore faith alone justifies.

IV. So faith is nothing else than trust in God's mercy promised in Christ, no matter the sign attached to this promise. This trust in the kindness or mercy of God first calms the heart, and then it inflames us to give thanks to God for his mercy so that we do the Law willingly and happily. Otherwise, insofar as we do not have faith, there is no sense of God's mercy in our heart. Where there is no sense of God's mercy, there is either contempt for or hatred of God. Therefore every work done outside of faith is sin. This is what Paul says in Romans, "Whatever is not of faith is sin" [Romans 14:23]. This passage explains the power and nature of faith very clearly. For whatever is done is done by nature or in hatred of God. And works of this kind belong to those who do good works unwillingly and out of fear of the Law and its punishments. For when we simulate good works outside of faith, our heart thinks in the following way: "I have done what I can, but I don't know whether God approves or disapproves of my works. The Judge is severe. I do not know whether he has had mercy on me or not." With this kind of thinking, how can we not be angry with the judgment of God? And most men live in this hypocrisy with great anxiety of heart. But they should not contemplate their own works but the promise of God's mercy. This one point makes it clear how corrupt their judgment is. For what could be more sinful than to judge the will of God according to our works instead of according to how he himself has declared it to us in his Word? And yet so many men live with contempt for God and will live and act this way even though it is displeasing to God. Their works are done without faith, that is, they are done with hatred of or contempt for God. Therefore, it is very beautifully stated in Ecclesiasticus 32:[27], "In your every work, believe from the faith of your soul. For this is the keeping of the commandments."[9] Whatever works you do, whether drinking, eating, manual labor, teaching, even if, I might add, they are open sins, you should not look at your works. Look at the promise of God's mercy. Trusting in him, do not doubt that you no longer have a Judge in heaven, but a Father to whom you are as precious as sons are to human parents. But if there were no other indication of God's goodwill toward us than this prayer that we say daily and in which he wants to be called Father, this alone would be proof enough that nothing is required of us beyond faith. Now since God demands this faith of us so often, since he praises this one thing so many times, since he commended it to us with the richest promises and even with the death of his Son, what reason is there not to commit ourselves to such great mercy and trust in it? Instead of faith, which is the anchor of consciences, Scholastic theology has taught the works and satisfactions of men. May God completely eradicate this infamous scandal to his Church!

V. Now you understand how Scripture uses the word "faith," namely to designate trust in the gracious mercy of God without respect to our works, whether good or evil. For by faith we all partake of the fullness of Christ. Now those who have this faith truly assent to every Word of God, both to the threats and to the promises of the divine history. The faith of the Scholastics is nothing but a dead opinion. For how do those who do not believe in the promised forgiveness of sins believe in every Word of God? Nor do the sophists make any sense when they say that the godless believe that the forgiveness of sins applies to others but not to themselves.[10] Tell me, was the forgiveness of sins not also promised to these godless

---

[9] This is the only citation from the Apocrypha in this work. The absence is deliberate, as is Melanchthon's stress on the *canonical* Scripture (see pp. 20, 21, 27, and 66). The Lutheran stress on Scripture as the only truly dependable source of doctrine, combined with the humanist motto *ad fontes* ("to the sources"), entailed a reexamination of the Apocrypha's canonicity. Since the Apocrypha included books with information of doubtful veracity and since it was not historically accepted as equal to the rest of Scripture, Melanchthon does not cite it here as a source of doctrine, though the books of the Apocrypha continued to be held in high regard in Lutheran circles. Cf. Melanchthon's *Defense against Eck* of 1519: "There is therefore a distinction among the books of the Church, for the Church receives some in one way, and some in another. It is therefore nonsensical to say: 'This book is counted among our books. It is therefore a writing of the Holy Spirit' " (*CR* 1:117).

[10] Melanchthon is again alluding to the distinction between formed and unformed faith, for which see p. 116, n. 3.

people? But we have determined not to argue this point, content instead to have briefly shown what the word "faith" means. Luther's little book *On Christian Freedom* is extant, and whoever wishes may seek from it further praises of faith.[11] Moving on, I think that we will learn the power of faith more clearly from examples in Scripture.

In Genesis 15:[1], God promises his mercy to Abraham with magnificent words: "Do not fear, Abraham. I am your protector and your exceedingly great reward." A little later he also promises him descendants. And then follow these words: "Abraham believed God and it was accounted to him as righteousness" [Genesis 15:6]. What then did Abraham believe? Not merely that God exists! No, he also believed God's promise, and then he proved his faith with an excellent example, since he was ready to sacrifice his son, not doubting that God would give him descendants even if this son were killed. Now since faith is assent to the Word of God, the object of Abraham's faith is clear enough from God's promise to be his protector. Therefore, those have faith who consider God their protector and Father, and not simply their judge.

In Exodus 14 the Israelites grumble in unbelief when the sea and mountains cut off their flight and their enemy is right behind them. Moses orders them to stand still and says that they are about to see the great works of God. And he adds a promise: "The Lord will fight for you, and you will be still" [v. 14]. What if the Israelites had argued like our schools at this point, insisting that it is enough that they believe the history—that God exists, that he punishes the evil and rewards the good, that they also are evil and it may happen that God will want to punish both the Egyptians and Israel? Instead, they believed God's word and his miracles. They trusted in God's mercy. Despite the fact that they also were very much deserving of death, they entrusted themselves to the seafloor by faith. And now having witnessed God's goodwill toward them by this example, when they saw that they had been saved and that the Egyptian force had perished in the waves, it is recorded that "they feared the Lord and believed in the Lord and his servant Moses" [v. 31]. Now these examples have been given to us so that we may learn to believe, not with the faith of the sophists, but with trust in the Word of God. This is the kind of trust that you see present in Moses both in this passage and elsewhere.

---

[11] AE 31:327–77; WA 7:49–73.

What kind of faith does God demand in Numbers 14:[11], when the people are despairing over the occupation of Palestine? For the Lord says, "How long will this people draw away from me? How long will they not believe in me and in all the signs that I have done in their sight?" And in chapter 20:[12], God becomes angry with Moses and Aaron because they had not believed that the water would flow from the rock. Of course Aaron and Moses believed that God existed, but they doubted the word of God that promised water from the rock. The Lord rebukes this unbelief.

Moses speaks of this faith in Deuteronomy 1:[31–33], "As a man bears his little son, so your God carried you the entire way, wherever you walked until you came to this land. And not even so have you believed in the Lord your God, who went before you on the way," etc. They certainly had an "unformed faith" and an "acquired faith," but they did not trust in the promises of God's mercy and their hearts were not animated by trust in the mercy of God. Rather, they lived in unbelief, despising God's word and displeased with God's work in leading them out of Egypt. Although they were undoubtedly good men in outward appearance, they suffered the penalty for their unbelief. This is the hypocrisy of men who are thus painted over with good works, but whose heart has not been animated by trust and happiness in God. But God requires this trust alone. For he has given his Son to confirm this one thing, that we might not doubt his goodwill toward us but place our hope in God, not forgetting his works, but seeking to obey his commandments (Psalm 78:[7]). So also in 1 Chronicles 5:[20], "They called on the Lord when they were in the battle, and God heard them because they believed in him." And in 2 Chronicles 16:[9], "The eyes of the Lord look over the entire world and provide strength to those who believe in him with a perfect heart." In this passage the prophet Hanani is rebuking Asa, king of Judah, for trusting in the aid of the Syrians. But I do not know whether Scripture ever gives a better example of the power of faith than what is recorded about Jehoshaphat. We read in 2 Chronicles 20:[21–22] that when he scattered the Ammonites and the Moabites with a mere song, he had no command for his army except that they take their stand in faith. A similar example can be found in Hezekiah [2 Kings 20:1–6]. Further, Isaiah requires this faith of Ahaz when he forbids him from calling on the aid of the Assyrians and promises

God's assistance, adding, "If you do not believe, you will not endure" (Isaiah 7:[9]).

All the sacred histories are full of such examples. Therefore, the godly and studious reader should take it upon himself to collect examples, both to learn the nature of faith and to strengthen his conscience. In addition, we will cite several passages from the writings of the New Testament to make it clear that the Spirit of the accounts in each testament is the same.[12]

So I will begin with Acts 15:[7–11], where Peter says that the Fathers were justified not by the works of the Law (although they lived under the Law), but by faith. He also adds that their hearts were purified by faith. And you are utterly mistaken if you do not understand this passage to be dealing with trust in God's grace and mercy, as Peter himself explains it. For how could the faith of the Scholastics purify hearts? Therefore, Peter means to say that all the works of the fathers were sins, including the works of David, Isaiah, and Jeremiah, but that they were justified by trust alone in God's mercy promised in Christ. The prophets often say the same thing about themselves. This trust in God's goodwill permeates the entire life, including all works and all trials, whether bodily or spiritual.

VI. The faith by which we believe in God and that by which we trust in his goodness throughout every trial is one and the same. The sinful woman of Luke 7 had a spiritual trial, but Christ strengthened her by saying, "Your sins are forgiven you" [v. 48], and again, "Your faith has saved you. Go in peace" [v. 50]. There are many examples of bodily afflictions in Jesus' healing of the sick. And in Matthew 16:[8], Christ rebukes his disciples for their lack of faith concerning material things when they were worried about bread. For he chides them with the following words: "What are you thinking within yourselves, O you of little faith," etc. How often does he stress his Father's care for his people's bodily needs? In Matthew 6:[32], he declares, "Your Father knows that you need all these things." And in Matthew 10:[31], "You are worth more than many sparrows." Since these are fundamental lessons for exercising faith, we should not ignore such examples of bodily trials.

---

[12] Another insistence of the Lutheran hermeneutic is on the unity of Scripture. Melanchthon and Luther take it as given that Scripture consistently and purposefully relates the same message of the forgiveness of sins for Christ's sake, since each testament has the same Author.

VII. I am calling attention to these examples so that we do not have trouble distinguishing between the promises of God. For some of his promises concern material things. These are all the promises of the Old Testament. Other promises are spiritual, and these properly pertain to the New Testament. Now I do not think that anyone believes in material promises from the heart unless he has already been justified. And I think that God declared his mercy through the promise of material things, because the saints could easily conclude that if God cared for their bodies, he cared much more for their souls. Nor could they deny that God was the Father of their souls when he had already acted as a father to their bodies. As I said before, even promises of material blessings were of themselves a promise of grace. The promise was dim, of course, but still recognizable enough to those who had the Spirit of God. Already in Numbers 14:[19], when Moses is praying for the sin of the people, their sin is forgiven. Even the Law was given with a promise of grace: "I am the Lord your God, having mercy on thousands of those who love me and keep my commandments" (Exodus 20:[5–6]). Sacrifices for sin were also offered, and we must confess that these were signs to the faithful of the forgiveness of their sins.

I am not looking for allegories here. Rather, I mean to say that the historical accounts speak of the promised mercy in and of themselves precisely because material blessings have been promised. Very many historical accounts square beautifully with this. For example, Jacob says in Genesis 28:[20–21], "If the Lord is with me and guards me on the way through which I walk, and if he gives me bread to eat and clothing to wear . . . the Lord will be my God." Moses points us to faith in God's mercy and goodness very effectively by pointing to the works and material promises of God: "He afflicted you with scarcity and then gave you manna for food, which neither you nor your fathers recognized, so that he might show you that man does not live on bread alone, but on every word that proceeds from the mouth of God" (Deuteronomy 8:[3]). And the word of life is any word by which the human heart learns of God's mercy. Examples of this kind of faith are recounted in Hebrews 11, and many of these examples pertain to material things. Why not use this entire chapter of Hebrews to illustrate this topic?

At the very start Hebrews 11 defines faith as follows: "Faith is the foundation of things hoped for," that is, the sure expectation of things that are not seen [v. 1a]. In their glosses, the sophists have twisted this description (ὑπογραφὴν) of faith to fit their fancies and to match that insignificant, carnal opinion that they call faith, proving that they do not understand the apostolic meaning. Therefore, we will repeat these simplest of words with the simplest of meanings: "Faith is certitude concerning those things that are not seen" [v. 1b]. Tell me, what is certitude? Our nature does not consider divine or spiritual matters certain unless it is enlightened by the Holy Spirit. Now he also calls faith "the expectation of things hoped for" [v. 1a]. Faith is not, therefore, a mere belief in threats. No. Rather, Scripture calls belief in threats "fear." But faith consists also in believing the promises, that is, in trusting God's mercy and goodness against the assault of the world, sin, death, and even the gates of hell. Do you see that faith is called "the expectation of things hoped for"? Therefore, those do not believe who are not expecting the promised salvation. "Yet," you will say, "I believe in the promised salvation, but only that it will come to others." For so the flesh opines. But listen: Have these things not been promised to you too? Has the Gospel not been preached to all nations? You do not believe, then, if you do not believe that salvation has also been promised to you. It is surely godlessness and unbelief not to believe every word of God and to be unable to believe that the forgiveness of sins has also been promised to you.

Moreover, the Epistle to the Hebrews adds examples to illustrate its definition: "By faith we understand that the world was created by the word of God," so that the invisibility of God's divinity and power might be made visible, and this, of course, by the work of God's power [v. 3]. So this passage agrees with that found in Romans [1:20]. But at this the sophists will foolishly clamor that another faith is demanded of us besides historical faith, since the Epistle to the Hebrews speaks here only of history, that is, the creation of the world. But listen: If this example pertains to historical faith only, how will it square with the definition of faith just given? Besides, he calls faith in the history of the world's creation not merely some common opinion held also by gentiles and Muslims, but knowledge of God's power and goodness, which are understood from his creative work. This faith is no different from Peter's or Paul's. For Peter understands the power of God with reference to Christ's resurrection, and he understands his mercy and goodness because he believes that Christ became a victim and satisfaction for him, and this without any work of his own. He simply trusts in the mercy that God promised in Christ. So also he who by the Spirit assesses the creation of the universe also sees the power of God who is the Creator of these things. He also sees his goodness, since he realizes that he receives everything from the hands of his Creator, including life, food, and children. And he commends all these things to his Creator to govern, rule, manage, and supply as it pleases him and according to his goodness. This faith in the creation of the universe is no idle opinion, but a most tenacious recognition of God's power and goodness, which pours itself out on all creatures, and rules and governs them. If I could explain God's goodness as the matter deserves and demands, how many pages I would use up on this one point! But he who truly believes will easily judge, by the Spirit's guidance, what this faith in the creation of the universe is.

Perhaps the sophists will laugh at this. But let them laugh. For they cannot refute what I know is so sure that even the gates of hell cannot overthrow it. Paul calls faith in creation something more noble and fervent than mere Scholastic opinion when he says in Romans 1:[20], "The visible things of God, namely his eternal power and divinity, are seen through visible things." But what are God's power and divinity other than his might and goodness? We also read in Acts 14:[17], "He has not left himself without a witness, since he does good and gives rain from heaven and fruitful seasons." And how delightfully David occupies himself as he contemplates creation in Psalm 104: "You have made all things in your wisdom. The earth is full of your possessions" [v. 24]. And again, "All wait for you, that you may give them their food in due time. When you give it to them they will gather it and when you open up your hand all will be filled with your goodness" [vv. 27–28]. Now tell me, can the flesh discuss the mystery of creation like this? Or can philosophy, that chaos of carnal dreams? But since it assumes that all things happen contingently, philosophy clearly denies the work of creation.[13]

---

[13] What Melanchthon calls "philosophy" here is closer to what we today call "science." It takes no account of God's continued working in his creation (*creatio continua*), because it cannot see God's invisible hand. Instead it judges by observable causes and effects according to scientific principles. Melanchthon writes in the 1559 edition of his *Loci*: "Philosophy teaches that we should doubt whatever has not been experienced by the senses, is not a principle, and has not been proved through experimentation. So, for instance, one can doubt or suspend judgment on whether the concavity of a cloud is the only reason a rainbow is an arch. But we must understand

In the same manner the people of the Law knew the power and goodness of God from the fact that he redeemed them from slavery in Egypt. In fact, this is what Exodus 20:[2] says, "I am the Lord your God who led you out of the land of Egypt from the house of slavery," etc. And before the Law was given, the Fathers knew the power and goodness of God by the things that God had done with Abraham, Isaac, and Jacob. This is why they call him the God of Abraham, etc. So also before the Fathers, the creation of the universe was a sure sign and stamp by which they could recognize God. In this way Abel and others believed, though the promise that the serpent's head would be crushed by the seed of Eve also awakened faith in them. Therefore, the Epistle to the Hebrews adds, "By faith Abel offered a better sacrifice than Cain" [11:4]. There is no doubt that both Abel and Cain had knowledge of history. Otherwise, why would Cain even make an offering? Therefore when he attributes faith to Abel and not to Cain, he is designating not some historical opinion but the faith that gives glory to God, thinks well of God, trusts in his mercy, etc. By this faith Abel was victorious and through this faith he obtained the witness that he was righteous. The author diligently notes this very thing in his epistle, and he does so to teach that faith is what is accounted for righteousness, not a sacrifice or any work. "By faith Enoch was taken up so that he might not see death," that is, because Enoch believed God was pleased with him [v. 5]. And God wanted to show the Fathers both proof and hope of a better life in Enoch by taking him up. For there is no need to ask where he was taken, so long as we understand that in him an example of life and the surest proof of immortality was given to the Fathers to strengthen their faith.

And the chapter continues, "Without faith it is impossible to please God. For he who approaches God must believe in him, both that he exists and that he rewards those who seek him" [v. 6]. You see that this cannot be understood of the Scholastics' faith, since it is clear enough that hypocrites do not trust in God, his mercy, his goodwill, or his salvation. For if you interrogate their hearts, they will respond something like this: "I do not know whether my works have been accepted by God. I do not know whether I can be saved. I know,

___

that the doctrine of the Church that God has given us is certain and immovable, even if it is not comprehended by the senses or innate to us like principles or discovered by experimentation. But the cause of certainty is God's revelation, which is true" (*SA* 2:169).

of course, that salvation has been promised. I know that God is merciful. But perhaps he will not act according to his mercy with me. His majesty does not take account of me." They say many similarly godless things besides. But not even what the unbelievers say about the judgment of God proceeds from a sincere heart. For they despise God's judgment and do not fear it until they are confounded by God. But we would be utterly won over if our heart could conceive the greatness of God's goodness and the fullness of his grace, and if our heart could confess with trust: "God has not forgotten me. So great is his mercy that if you should trust him, he would save, protect, and heal you. Trust therefore." Hearts that have been strengthened in this way by recognition of God's goodness, believing that what God has promised will come to them, these are the hearts that truly believe that God is their Rewarder. No, more than that, these are the hearts that truly believe in God. For the godless do not believe but are gripped by a cold opinion which does not consent from the bottom of the heart.

"By faith Noah, after receiving a divine message and in fear of things not yet seen, built an ark to save his household" [v. 7]. Look how the faith of Noah embraces two things—the threats and the promise. This is what I meant before when I said that the godless do not believe in the Word of God at all, neither its threats nor its promises. Noah gave glory to God by acknowledging the truth of his words. Therefore, he both feared God's threats and trusted in his promise of salvation and mercy. You should have no doubt that many, even in those times, were hypocrites who acted like they had faith that God exists, punishes evildoers, and saves the righteous. But those threats of God had not moved them. Why? Because they would not believe with a sincere heart. Nor did the promise of salvation through the ark move them since they did not trust God's mercy for them. Therefore, the faith of the sophists is nothing but pure imposture, sheer mockery of souls, and still these impious and godless sophists teach that their fictitious faith is enough to be considered a good work! But what proceeds from hatred of or contempt for God is no good work. Whatever does not proceed from trust in God's mercy and goodness proceeds from hatred of and contempt for God. This is exactly what Paul says, "Whatever is not of faith is sin" [Romans 14:23]. And the author of Hebrews says, "Through the ark he condemned the world" [11:7]. It follows that if faith saved the one, then unbelief destroyed the others. And how anxiously he insists that faith in God's mercy and grace is the height of righteousness when he adds, "And he was made an heir of the righteousness that comes through faith" [v. 7]. I am not talking about figures here, nor am I seeking after allegories.[14] Rather I am concerning myself with the very simple, historical narrative. Noah is justified not by any work of his own but by faith alone in the mercy of God. This faith had arisen in Noah both from this promise of rescue from the flood and from the promise that had been handed down from his fathers concerning the head of the serpent, that is, concerning the crushing of death's sting.

"By faith Abraham obeyed when he was called to depart to a place that he would receive for his inheritance, and he left not knowing where he was going" [v. 8]. Abraham trusted in God's mercy and goodness, not doubting that wherever he was, God would be there for him as his Protector and Savior. Therefore, leaving his fatherland, he entrusted himself to God's voice, just as the Israelites entrusted themselves to Moses' voice when they entered the seafloor of the Red Sea. And how great was Abraham's faith! For it was not shaken even though he wandered his entire life in unknown places. Because he was living his life under the shade of God's wings, he thought that he was able enough, rich enough, and living in a place that was safe enough. And because he saw that neither he nor his son would obtain a sure home in Canaan and knew that he was a stranger in this land, he had hope that he would be a citizen in the eternal city. "By faith Sarah received the ability to conceive" [v. 11]. For the word of God creates and gives life to all things. When Sarah trusted in this word, that is, the promise of offspring, how could it not happen that she become fertile, though previously infertile and barren? "For all things are possible to the one who believes" [Mark 9:23]. But how the faith of Abraham was attacked, how it was struck with a strong ram when he was commanded to sacrifice Isaac, in whom he knew his posterity had been promised![15] And how strong was the young man Isaac's faith when he did not hesitate to obey his father's command and so to obey the will of God! Do you think that the father could have carried out the cruel command against his son, the one in whom his posterity had been promised, and do you think that the son would

---

[14] See p. 76, n. 28.

[15] The pun on the battering ram and the animal ram is the same in Latin (*aries*) as it is in English. Melanchthon undoubtedly uses the word here to allude to the ram offered instead of Isaac.

have obeyed his father, unless each trusted in God's mercy and entrusted themselves to it? Nor did faith fail. The son was saved and restored to his father while the father's obedience was praised. You see here a prelude to sin and death and justification and resurrection and thus to the entire New Testament. Surely not only Abraham and Isaac, but also all the godly who lived before the revelation of the Gospel learned here to hope in God's goodwill when facing death. Surely from this example the Fathers took hold of faith in the victory over death and saw here a prelude to Christ who would crush the head of the serpent and the sting of death.

"By faith Isaac blessed Jacob and Esau," believing that they would finally occupy the promised land [Hebrews 11:20]. But more remarkable than this is that he wanted the blessing of Jacob confirmed, the blessing stolen from his older brother to whom it was due by the custom of the Gentiles. He did this, no doubt, because of his faith in God's word: "The older will serve the younger" [Genesis 25:23]. "By faith Jacob blessed the sons of Joseph," although they were then exiles [Hebrews 11:21]. But Jacob did not doubt that they would return to Canaan and be the beginnings of great nations. Nor did the parents of Moses doubt that they would return to Palestine, and it was for this reason that they hid the infant, the hope of their race [v. 23]. This is also why they exposed him to divine mercy instead of killing him.

If you want to add further examples, you certainly could. We have simply pointed out the way to treat these examples. We have not taught the hypocrisy of the sophists, but the faith spoken of by the author of the Epistle to the Hebrews, that is, trust in God's mercy and grace. You do not see here a distinction between the promises of God. Rather, note that the word that faith trusts is simply the promise of God's mercy and grace, whether it deals with eternal or temporal matters. But in general, promises of spiritual things can be inferred from material promises, and I do not mean only through allegory but by the clear and obvious testimony of the Spirit. The sacrifice of his son clearly teaches Abraham what he should hope for when facing death. A further reason not to distinguish between promises is that all other promises point to the first promise concerning the seed of Eve, that is, Christ. Posterity was expected because that Seed was expected, namely Christ. And so the promise made to Eve was renewed in the promise made to Abraham, when God says in Genesis 22:[18], "In your seed all the nations of the earth will be blessed," which cannot be explained except concerning Christ. So the apostle interprets it in Galatians 3:16, " 'In your seed,' who is Christ." In Genesis 49:[10], Jacob makes it plain enough that posterity was expected and a kingdom was expected because of the promised Christ: "The scepter will not depart from Judah nor a leader from his loins, until the one who is to be sent comes, and he will be the expectation of the nations." What else did he mean here except that the promise of a kingdom and all the promises of material things refer to Christ and are fulfilled in Christ? This is why Paul cites all the promises made to Abraham without distinction. In Galatians 3:[8], he cites the promise found in Genesis 12:[3], "In you all the nations will be blessed." And in Romans 4:[13–25] he says that the inheritance of the world was promised to Abraham in that the sons of Abraham are those from all nations who have believed, and because all believers are kings in Christ their King. In the same way the Psalm says, "You have put all things under his feet" [Psalm 8:6].

Moreover, now that the Gospel has been clearly revealed, those who believe in Christ have all material blessings in him: "For if God did not spare his own Son, but delivered him up for us all, how will he not give us all things in him?" [Romans 8:32]. And this very promise is evident from the nature of the kingdom, because if all creatures have been subjected to Christ, then they have also been subjected to his brothers, whether death, famine, sword, powers, height, depth, sin, or whatever else human infirmity fears—it is all under our power, subjected under our feet, unless we do not believe that Christ is reigning. What I said above also applies here—faith permeates every circumstance of our life and death. This is the case because we cannot use any created thing rightly except by faith. We abuse all created things by our unbelief, that is, by not believing that our use of the created thing is pleasing to God and by despairing of God's mercy and kindness toward us when we use created things. He who does not believe that poverty, death, and other adverse circumstances are the works of God's mercy abuses them. He does not trust when he is in these circumstances, but flees to the aid of men and doubts that he can overcome his misfortunes in Christ. So Abraham would have abused that most tragic command to slaughter his son, unless he had freely and obediently committed himself to God's mercy, trusting that God always dealt with him according to his fatherly love. In the same way, he who does not acknowledge that money, life, and favorable circumstances are gifts of God's mercy and does not use them in faith as if they were gifts belonging to someone else abuses them.

In summary, he who has Christ has all things and can do all things. Here is righteousness, peace, life, and salvation. So you see that in this way God's promises are united. For these promises are really individual significations and testimonies of God's goodwill toward us that he by one act or another, by one gift or another, commends and makes known to us. Therefore by means of the whole narrative of Scripture, God devotes himself entirely to the task of teaching and persuading us to trust in his goodness. Now if anyone contemplates the goodness of God, which has been illustrated so often with so many promises, how will he be able to restrain himself from surrendering his soul and spirit to the care of such great mercy? Moreover, Christ has merited God's goodwill, and it is Christ whom God has given to be an intercessor for us, to be our sacrifice, and to make satisfaction for us: "For God so loved the world that he gave his only begotten Son for the world" [John 3:16]. Because he favors Christ, he favors us. Because he has put all things under Christ, he has put all things under us. And so all the promises must be referred to Christ, who has merited for us his Father's mercy and reconciled him to us. This is what John 1:[16] says, "From his fullness we all have received, and grace for grace." This means that God shows favor toward us for the sake of his favor toward Christ. You will exercise your spirit well by meditation on the promises, because Christ cannot be known except from the promises. But unless you know Christ, you will not know the Father. Therefore direct all the thoughts of your spirit to this end and strive to learn from the promises what has been given to you in Christ. But tell me, where has Scholastic theology acknowledged the promises, even with a single word? And so it has come about that Scholastic theology has obscured Christ, and instead of offering him as the guarantee of God's mercy, it has made him into a lawgiver and exactor far more severe than Moses ever seemed to be.

So far concerning the promises, all of which should be traced back to that first promise made to Eve, by which God confirmed to Adam and Eve that sin and death, the punishment for sin, would be destroyed when the offspring of Eve would crush the head of that infamous serpent. For what do the head of the serpent and the intrigue of the serpent signify except the reign of sin and death? If you refer the other promises to this promise, you will see that the Gospel, which is simply the forgiveness of sins on account of Christ or the preaching of grace, marvelously permeates all of Scripture. But, as I said before, all the promises, even those concerning material blessings, are testimonies of God's goodwill and mercy. And whoever believes in these promises is righteous because he thinks well of God and praises him for his mercy and goodness. He who only hears the threats and professes the history does not yet believe God's every word. Only he does this who believes the promises in addition to the threats and history. But faith is not belief in the history of Christ, as the godless think, but belief in the purpose of Christ's incarnation, crucifixion, and resurrection. For he took on flesh, was crucified, and rose from the dead in order to justify all who would believe in him. If you believe that these things were done for your good and for your salvation, your faith is fruitful. Whatever they call faith outside of this faith is a sham, a lie, and deceptive madness.

Why then is justification attributed to faith alone? My answer is that since we are justified by God's mercy alone and since faith is clearly the recognition of this mercy (regardless of which promise you have taken hold of), justification is attributed to faith alone. Those who wonder why justification is attributed to faith alone are the same ones who wonder why justification is attributed to God's mercy alone and not to human merits. For trusting in God's mercy means believing without any regard to our own works. Whoever denies that the saints are justified by faith insults the mercy of God. For since our justification is the work of God's mercy alone, our works do not earn it. Paul teaches this clearly in Romans 11:[6]. It is necessary that justification be attributed to faith because we receive the promised mercy by faith alone.

What then about the works that precede justification, the works of the free will? These are all cursed fruits of a cursed tree. And though they be examples of the most beautiful virtues, such as the righteous works of Paul before his conversion, they are nothing but a sham and a lie proceeding from an impure heart. Impurity of the heart and ignorance of God consist in not fearing God, not trusting in him, and not seeking after him, as we stressed above. For the flesh seeks after nothing but carnal things, as Romans 8:[5] says, "The flesh desires the things of the flesh." And 1 Corinthians 2:[14, 16], "Natural man does not perceive the things of the Spirit of God. . . . Who has learned the mind of the Lord?" Human nature understands, seeks after, and desires glory, wealth, tranquility of life, and honor. The philosophers count many such things among the goals of good people, one claiming tranquility of mind (εὐθυμίαν) should be our aspiration, with another claiming freedom from pain (ἀναλγησίαν) as the objective.[16] But it is clear that human nature wants nothing to do with God. For it neither fears the Word of God nor is it given to trust in it. Now what are the fruits of such a tree except sin?

But the works that follow justification, although they proceed from the Spirit of God who fills the hearts of the justified, are still impure themselves, since they are done in flesh that is still impure. For justification has begun but is not finished.[17] We have received the firstfruits of the Spirit, but we do not have the full inheritance yet. We still wait for the redemption of our body with groaning, as Romans 8:[23] says. Moreover, since there is a certain impurity even in these works, they do not merit the name "righteousness." No matter where you turn, whether to the works that come before justification or to those that follow justification, there is no place for our merit. Therefore, justification must be the work of God's mercy alone. This is what Paul says in Galatians 2:[20], "The life that I now live in the flesh I live by faith in the Son of God, who loved me and gave himself for me." He does not say, "Now I live in my good works," but, "I live by faith in the mercy of God." Because of faith, moreover,

---

[16] Melanchthon has Stoicism and Epicureanism in mind, respectively, though earlier philosophers, for example Plato, expressed similar views. But this is not simply a reference to discarded and arcane philosophy. The humanists, especially Erasmus, had revived and endorsed these ancient philosophers, promoting emotional and mental tranquility through human virtues. Cf. Albert Salomon's summarization of Erasmus's philosophy: "Moral learning and spiritual learning as a way of life lead to Christian liberty, tranquility of mind, and peace of conscience—ideals of human perfection on which pagans and Christians, Epicurus and Christ, agree" (*In Praise of Enlightenment* [Cleveland, 1963], 43).

[17] Melanchthon uses the word *iustificatio* ("justification") in its broader sense of *iustitia* ("righteousness"), denoting an ethical righteousness. Use of "justification" for "righteousness" is a holdover from humanist usage. Melanchthon uses *iustificatio* elsewhere in this work to mean "righteousness," e.g., when citing the Vulgate translation of Romans 8:4: "Paul says that the righteousness (*iustificatio*) of the law could not be fulfilled by the flesh" (p. 58). The context of his use of the word here shows that he is speaking of the ongoing sanctification of the Christian. See p. 159, n. 13 below. For a good treatment of Melanchthon's use of the term *iustificatio* in this work, see Michael Rogness, *Philip Melanchthon: Reformer without Honor* (Minneapolis: Augsburg, 1969), 36–43.

the works that follow justification are not imputed as sins. This point will be treated shortly.

Therefore when justification is attributed to faith, it is attributed to the mercy of God and denied to human endeavors, works, and merits. The beginning and continuation of righteousness belong to God's mercy, with the result that there is no righteousness in all one's life besides faith. This is why the prophet Isaiah calls Christ's kingdom a kingdom of mercy: "And his throne will be established in mercy," etc. (Isaiah 16:[5]). For if we were justified by our own works, the kingdom would no longer be Christ's but ours. It would no longer be the kingdom of Christ and the kingdom of mercy but our kingdom and the kingdom of our works. Hosea 2:[19–20] says the same thing: "I will betroth you to me forever, and I will betroth you to me in righteousness and justice, in mercy and in compassion, and I will betroth you to me in faith. And you will know that I am the Lord." And Psalm 89:[14], "Mercy and truth go before your face." This mercy is favor that is given freely and pays no regard to merit. This truth is the work of God who justifies us in truth and without hypocrisy (ὑποκριτικῶς). But why cite so many passages when the prophet Isaiah openly condemns all our righteousness when he says, "We all like sheep have gone astray, each one has turned aside to his own way. And the Lord has put on him the iniquity of us all" (Isaiah 53:[6])? A little later he says that our justification is not of our own works, not of the noble endeavors of our will, not by our counsels, but rather that Christ himself will justify many by knowledge of himself. You see that knowledge of Christ is justification. Moreover, knowledge is nothing other than faith. The diligent reader will note other passages of this kind on his own. For I seem not to have the ability to explain with words the nature and power of faith as I had hoped. Those who know the power of sin and whose consciences have been struck by the knowledge of their sin finally have the desire to hear the teaching about faith. "But our Gospel has been hidden from the hypocrites whose unbelieving minds the god of this world has blinded so that the light of the Gospel of Christ's glory, who is the image of God, might not shine on them" [2 Corinthians 4:3–4].

You will say, "Do we merit nothing then? Why then does Scripture use the word "reward" so often?" My response is that there is a reward, yet it is owed not because of any merit of our own but because the Father promised it. He has, as it were, bound himself to us and made himself a debtor to those who had merited no such thing. For what could be said more clearly against our merits than the passage in Luke 17:[9–10], "Does he then thank that servant because he did what he had commanded? I don't think so. So you also, when you have done all that has been commanded of you, say: 'We are unprofitable servants. We have done what we were supposed to do.' "[18] And Paul states in Romans 6:[23], "The wage of sin is death, but the gift of God is eternal life." He calls eternal life a gift, not a debt, though it *is* a debt because the Father promised it and has bound himself in faithfulness to us.

Nor do those passages of Scripture that seem to teach the merits of works give any offense. Examples of such passages include Romans 2:[10], "Glory and honor to everyone who does good," and Matthew 25:[35], "I was hungry and you gave me something to eat," etc. There are many such passages in the Scriptures. My response is short—Scripture is not speaking about the outward aspect or appearance of the work only, but about the entire work, that is, both the outward appearance and especially the will or the affection, which is the origin of the work. Scripture does not call the mere outward aspect of a work a good work, but the entire work, that is, the good affection and the fruit of this affection. This is the ordinary, commonsense way of speaking. After all, when someone knows that a work has been perpetrated with evil motive, does he call it a good work? Thus when Paul says, "Glory and honor to everyone who does good," I do not see why we need any gloss here to prevent us from understanding this passage as simply as possible, as it reads. For Paul does not say, "to the one pretending to do good," but "to the one who works" from the heart, from his affection, as well as with his hands and in the external work. Therefore, those who interpret the apostle's words as if he is speaking not about the entire work, not about the life and soul of the work, but about the outward appearance of the work, are corrupting the apostle's statement, which was spoken so simply and correctly. It is a commonly accepted opinion in the schools and natural common sense also teaches that the goodness of a work cannot be assessed outside of the affections. Those who interpret

---

[18] Melanchthon cites the same passage in AC VI, *On Good Works*, to show that Scripture attributes no justifying merit to our good works.

Scripture concerning only a part of the work and not concerning the entire work should consult common sense.

What of the fact that Paul, in the very same passage, most beautifully assigns a life of good works to faith and teaches that good works arise from faith as from a spring? For he says, "To those seeking glory and honor through perseverance in doing good ..." [Romans 2:7]. Now this "seeking" is nothing else than what is written in Hebrews 11:[6], "He who approaches God must believe in him, both that he exists and that he rewards those who seek him." Those seek who believe and are drawn to glory by trust in God's Word. Moreover, how can the power and nature of faith be expressed more clearly than with the word "perseverance"? For amid so many enticements of the flesh and the world, amid so many afflictions, nobody without great faith can remain firm and endure in good works. More than this, in the same passage Paul assigns a life of wickedness to unbelief, saying, "To the contentious and those who do not assent to the truth" [Romans 2:8]. What is refusal to assent to the truth except unbelief? And those are contentious who are opposed to the truth, who follow the judgment of the flesh. For whoever openly sins does so either out of contempt for God or because he despairs of God's mercy. In 2 Kings 18, Sennacherib took up his godless arms against Israel because he considered God to be nothing. Cain, because he despaired of God's mercy, was not afraid to do something wicked afterwards. For no one who trusted God's mercy would fail to follow God's Law with the utmost eagerness. But because we are contentious, we deliberate within ourselves and imagine that God's anger and his mercy are less extensive than they are in reality. Then, in contempt for God's anger and his mercy, we turn to our own desires. Godless, blind, and insane, we attempt nothing except out of love for glory, possessions, or pleasures. What a pathetic spectacle it would be to see that godless insanity and insane godlessness of your heart!

You see, then, how appropriately Paul assigned a life of good works to faith and a life of wickedness to unbelief. In the same way, the context supplies the meaning for other, similar passages, so that there is no need for foreign glosses. I leave the treatment of these passages to the industry of spiritual readers. By spiritual readers, I do not mean those terribly idle sophists, for nothing has been said so well or so simply that they could not pervert, divide, and dissect it into a thousand different meanings. If you judge the matter correctly, there is certainly no obscurity in the passage from Matthew that we cited. Not to press the argument, but it cannot be denied that when Christ calls them blessed of his Father, he means that salvation depends on God's blessing, not on our merits. Of course Christ is talking about the works of faith when he says, "I was hungry and you gave me something to eat," and a little later, "What you have done to the least of these my brothers, you have done to me" [Matthew 25:40]. Because the just believe that what they do for the brothers they do for Christ, they act righteously. This faith marks the distinction between good works and evil works. Hypocrites give food and drink to themselves, not to Christ. For they serve their own glory no matter how much they show off with the appearance of the most admirable virtues.

These examples will have to be enough for the studious to have a model for treating similar passages. For my part, I need to moderate the scope of my commentary.

THE EFFICACY OF FAITH

Now we also have to consider that works are fruits of the Spirit, that is, indications, testimonies, and signs of the Spirit's work, as Christ says, "From their fruits you will know them" [Matthew 7:16]. For hypocrisy cannot deceive forever, just as it is impossible for faith not to pour itself out and serve God in all his creatures with the utmost eagerness, as a pious son serves his pious father. For when by faith we have tasted God's mercy and come to know his goodness through the word of the Gospel, which forgives us our sins and promises God's favor despite our sin, our soul cannot but love God in return and rejoice in him. Thus it gives a sort of testament to its thankfulness for such great mercy by reciprocating some kind and dutiful work. Paul expressed this so meaningfully when he said that by faith we cry out, "Abba, Father" [Romans 8:15]. Now because such a mind truly submits itself to God, ambition, jealousy, malice, envy, greed, sinful pleasures, and the fruits of these vices are strangled. This mind desires humble things, hates itself, and detests all its sinful desires. Paul says it so well in Romans 6:[21], stating that the converted mind is now ashamed of those things in which we used to revel. It therefore pours itself out for all its neighbors, serves them, makes itself available for their use, considers their need its own, and does all things with all people honestly, sincerely, and without ambition or malice. This is the efficacy of faith. Therefore, from these fruits it is clear in whose hearts true faith resides.

Concerning such faith Galatians 5:[6] speaks, "In Christ Jesus neither circumcision nor uncircumcision avails anything, but faith that is efficacious through love." It says that faith in Christ avails, then describes this faith as pouring itself out in love for the benefit of its neighbor. John, in 1 John 4:[7–8], expresses the same thing admirably: "Everyone who loves his brother has been born of God and knows God. He who does not love does not know God, because God is love." And 2 Peter 1:[5–8] states, "Furnish your faith with virtue, your virtue with knowledge, your knowledge with self-control, your self-control with patience, your patience with godliness, your godliness with affection for your brother, your affection for your brother with love. For if these things belong to you, they will make it so that your knowledge of our Lord Jesus Christ is not unfruitful." By this progression Peter grafts other virtues into faith, like most beautiful branches into their root, so that virtue, that is, the fervent passion to mortify the flesh, is joined to faith. But knowledge should govern this passion so that the body is also given care. Some consideration should be given so that the subjugated body may serve the Spirit readily (εὐπροσέδρως),[19] to use the Pauline term, and not be killed. But it should not serve the needs of the body to the point of luxury, but so that it possesses self-control. Now besides self-control, there should also be endurance of evils. For many possess self-control but cannot handle offense. Godliness should accompany endurance. This means that we should not only patiently accept adverse circumstances before men but also before God. We should give thanks to him for mortifying us, not despising his will as the Israelites did, who grumbled against the will of God and perished in the wilderness. Godliness should bring about affection for our brothers. This means that we should think well even of those who persecute us and that we should treat our enemies with kindness. Finally, all this should come from a sincere heart, so that we love all people equally and sincerely. This faith with its fruits is the sum of the entire Christian life. Nor is it necessary to divide the virtues into types and categories like the philosophers and Scholastics, or, like Aquinas and

---

[19] See 1 Corinthians 7:25.

his ilk, into moral virtues, theological virtues, gifts, and fruits.[20] What inanity! Faith stands alone as the recognition of God's mercy and as the source, life, and root of all good works.

LOVE AND HOPE

It is clear from what has just been discussed how love of God and love of our neighbor arise from faith. They call this love "charity" (*caritas*). For knowledge of God's mercy leads us to love God in return, leads us to subject ourselves willingly to all creatures and thus to love our neighbor. Hope, moreover, is also faith's working. For faith is that by which we believe the Word, and hope is that by which we expect what has been promised in the Word. Faith in the Word of God causes us to expect the promise, as Psalm 9:[12] states, "Let all who know your name hope in you." There is no reason to separate one from the other. Scripture, after all, uses the words "hope" and "faith," "expecting" and "enduring" interchangeably. And just as faith is trust in God's gracious mercy with no regard for our works, so hope is an expectation of salvation with no regard for our merits. In fact, hope has nothing to do with God if it is based on our merits. For how could anyone hope for mercy when he is asking for a reward as if it were owed to his own merits? The afflicted conscience rejoices, and the sinner who believes the Gospel rejoices that there is no regard for our merits. But the hypocrite is indignant. Therefore, Christ is an offense to the Jews and foolishness to the Gentiles, but to those who believe, he is wisdom and salvation [Romans 1:16].

First Corinthians 13:[2] is cited in opposition to those who defend the righteousness of faith: "If I have faith so great that I could move a mountain, but do not have love, I am nothing." But I must ask you, sophists, why, when you see that all of Scripture insists on teaching that justification is a work of mercy and that Paul so often repeats this in the clearest words, "The just lives by faith" [Romans 1:17], and, "The one who believes on him who justifies the ungodly, his faith is accounted for righteousness" [4:5], and, "It is believed with the heart unto righteousness" [10:10], and many other similar expressions, I ask you why you oppose this one passage from Corinthians to all of Scripture and to the constant preaching of all of Paul's epistles? So

---

[20] See *Summa* I–II, qq. 61–70, esp. qq. 68–70 where Aquinas distinguishes the gifts and fruits of the Spirit from the moral and theological virtues.

while you excuse all other passages with glosses, you are unwilling to interpret this one passage with some qualification? We will explain this passage without any gloss as simply as can be, since it is already very simply put. First of all, it is clear enough that Paul is speaking about love of our neighbor in this passage. Not even your schools attribute the beginning of justification to this kind of love. (I am not going to waste time here on that fiction that love of God and the neighbor is the same.)[21] Furthermore, it cannot be denied that he has here used the word "faith" to designate the gift or faculty of performing miracles. First Corinthians 12:[9] testifies to this, where it reads, "Faith to another by the same Spirit." But it is generally accepted that the gift (χάρισμα) of performing miracles can also be conferred on the godless, as can prophecy, knowledge of languages, and eloquence.[22]

Even if you do not separate justifying faith much from the gift of performing miracles, it is my opinion that Paul here requires love along with faith, just as he does throughout almost the entire epistle. In the same way, he requires good works from the believers, from those who have been justified, in every one of his epistles. Although faith does not of itself lack these fruits, he still commands them because of the weakness of our faith. And his judgment is correct when he says that the man who lacks love but has all the faith in the world is nothing. For although faith alone justifies, love is still required, namely the Second Table of the Law, as Romans 13:[9] says, "The entire law is summed up in this: 'love your neighbor as yourself.' " But love does not justify. For nobody loves as much as he should. Faith justifies. And faith trusts in God's mercy, not in its own merit.

The passage in James [2:17] remains: "Faith without works is dead." James has certainly spoken well here. He is censuring those who judge that faith consists in a historical opinion about Christ. Therefore, just as Paul distinguishes between feigned faith and true faith, so James distinguished between faith that is dead and faith that is alive. This living faith is a powerful and eager trust in God's mercy,

---

[21] Among others, Aquinas argues that love of God and love of neighbor are the same act, since the neighbor is only loved in and under God, just as it is the same act to see color and to see the light that makes seeing the color possible (*Summa* I–II, q. 25, art. 1).

[22] All listed as gifts of the Spirit in 1 Corinthians 12:7–10.

never failing to produce good fruit. This is what James means when he says, "Faith is perfected by works" [James 2:22]. Also, because Abraham's works showed that he had a living faith, therefore "Scripture was fulfilled where it says: 'Abraham believed God and it was accounted to him as righteousness' " [2:23]. James's whole point, then, is that a dead faith, that is, a cold Parisian opinion, does not justify. A living faith justifies. But a living faith abounds in works. This is why James says, "Show me your faith without works, and I will show you my faith from my works" [2:18]. Now what he does not say is, "I will show you my works without faith." What James says about faith, then, squares perfectly with what I have explained, "If faith does not have works, it is dead in itself" [2:17]. Therefore, it is quite clear that James is only teaching that faith is dead in those who do not produce the fruits of faith, even if they seem to believe in outward appearance.

It will be quite appropriate to treat a matter that I see is constantly debated, namely, how a man knows whether he is in God's grace or whether it can be known that faith is present in our hearts. The first question concerns God's will toward us, not our affections. The second deals with our affections alone. With utter shamelessness the Scholastics have falsely taught that neither can be known. Therefore, from this point alone it is quite clear that the Spirit was entirely absent from that whole clan. For why would the flesh, with its complete ignorance of God, care how it can know God's will toward it? And how will the flesh make judgments about spiritual affections when it is not even well-acquainted with its own affections? "For man's heart is corrupt and inscrutable" [Jeremiah 17:9]. Therefore, the Scholastics imagined that there lay snoring in man's soul several qualities of which we ourselves were ignorant. More than this, they have maintained that God does not want us even to ask about these things, with the result that the conscience is restless within itself and in perpetual uncertainty.[23] But what are they teaching here except despair? As far as I can tell, that is exactly what they are doing.

---

[23] Melanchthon again echoes Luther in maintaining that Christians can be certain of their salvation because their confidence lies not in their own works or latent virtues, but in the sure promise of forgiveness for Christ's sake. Luther's insistence that faith is no mere opinion but the Christian's absolute certainty that God is merciful to him can be seen clearly in his commentary on the Psalms (1519–21): "But there cannot be any faith besides that living and undoubting judgment by which a man is certain

Now as concerns God's will, faith is nothing less than a certain and constant trust in God's goodwill toward us. God's will is known, but it is known by faith from the promise or the Gospel. For you are not crediting God the glory of telling the truth unless you believe that his will accords with what he declares in the Gospel. Those who believe the Word of God and assess God's will according to his Word—and not according to our merits—know that they are in God's grace and that they have a benevolent God. Paul therefore uses many arguments in Romans 4 to teach that righteousness belongs to faith. Finally he adds this most effective line of reasoning: If justification belongs to our works rather than to faith, the conscience could never rest, since our lives and works lack now this and now that, so that nothing could be done except to despair. This is why he says that it is not of works "so that the promise according to grace may be secure" [Romans 4:16]. How often the prophets rejoice in this security! For example, Hosea 2:[18], "I will make them sleep securely." And Jeremiah 23:[6], "In those days Judah will be saved, and Israel will live in confidence." Now what else do the words "securely," "in confidence," and others like them designate except security? Micah [4:4] expresses this security so beautifully, "A man will sit under his vine and under his fig tree." There is nothing obscure in Isaiah's description, "And the work of righteousness will be peace, and the cultivation of righteousness will be tranquility and security forever. And my people will sit in the beauty of peace and in secure tents and in opulent rest" (Isaiah 32:[17–18]). In this way, the prophets describe the kingdom of Christ as a kingdom of security. But where is the security if consciences are constantly in doubt about God's will? Therefore, we must be certain of God's favor and goodwill toward us. This is what the Lord says in Jeremiah 9:[24], "Let him who glories glory in this, that he understands and knows me." God wants his will to be known, and he wants us to rejoice in it. What then is more godless than to assert that the will of God either cannot be known or ought not be known? Indeed, nothing could be more godless, since God has revealed his will in his Word.

Now let us ask the sophists whether they believe what the Apostles' Creed states about the forgiveness of sins. And do they believe the declaration of the priest when they are absolved? Now if

above all certainty that he is pleasing to God, that God is propitious and merciful to him" (WA 5:395).

143

they believe it, then they must acknowledge that they are in God's grace. But if they do not believe it, why do they confess their sins? Vile Rome and Eck, the author of the Roman bull, have condemned a particular statement of Luther's on faith, which teaches that we must believe the absolution.[24] Let them answer, then, why they go to hear the absolution if they do not believe it. This is a strange piety and more pernicious than anyone would have imagined. I do not doubt that it has killed many souls, which have been led to despair because of this carnal, sophistic, Parisian teaching. May the Lord destroy all lips that speak a lie! With experience as its teacher, the Christian mind will easily learn that Christianity is nothing but a life certain of God's mercy. In Romans 12:[2], Paul says, "So that you may learn what is the good, perfect, and well-pleasing will of God," etc. Therefore, the sophists will say, is there nothing that we should fear? Exactly. If fear lacks faith, it is a godless fear. But the fear that is joined with faith is not ignorant of God's mercy but declares with Job, "I was afraid of all my works" [Job 9:28]. Saints fear because of their own works, but they trust in God's mercy. Hypocrites trust their own works, but they have no knowledge of God's mercy. More than this, they have no knowledge of the fear of God. And so the prophet has said, "The fear of God is not before their eyes" [Psalm 36:1]. This phenomenon is evident in the hypocrite of Luke 18:[9–14]. But experience with Scripture will teach the relation of fear and faith. For now, it is enough to have stressed that we should reserve fear for our own works and faith for God's mercy. Faith produces a holy fear. If fear lacks trust in God's goodness, it must be a godless fear.

But they cite Ecclesiastes 9:[1], "Man does not know whether he deserves love or hate, but everything is reserved for the future." This does not mean that man does not know whether or not God forgives his iniquity. If they insist on this meaning, I could just as well get it to say that man does not know whether or not God is angry with sin. I cannot marvel enough at the deception that Satan has perpetrated in his cunning abuse of this passage of Scripture, for I see that by so doing he has snatched not only faith but also fear from the hearts of

---

[24] Luther writes in the tenth of the articles condemned by Pope Leo X's bull, "No one has his sins forgiven unless he believes that he has been forgiven when the priest forgives him. In fact, sin would remain if he did not believe that it was forgiven. For forgiveness of sin and the gift of grace are not enough, but belief in this forgiveness is necessary" (WA 7:119; AE 32:44–55).

men. What else does Paul call "the cunning" and "craftiness leading to the schemes of deceit"[25] if not the theology of Paris, which so skillfully overturns Scripture? Throughout his entire work, Solomon insists that God's judgments must not be assessed according to human arguments, and he thereby refutes the slanders of godless philosophy against the judgments of God. I wish that instead of this noxious philosophy Solomon's work were offered to the youth for instruction, so that their feeble hearts could be established by trust in and fear of God. At present philosophical godlessness and the godless judgments of poets and orators exacerbate the godlessness of our nature, which should have been repressed and removed in every way possible by the Word of God.[26]

Therefore, Solomon writes that though "they are just and wise," there is still no way that they can trust in their righteousness or wisdom, "For their works are in God's hand." See how magnificently Solomon has taught both fear and faith in only one verse! For he forbids us to trust in our own righteousness or wisdom. Furthermore, since the works of the wise and just are in God's hand, he commands them to trust in him who has the spirit of the wise and just in his power. Afterwards, Solomon says that there are those whom God loves and those whom he opposes, but man cannot know them from their appearance, but everything is reserved for the future. That is, human reason judges that those whom God loads with gifts, riches, wisdom, righteousness, and glory have been accepted by him. Moreover, it thinks that God hates those who lack these things. But when it reasons this way, it judges falsely. For maybe God especially loves those who are poor, miserable, base, and abject, while he perhaps especially despises those on whom he heaps excessive blessings. You have an example of each scenario in the children of Israel and in Pharaoh. This drives home the point that we cannot, as human reason supposes, distinguish between the godly and godless by looking at external events.

For if you would interpret Solomon as speaking about the judgment of the individual conscience, I do not see how a sinner

---

[25] Greek: κυβείαν et πανουργίαν πρὸς τὴν μεθοδείαν τῆς πλάνης. See Ephesians 4:14.

[26] The use of polyptoton, or the repetition of the same root word (here, "godless") in one statement, stresses the inescapable grasp of sin on fallen man, whose nature itself is godless and who then must face the godless influence of the world.

could be ignorant of God's anger, since nothing is more certain than that God is offended by sin. Therefore, even if we should simply grant to you that Solomon ought to be understood as speaking about the judgment of the saints' conscience, you would only be making him say that the saints are secure only insofar as they have faith. And this is what Romans 8:[24] says, "We have been saved by hope." Indeed, faith alone is clearly the saints' only security. But just as they know God's mercy by faith, so also with trusting fear they permit themselves to be judged and condemned by God's will in order to give glory to God. For so we pray, "Thy will be done." You have the example of David in 2 Samuel 15:[25–26], "If I find favor in the eyes of the Lord, he will lead me back and will show me both the ark and his tabernacle. But if he says, 'You are not pleasing to me,' then I am here, let him do what is good in his eyes." For fear cannot be separated from faith. Faith looks at God's mercy alone, but fear looks at God's judgment and our own works. So Paul enjoins in Romans 11:[20], "You stand by faith; do not be arrogant, but fear." So also Solomon's entire book is concerned with teaching that the flesh must not judge God's counsels, but that, denying ourselves, we should fear God and trust in him. Therefore, this little book can be seen, wisely I think, to be issuing a warning that we do not know whom God has chosen and whom he has rejected, and that saints should not be arrogant and sinners should not despair.

But as I understand them, Solomon's words carry the following meaning: Every man is ignorant of both God's love and his hate according to their outward appearance, because all things happen indifferently to the righteous and the godless. Therefore, it is clear enough that Solomon is not speaking about the judgment of individual consciences but about the matter of distinguishing the godly from the godless and the godly from one another by mere outward observation. The added phrase in Latin, "Everything is reserved for the future," seems to have been added by the translator for clarification. It is not in the Hebrew, as far as I know, nor in the Greek codices.[27] But this needs a longer treatment elsewhere.

Let this judgment stand most certain that we should always be most certain of the forgiveness of sin and God's goodwill toward us

---

[27] The Vulgate adds at the beginning of Ecclesiastes 9:2, *sed omnia in futuro servantur incerta* ("But all things are kept uncertain for the future"). Neither the Hebrew nor the Septuagint manuscripts have this sentence.

who have been justified.[28] Therefore, sacraments or signs of God's mercy have been added to the promises, as I will soon explain, and they give a most certain testimony that God's goodwill applies to us. As the lender is certain that he will receive money from him whose signature and autograph he has on the contract, so also the signs of Baptism and participation in the Lord's Supper have been added to the promises as the autographs of Christ (αὐτογράφοις *Christi*), so that Christians may be certain that their sins are forgiven. And the saints know by faith that they are most certainly in God's grace and that their sins have been forgiven. For God does not deceive, and he has promised that he will forgive the sins of those who believe, even if they are uncertain as to whether they will persevere.

Up to this point I have said that we should be certain of God's goodwill toward us. But what about the works of God in us? Can we know whether we, in our sin, have taken hold of the Spirit of God? My response is that the fruits of the Holy Spirit witness to us that he resides in our heart, as Paul says in Galatians 5:[24], "Those who are of Christ have crucified the flesh," etc. But each individual senses whether he hates and despises sin truly and from the heart, for this is what it means to crucify the flesh. Each individual senses whether he fears God and whether he believes in God. Hypocrisy mimics the Spirit of God, but trial will show the truth, since in affliction only the faithful endure. Besides, hypocrisy is not even able to hate vices. Whatever kind of person you think you are, see to it above all that you believe. For God wants the glory of telling the truth attributed to himself.

Now let us summarize this entire conversation on the Law, the Gospel, and faith with some headings:

I. The Law is the teaching that commands what must be done and what must not be done.

II. The Gospel is the promise of God's favor.

III. As Romans 8:[3] teaches, the Law demands the impossible, that is, love of God and the neighbor.

---

[28] Polyptoton. This repetition of the word "most certain" to describe both the confession of our certainty and our certainty itself is the start of Melanchthon's rhetorical recapitulation against the uncertainty taught by the Scholastics. He repeats the superlative of *certus* ("certain") four times in this paragraph.

IV. Those who try to fulfill the Law through the powers of human nature or the free will merely simulate outward actions, but do not elicit the affections demanded by the Law.

V. Therefore, they do not satisfy the Law but are hypocrites, "whitewashed tombs," as Christ calls them [Matthew 23:27]. And according to Galatians 3:[10], "Those who are of the works of the Law are under the curse."

VI. Therefore, justification is not the work of the Law.

VII. But the proper work of the Law is to reveal sin and especially to confound the conscience. According to Romans 3:[20], "Through the law is the knowledge of sin."

VIII. The Gospel reveals Christ to the conscience that has acknowledged its sin and is confounded by the Law.

IX. So John, when he preaches repentance, points to Christ at the same time: "Behold, the Lamb of God who takes away the sins of the world" (John 1:[29]).

X. Faith is our righteousness. For by faith we believe the Gospel that reveals Christ to us, and by faith we accept Christ as the one who has placated the Father and through whom grace is bestowed. John 1:[12], "As many as received him, to them he gave the power to become children of God."

XI. Since this faith alone justifies, justification has nothing to do with our merits or works but regards Christ's merits alone.

XII. This faith gives peace and joy to the heart, according to Romans 5:[1], "Since we have been justified through faith, we have peace."

XIII. Faith causes us to love God in return for such great kindness, for the forgiveness of sins on account of Christ. Therefore, love of God is the fruit of faith.

XIV. The same faith causes us to regret offending so kind and so gracious a Father.

XV. Therefore, it causes us to hate our flesh along with its desires.

XVI. Human reason does not fear God, nor does it believe in him, but it is utterly ignorant of God and despises him, according to the Psalm, "The fool has said in his heart: 'There is no God' " [Psalm 14:1]. Also Luke 16:[31], "If they do not believe Moses and the prophets, neither will they believe if someone rises from the dead." Here Christ shows that the human heart does not believe the Word of

God. Solomon rails against this madness of the human heart throughout all of Ecclesiastes, as in chapter 8:[11], "Because judgment is not quickly brought against the evil, the children of men perpetrate wickedness without any fear."

XVII. Because the human heart is thoroughly ignorant of God, it turns away to its own counsels and desires and sets itself up as its own god.

XVIII. When God confounds the human heart through the Law and thus makes it recognize its own sin, it still does not know God because it does not know his goodness. Therefore, it hates him as if he were an executioner.

XIX. When God strengthens and comforts the human heart through the Gospel and the revelation of Christ, then it finally knows God since it knows both his power and his goodness. This is what Jeremiah meant, "Let him glory in this, that he knows me" [Jeremiah 9:24].

XX. He who believes the Gospel and therefore knows the goodness of God has already been strengthened in his heart to trust in and fear God and therefore to despise the counsels of the human heart.

XXI. Therefore, Peter spoke very appropriately when he said that our hearts are purified by faith (Acts [15:9]).

XXII. Mercy is revealed by the promises.

XXIII. Sometimes material blessings are promised and sometimes spiritual.

XXIV. In the Law, material blessings have been promised, such as the land of Canaan, a kingdom, etc.

XXV. The Gospel is the promise of grace or the forgiveness of sins for Christ's sake.

XXVI. All the material promises depend on the promise of Christ.

XXVII. For the first promise was a promise of grace or a promise of Christ: "Her seed will crush your head" (Genesis 3:[15]), that is, the Seed of Eve will destroy the kingdom of the serpent who lies in ambush against our heel. This kingdom, then, is sin and death.

XXVIII. This promise was renewed in the promise given to Abraham, "In your seed all nations will be blessed" [Genesis 12:3; 22:18].

XXIX. Further, since Christ was to be born from the posterity of Abraham, the promises added to the Law about possessing land, and so forth, are dim promises of the Christ who was to come. For those material blessings were promised to the people so that they would not die off before the promised Seed was born, and so that God could show them his mercy in the meantime by material blessings and so exercise their faith.

XXX. When Christ was born, the promises were fulfilled together with the people of Israel,[29] and remission of sin, on account of which Christ had to be born, was made known openly.

XXXI. The promises of the Old Testament point to the Christ who was to come, and therefore they are promises of the grace that would, in the future, be made known to all. The Gospel is this very promise of grace now openly made known.

XXXII. Just as he does not know God who simply knows that God exists but does not know either his power or his mercy, so also he does not believe in God who merely believes that God exists but does not believe in God's power and mercy.

XXXIII. Therefore, he truly believes who besides the threats of the Law also believes the Gospel and fixes his eyes on the mercy of God or on Christ, who is the guarantee of God's mercy.

So far concerning faith. We will add a few more things about love a little later when we have completed this next section on the distinction between the Law and the Gospel.

---

[29] That is, the reason for which God had chosen the children of Israel as his people was fulfilled.

THE DISTINCTION BETWEEN
THE OLD AND NEW TESTAMENT
AND THE ABROGATION OF THE LAW

From what we have said about the Law and the Gospel and their respective functions, one can easily figure out the difference between the Old and New Testament. And just as they mess up the distinction between Law and Gospel, so the schools flounder here. For they call the Old Testament a law that requires external works and the New Testament a law that requires the affections in addition to external works.[1] Because of this, the greatness and fullness of grace have been obscured. Yet it is grace that should have been given a noble place and displayed conspicuously everywhere and to all. I would even say that it alone should be preached. But we will resolve the matter with a few words. You can find out what the Law is and what the Gospel is from the preceding chapters. Here we are simply dealing with the usage of the terms.

It seems to me that those who call the Old Testament simply that which contains the Law are following popular usage rather than the proper manner of speaking (*rationem loquendi*).[2] They use the word "testament" according to its popular usage to denote a constitution or ordinance. I call the Old Testament the promise of material blessings joined with the demands of the Law. For God demands righteousness through the Law and also promises a reward for it, such as the land of Canaan, wealth, etc. This is clear from Deuteronomy 29:[10–13], "You stand together today before the Lord your God, your princes and tribes and elders and teachers, all the people of Israel, your children and your wives and the foreigners who stay with you in your camp, besides those following the camp, so that you may cross into a

---

[1] See p. 95, n. 7 above.

[2] According to Quintilian, the *ratio loquendi*, or *recte loquendi scientia* (science of speaking correctly), includes knowledge of both grammar and rhetoric (*Institutio* 1.4.2; cf. 1.9.1). Melanchthon is again insinuating that lack of humanist training has handicapped Scholastic studies.

pact with the Lord your God and into the oath which the Lord today strikes with you, so that he may raise you up to be his people and that he himself may be your Lord, just as he has spoken to you," etc. The New Testament, on the other hand, is nothing else than the promise of all good things outside of the Law, with no regard for our own righteousness. In the Old Testament, good things were promised, but at the same time, the people were commanded to fulfill the Law. In the New Testament good things are promised without condition, and we are commanded to do nothing in return. Here you see what this fullness of grace is and what this prodigality of divine mercy is. In short, you see what the glory of the Gospel is. It bestows salvation freely, without any regard for our righteousness or our works. Should not the human heart cry out at such an outpouring of grace? Who could believe this report? Yet even Jeremiah 31:[31–34] declares this difference between the Old and New Testament. But for a clearer understanding of this distinction, we need to discuss the abrogation of the Law.

Now since there are three parts to the Law, let us consider to what extent each has been abolished, especially since it seems that they have not all been abrogated in the same way. The consensus of authors on this topic has held that the judicial and ceremonial laws have become obsolete but that the moral laws have been renewed. We will speak first about the moral laws.

The part of the Law that they call the Decalogue or the moral commandments has been abolished by the New Testament. The proof for this, first of all, is provided by the Epistle to the Hebrews, which quotes from Jeremiah [31:31–34] where the prophet argues that the Law is to be abolished by God because the people have rendered it invalid. Now Israel did not sin against ceremonies only, but also against the Decalogue, which is, according to Christ's testimony in the Gospel, the highest part of the Law. Also, when the prophet calls the Gospel a new covenant, he is asserting that the old covenant is antiquated, as the author of Hebrews argues, "Since he speaks of a new covenant, he has made the first obsolete" (Hebrews 8:[13]). And we read in 1 Timothy [1:9], "The law has not been given for the righteous person." There are many such testimonies of freedom from the Law in Romans as well as in Galatians. For who does not know the popular passage in Galatians: "You are free, but do not use your freedom as an opportunity for the flesh" [Galatians 5:13]? No, that would be a most pathetic Christian freedom, worse than slavery, if it should abolish only the ceremonial laws, since this is the part of the Law that is easiest to endure. For it is much easier to beat your breast than it is to rule over your anger, love, or similar desires. Therefore, it must be confessed that the Decalogue has also been abolished.

Is everything then permissible? To kill the innocent? To lie? The same question is posited by Paul in Romans 6:[15], when he says, "Since we are not under the law, shall we therefore sin?" But our freedom consists in this, that every right of accusing and condemning us has been removed from the Law. The Law curses those who fail to keep it entirely and constantly. But the entire Law demands perfect love of God and exacts the most vehement fear of God, does it not? And since our entire nature is thoroughly inimical to these commands, although we present the greatest and most attractive pharisaism, we are nevertheless guilty and deserving of the curse. Christ has taken away this curse and right of the Law, so that although you have sinned and although you have sin even now—for we should use the terminology of Scripture—you are nevertheless saved.[3] Our Samson has crushed the power of death, the power of sin, and the gates of hell. This is what Paul writes to the Galatians, "Christ has redeemed us from the curse of the law, having become a curse for us" [Galatians 3:13]. And again, "When the fullness of time had come, God sent his Son, born of a woman, born under the law, to redeem those who were under the law" [Galatians 4:4–5]. And in Romans 6:[14], he writes, "Sin will not have dominion over you, for you are not under the law, but under grace." This is the security that the prophets loudly and constantly celebrate, that those who are in Christ are above all the power of the Law. That is, even though you have sinned, even though you have sin, you cannot be condemned, as Scripture decrees, "Death has been swallowed up in victory. Where, O death is your victory?" etc. [1 Corinthians 15:55]. These passages should always be impressed upon Christians, but especially when they are about to die, since to them this one truly sacred anchor alone is left, as the proverb says.[4]

---

[3] 1 John 1:8–10; cf. Romans 5:6.

[4] The proverb referring to a "sacred anchor" as a person's last hope derives from the heavier than normal anchor that was kept on ancient ships for times of emergency and storm. It was called sacred because it was consecrated to one god or another. This anchor was meant to stay the boat against overwhelming winds and waves.

And this is the freedom that Paul preaches everywhere. In contrast, he barely even discusses ceremonies except in one or two places. But the New Testament is nothing else than the proclamation of this freedom. What the prophet foretold in Psalm 2:[6] is applicable here: "I have set my king on holy Mount Zion." Here the Father says that he will elect a king for Mount Zion. Afterwards he reveals what kind of kingdom this will be, a kingdom where God will reign with his Word, not with human strength or the power of the world. Therefore he adds, "I will preach the decree, the Lord has said to me: 'You are my Son' " [Psalm 2:7]. What will this new preaching be? Was not the Word of God that had already been preached on Mount Zion the Law? But this is now replaced by a new preaching that speaks of God's Son, Christ. But if nothing else is preached except that the Son is Christ, it follows that the works and righteousness of the Law are not demanded, nor is anything commanded except that we kiss that Son. And this is what he says more clearly a little later: "Blessed are all those who trust in him" [Psalm 2:12]. Your righteousness will not save you, your wisdom will not save you, but this Son will save you, your King, your strong Defense, etc. There are many such passages in Scripture that commend this freedom to us. In short, what is the Gospel other than the preaching of this freedom?

Finally, Christianity is freedom because those who do not have the Spirit of Christ cannot keep the Law at all and are under the curses of the Law. Those who have been renewed by the Spirit of Christ are moved to do what the Law commands by their own will and without the Law's encouragement. The Law is the will of God. And the Holy Spirit is nothing else than the living will and movement of God. Therefore when we have been reborn by the Spirit of God, who is the living will of God, we willingly desire exactly what the Law used to demand of us. Paul expresses the same judgment when he says that the Law was not given for the righteous [1 Timothy 1:9]. In Romans 8:[2] he says, "The law of the Spirit of life," that is, the Law understood as the movement of the Spirit who gives life, "has freed me from the law of sin and death." Augustine gives a full

---

Already in ancient times the "sacred anchor" was made proverbial for a last resort (cf. Plutach, *Gaius Marcius Coriolanus*, 32). Christians, as Chrysostom's frequent use of the proverb shows, accommodated the proverb to refer to Christ. Erasmus deals with the saying in his *Adages* I.i.24.

treatment of Christian freedom along the same lines in his book *On the Spirit and the Letter*.[5] And Jeremiah writes, "Behold, the days will come, says the Lord, when I will strike a new covenant with the house of Israel and the house of Judah, not according to the covenant that I struck with your fathers in the day when I took their hand to lead them out of the land of Egypt, a covenant which they made void and I was angry with them, says the Lord. But this will be the covenant that I will strike with the house of Israel: After those days, says the Lord, I will put my law inside them and I will write it on their heart and I will be their God and they will be my people. And no longer will a man teach his neighbor and a man his brother saying: 'Know the Lord.' For all will know me, from the least of them to the greatest, says the Lord, because I will forgive their iniquity and remember their sin no more" [Jeremiah 31:31–34]. In this passage the prophet makes mention of a twofold covenant, the old and the new. He says that the old covenant, justification by the Law, has been made void. For who could keep the Law? Therefore, he says that now that the exaction of the Law has been removed, the Law must be inscribed on our hearts, so that it can be kept. Therefore, freedom does not consist in this, that we do not keep the Law, but rather that we willingly and heartily will and desire what the Law demands. No one could do this before. Ezekiel 11:[19–20] says the same thing: "I will remove the heart of stone from their flesh and I will give them a heart of flesh so that they may walk in my commandments and may guard and keep my judgments and be my people."

You now understand to what extent we are free from the Decalogue. First, we are free because it cannot damn those who are in Christ even though they are sinners. Then we are also free because those who are in Christ are led by the Spirit to keep the Law. For by the Spirit they keep the Law, love and fear God, apply themselves to their neighbors' needs, and desire the very things the Law used to demand of them. And they would do them even if no Law had been given. Their will, the Spirit, is nothing other than the living Law.

In the same way, the fathers who possessed the Spirit of Christ before his incarnation were also free. Peter acknowledges this in Acts 15 when he says that they were not able to keep the Law, which

---

[5] "It is the Spirit of God by whose gift we are justified, and in the process it happens within us that we no longer desire to sin, which is freedom" (*On the Spirit and the Letter*, 16; *MPL* 44:218).

"neither we nor our fathers could bear" [v. 10]. But they were justified by faith. That is, since the fathers could not keep the Law, they understood that they were also free through Christ, and they were justified by faith in Christ, not by the merits of their works or their own righteous deeds. In this passage from Acts, Peter is speaking not only of ceremonies but of the entire Law. For the ceremonial law cannot be kept at all unless you also keep the Decalogue. After all, the ceremonies are not even done in God's eyes unless they are done with a believing and willing heart. Peter was certainly not saying that the external actions of the ceremonies could not be done. For what could be easier than performing a few little ceremonies? If you should count them, you would see many more papistic rituals in the Church today than there were ceremonies in Moses' time. And you could embrace the general content of all the Mosaic ceremonies in a few short verses, while huge volumes of decrees and decretals do not suffice to record all of the papists' ceremonies![6] How different are the Roman popes from Peter, whom they boast as their predecessor! Peter abrogated a few little ceremonies that had been given by divine right, but these popes have devised new and stupid ones in every age. It can be seen, then, that Peter was speaking not only about ceremonies in Acts but about the entire Law.

In Romans 6, 7, and 8 the apostle discusses this freedom in more depth, teaching that only the new man is free. Thus, insofar as we have been renewed by the Spirit we are free, and insofar as we are flesh and old man, we are under the Law. But whatever is left of the old man is forgiven to believers because of their faith. In short, we are free insofar as we believe, and we are under the Law insofar as we do not believe. In his *Against Latomus*, Luther has thoroughly discussed the sins of saints and the remnants of the old man in the regenerate, so there is no need for me to give a long treatment of the matter here, especially since Paul states so clearly that he is still a captive to sin

---

[6] This is recognized even by the Scholastics, as Biel, quoting Scotus, maintains, "Christian law has fewer burdens insofar as it was taught by Christ, but perhaps more burdens insofar as others have been added by those who have charge of ruling over the Christian people" (*In sent*. III, dist. 40, q. unic., art. 1).

[Romans 7:23].[7] Augustine and Cyprian say the same thing in many places. For though our justification has begun here on earth, we have not yet completed it.[8] So Paul constantly commands us to be restored in the newness of our understanding.[9] And to the Philippians, he says that he has not yet attained it, that he is not yet perfect, but that he presses on to obtain it [Philippians 3:12]. Therefore when we discuss the abrogation of the Law, we must concern ourselves with the question to what extent the Gospel has abrogated the Decalogue, rather than with the fact that ceremonies and judicial laws have been abolished. For from the abrogation of the Decalogue the fullness of grace can be known most intimately, since it proves that those who believe are saved apart from the Law's demands and with no regard for our works. Therefore, the Law has been abolished, not so that it may not be kept, but so that it may not condemn when it is not kept, and also so that it can be kept.

I wish those who have maintained that our freedom only applies to judicial and ceremonial laws had used more precise arguments. As far as these laws are concerned, we should again carefully observe what Paul says, "Circumcision is nothing" [1 Corinthians 7:19]. Again he says in Galatians [5:6], "In Christ Jesus neither circumcision nor uncircumcision avails," but a new creature. He also says the following in 1 Corinthians [10:26], "The earth and all its fullness are the Lord's." These passages prove that Christian freedom consists in this, that you can either use external things of this nature or not. So Paul has one man circumcised and leaves the other uncircumcised.[10] Sometimes he conformed himself to those who observe Jewish rites; at other times he opposed them. Let us practice the same freedom. Neither those who are circumcised nor those who refuse circumcision sin in so doing. Therefore, what Jerome claimed concerning abolished ceremonies was too harsh.[11] Yet today's theologians generally follow

---

[7] Luther wrote *Against Latomus* (WA 8:36–128; AE 32:137–260) in the spring of 1521 in response to Latomus, a professor and theologian at the University of Louvain who had publicly condemned the Reformation's teachings on sin and the free will.

[8] Melanchthon uses the word "justification" (*iustificatio*) to mean righteousness (*iustitia*). See p. 134, n. 17 above.

[9] E.g., 2 Corinthians 4:16; Ephesians 4:23; Colossians 3:10.

[10] Paul had Timothy circumcised (Acts 16:3), but not Titus (Galatians 2:3).

[11] See Jerome's letter to Augustine, in which he argues that observance of Jewish rites is harmful for the Christian (*Epistle* 112, esp. 12–18; MPL 22:923–8).

him. On the other hand, those do sin who imagine that circumcision is necessary, who are circumcised in order to be justified, in order to do a good work. Moreover, they also sin who refuse circumcision in order to be justified. For just as Jerome errs when he forbids circumcision, so also the Jews erred when they required circumcision. If anyone makes it a command that we eat pork, he errs, just as he errs who forbids us to eat it. This was Paul's reasoning also. He did not want to circumcise Titus because he saw that the Jews were requiring circumcision and that the teaching of faith was therefore being obscured by the attribution of justification to circumcision instead of to faith. We should be on guard against the same thing when it come to moral works. Just as you do not eat or drink in order to be justified, so you should not give alms in order to be justified. Rather, just as you eat and drink to serve your bodily need, so you should give alms, love your brother, and so on, in order to serve the public need; so also you should restrain your desire, in order to subject your body to the Spirit, etc. Just as eating, drinking, sleeping, standing, and sitting do not justify, so also, neither circumcision nor those works of morality—chastity, serving the needs of the brethren, and the like— justify. For faith alone justifies, as Scripture declares, "The just shall live by his faith" [Romans 1:17]. Moreover this freedom in moral matters is not only necessary to know but also hard to grasp, so that it cannot be understood except by those who have the Spirit.

Therefore, what we have said must stand strong, that judicial and ceremonial observances have not been abolished in such a way that someone sins if he observes them. Because Christianity is freedom, it is up to us whether we observe them or not, just as it is up to us whether we eat or drink. But I would prefer that Christians use the code of judicial laws that Moses prescribes as well as most of the Mosaic ceremonies. For since the contingencies of this life cannot do without judicial laws, nor, I think, without ceremonies, it would be better to use those of Moses than Gentile laws and papistic ceremonies.[12]

Now for a closer examination of the matter. The reason is one and the same why the entire Law has been abolished, not only the ceremonies and judicial codes, but also the Decalogue—it could not

---

[12] Contrast Melanchthon's confession in the *Apology*, where he calls Carlstadt insane because he tried to "impose on us the judicial laws of Moses" (Ap XVI.55).

be kept. Both Peter in Acts and the prophet Jeremiah have given this one reason for the abrogation of the Law. For Jeremiah taught that the new covenant entered in because we had rendered the old covenant void. And in the passage cited from Jeremiah above, he excludes no part of the Law, so it is clear enough that he is speaking about the entire Law. But the old covenant is abolished only in those who have believed the new covenant, that is, the Gospel. Therefore, those who have the Spirit of Christ are completely free from every Law.

Moreover, the reason why the saints still keep the Decalogue is because it demands only a righteousness of heart and not specific distinctions between places, times, things, and people. The Spirit is this very righteousness (*iustificatio*) of the heart.[13] Now that the Law has been abolished, the Decalogue cannot but be kept. Just as the sun cannot help but shine when it rises, so also the Decalogue cannot but be kept when the Spirit is poured out into the hearts of the saints. But the spiritual man is so free that if the Spirit did not bring with him the fulfillment of the Decalogue by his very nature, we would not even be obligated to do it. Now since the Spirit brings the very will that is the fulfillment of the Decalogue, the Law is kept. But this is not because it is forced from us, but because a spiritual man can do nothing else.

Judicial laws and ceremonies are external observances limited to things, persons, places, and times, and as such have nothing to do with the righteousness of the heart. Since the Spirit does not necessarily bind himself to these observances, there is no reason why we should perform them. The Spirit of God cannot reside in the human heart without it keeping the Decalogue. Therefore, the Decalogue is kept by necessity. But the Spirit can be in the human heart without these external observances. Therefore, it is not necessary that judicial and ceremonial observances be kept. It is clear, then, why the Decalogue generally contains negative laws. It thereby shows that it requires the righteousness of the heart, not some specific work limited to persons, places, or times. Other laws distinguish and regulate external observances. But I leave it to more subtle spirits to meditate on freedom in these matters. I am content to have pointed out that the Decalogue has been abolished not so that it may not be kept, but so that it may not condemn us if we sin, and then also so that

---

[13] In this passage it is especially clear that Melanchthon is using the word "justification" (*iustificatio*) to mean righteousness (*iustitia*) when dealing with the doctrine of sanctification. See p. 134, n. 17 above.

it can be kept. Therefore, this is the freedom of the conscience that understands by faith that its sin has been forgiven.

Generally speaking, people hold that ceremonies have been abolished because they were shadows of the Gospel, and so there is no need of them now that the substance, that is, the Gospel has come. But I do not think Paul ever followed this reasoning. In Colossians [2:16–17], he says, "Let no one judge you in food or drink or regarding a festival or a new moon or sabbaths, which are shadows of what is to come, but the substance is of Christ." Now perhaps one could make the argument that Paul is discussing a type in this passage. But in Galatians he definitely rejects ceremonies on the grounds that they do not justify. The same argument is made throughout the entire Epistle to the Hebrews, namely that not just ceremonies have been abrogated, but the entire Law has been abolished because it could not justify, or, as we said above, because it could not be kept. For this is what is written in Hebrews 7:[18], "The rejection of the previous commandment because of its weakness and uselessness." In its extensive treatment of the priesthood, the Letter to the Hebrews establishes that the Levitical priesthood was abolished because it did not obtain the forgiveness of sins, whereas our High Priest, Christ, does obtain it. You see that Scripture stresses and insists on this one reason for the abrogation of the Law, that the Law was abolished because it did not justify or, what is the same, could not be kept.

The schools abolish only the ceremonies on the grounds that they were types of the Gospel. The Decalogue remains because it is considered something more than typological (τυπικὸς). But how does this reasoning commend to us the preaching of grace? Scripture so speaks of the abrogation of the Law that it always commends to us the fullness of grace in this abrogation. It does away with ceremonies to make it clear that the entire Law has been abrogated. It rejects ceremonies to make it clear that ceremonies are abolished because the Decalogue has been abolished. This is the single and greatest proclamation of grace. Therefore, ceremonies have been done away with not so that they may not be observed, but because they can be observed or not without danger to the conscience. For they do not condemn when they are left undone nor do they justify if you observe them. Let it suffice to have pointed out these matters. You can seek the proof for them from Galatians and Hebrews. In one of his works

Augustine inquires into the reason for the abrogation of the Law, but then deals with nothing but typology.[14] Scripture says that the Law has been abolished because it does not justify. Why then was the Law given? To show us our sin or, what is the same, to convict us of sin, to show us clearly that we need God's mercy.

As far as the judicial codes are concerned, I think that they were abolished for the same reason, because they are external observances no less than ceremonies are, and the Spirit is free to observe them or not. It is not permissible for Christians to go to court, but this is not the reason for the abrogation of the Law. For although those who go to court sin by so doing, we nevertheless need laws and judicial codes to restrain criminals. Nor do those sin who administer judgments or render a legal decision. Nor was the Law given to Moses so that citizens would have the occasion to go to court, but so that the magistrate would have a process by which to make judgments. Therefore, we should not argue whether someone who wants to go to court can use the Mosaic Law or any other law. In fact, whoever goes to court is not a Christian.[15] But should the Christian judge use only Mosaic Law? Here I respond that it is up to the judge whether or not to use the Law of Moses. For this, too, has to do with external observances, which pertain to Christianity no more than eating or drinking. Paul requires only that a judge be a wise man in whom the Spirit of Christ resides. He writes in 1 Corinthians 6:[2], "Or do you not know that the saints will judge the world?" And a little later, "Is there not a wise man among you who can judge," etc. [v. 5]. It is clear from these passages that he requires not any one specific law but rather the judgment of a man who has the Spirit.

Elsewhere, Paul also approves of the sword of the Gentiles, concerning which we will speak later, and calls it a divine ordinance. Moreover, laws are the most effective component of the sword. Therefore, Naaman the Syrian, Nebuchadnezzar, and other pious princes among the Gentiles employed the sword and laws of the Gentiles. Perhaps also Daniel and other Israelites among the

---

[14] *Against Faustus* 15–19 (*MPL* 42:301–18).

[15] Melanchthon qualifies his polemic against Christians going to court in his later works. In the *Apology*, he writes only that private vindication is prohibited to Christians and commends the public courts for Christian use. He also condemns Carlstadt's teaching that Christians may not go before a secular court to seek redress (Ap XVI 55–60).

Assyrians also used them. Surely the Roman garrison imposed on Judea wielded the sword of the Gentiles. And John grants his approval to them in Luke 3:[14], "Threaten no one and do not bring false accusations, and be content with your pay." Cornelius in Acts 10 was such a man and so was the proconsul Sergius in Acts 13:[6–12]. I have pointed these things out to make it clear that this civil and external arrangement of things has nothing to do with the righteousness of the Spirit, not any more than tilling a field, constructing a building, or stitching shoes. It is up to individual Christians whether or not they use the judicial laws of Moses, though I would prefer that they be used instead of the laws of the Gentiles, which are quite often imprudent. For we have been grafted into that olive tree, and the Word of God ought to be preferred to man-made constitutions.[16] Besides, almost no one uses the Roman law code today except to bring cases to court so that argumentative lawyers can make their living on lawsuits.

From what we have said, I think one can understand to some extent how far the Law has been abolished. But the Spirit will bestow a more complete understanding as you delve into Scripture. This freedom cannot be understood except by those who have the Spirit.

But, you will say, if those who have the Spirit are free, then were Moses and David also free? Of course! This is exactly what Peter says, "Neither we nor our fathers could bear it, but we believe that we are saved through the grace of our Lord Jesus Christ, just as they were" [Acts 15:10–11]. That is, the fathers acknowledged that all of their works were sins, that they did not merit salvation by any of their works, and that they needed God's mercy. Therefore, they believed, and they were saved by trust in God's mercy. And having received the Spirit of God, they understood that they were free from the curse of the Law and therefore from every burden and demand of the Law. But the reason that they did not stop performing the ceremonies was because this freedom had not yet been revealed, because the Gospel had not yet been made known to all. Therefore, they willingly kept the Law because they understood that they were justified by faith. You see also that they sometimes used this privilege of freedom, and rightly so. For example, in 1 Samuel 21, David ate the showbread, which no one was allowed to eat except the priest. And David speaks

---

[16] Cf. Romans 11:17.

beautifully about this freedom when he says, "The way was polluted, but it is sanctified by the vessels" [v. 5],[17] that is, they were clean because they had faith, and all things were therefore sanctified, whether food, works, and so on, by the faith of the saints. This is also what Paul says, "To the pure all things are pure, but nothing is pure to the defiled" [Titus 1:15].

In summary, we are free from the entire Law through faith. But this same faith that we have received, that very Spirit of Christ, mortifies the remnants of sin in our flesh. This is not because the Law demands it, but because it is the very nature of the Spirit to mortify the flesh. This is precisely what Paul says, "There is now no condemnation for those who are in Christ Jesus" [Romans 8:1]. That is, because they have been redeemed from the curse of the Law, those who believe are saved. But these same people do not walk according to the flesh. In other words, because the Spirit reigns in them, the remnants of the flesh are crucified. So, laws are given to believers so that through them the Spirit may mortify the flesh. For freedom has not yet been completed in them, though it is being secured as the Spirit increases and the flesh is killed. Now the Decalogue is of use in mortifying the flesh, but the ceremonial and judicial laws are not. So it is that believers have need of the Decalogue but not of the other laws. But the Spirit uses His judgment in the use of ceremonies and external observations.

THE OLD AND NEW MAN

I stated that our freedom has not yet been completed because sanctification has also not yet been completed in us. For we begin to be sanctified by the Spirit of God, and we continue to be sanctified until this flesh is completely killed off. So it is that the nature of the saints is twofold, spirit and flesh, new man and old man, inner man and outer man. The term "flesh" designates not merely the body, as was discussed above, but clearly signifies man in his entirety, or as Paul calls him, the natural man (φυσικόν),[18] who is subject to natural affections and emotions. The terms "old man" and "outer man" mean the same thing as "flesh." Moreover, "flesh" includes everything that

---

[17] Melanchthon translates here from the Septuagint.

[18] See 1 Corinthians 2:14.

belongs to natural human affections, not only hunger and thirst but also love of wealth, thirst for glory, and other similar desires. Clearly the flesh also includes the philosophical virtues, the endeavors of the free will, and the like. On the other hand, the word "spirit" refers both to the Holy Spirit himself and to his activity in us. The new man and the inner man are "spirit," because they have been reborn by the Holy Spirit. John 3:[6] states, "What is born of the Spirit is spirit." Therefore, we are saints insofar as we are spirit, insofar as we have been renewed. In the flesh, in the old man, in the outer man, there is still sin, as the apostle states, "The flesh strives (*concupiscit*) against the Spirit and the Spirit against the flesh" [Galatians 5:17].

The Parisian sophists say that concupiscence in the flesh of the saints is not sin but an infirmity. Luther has refuted them quite thoroughly in his *Against Latomus*.[19] What is more obvious than that sin is everything that is opposed to the Law of God?[20] The flesh strives (*concupiscit*) against the Law of God. Why, then, do they not call concupiscence sin? Do not saints also seek after their own benefit? Is there not love of life, glory, security, tranquility, and possessions in the saints? The reason that the Parisians do not call these things sins is because they pay no attention to the affections but imagine that sin is located in external actions. They do not see the root of the works. So it is that they foolishly judge the fruits. What work is so good that our nature does not seek its own advantage in doing it? Even if you have set aside your love for glory (κενοδοξίας), you have certainly not put aside your fear of punishment yet. Therefore, the flesh pollutes all the good works that you do. Now if you sin in no other way, do we not transgress terribly and wickedly in the inactivity and idleness of our spirit? We should be burning with love for God and trust in him, and we should be trembling with fear of God, as the First Commandment requires. But who succeeds in this? Let us then confess our reality—sin dwells in our flesh. But this

---

[19] In his *Against Latomus*, Luther bases his argument that concupiscence is sin on Paul's letter to the Romans, especially Romans 7, where Paul claims that he would not have known that concupiscence was sin unless the Law had told him (WA 8:36–128; AE 32:137–260). Melanchthon follows Luther closely in his argumentation here.

[20] This is, in fact, Aquinas' definition of sin also, that it is "against the eternal law" (*Summa* I–II, q. 71, art. 6). Citing Augustine, Aquinas calls opposition to the Law the "formal" component in sin, as opposed to the "material" component, namely, that it consists in a word, act, or desire.

is the glory of God's mercy, that he forgives the sin of those who believe. The abrogation of the Law consists in this alone, that Christ has taken away the Law's right to condemn sinners by the forgiveness of sins.

There are those who posit three parts of man—spirit, soul, and body.[21] I do not object to this formulation provided that they concede the reality that "spirit" is not properly a component of our nature, but a divine activity. The body and the soul, that is, human nature apart from the Spirit, can do nothing but sin. Nor do moral virtues compensate for sin. In Philippians [3:8], Paul says that he considers all his righteousness as loss and dung. And this is the righteousness that the endeavors of his nature had produced by the Law's encouragement. Why then do the blasphemous sophists still boast of the works of nature, and this to the great injury of the Gospel? For nothing so obscures the fullness of God's grace than that godless teaching about moral works. Paul rejoices to be found in Christ, not having his own righteousness from the Law, but the righteousness which is through faith in Christ, the righteousness which is from God. The sophists also place merit in the righteousness of the Law.

MORTAL AND DAILY SIN

We spoke above about sin and purposely omitted a treatment of the different types of sin. The Scholastics distinguish between mortal and venial sin.[22] But every work of man not done in Christ is a mortal sin, because it is the evil fruit of an evil tree—the flesh. Romans 8:[6] states, "But the affection of the flesh is death," and, "The affection of the flesh is enmity toward God" [v. 7], and again, "Those who are in the flesh cannot please God" [v. 8]. One has to interpret the word "flesh" in these passages as designating the entire nature of man and therefore the most impressive powers of our nature, as we pointed out above.[23]

---

[21] See p. 59, n. 43.

[22] See, Lombard *Sentences* II, dist. 42: "For if the sin is mortal it binds us to eternal punishment, and if venial it binds us to temporal punishment. For there are two kinds of sin, mortal and venial. Mortal sin is that through which man merits eternal death. For the offense, as Augustine says, is worthy of indictment and damnation. But a venial sin does not burden a man with the guilt of eternal death. It does merit punishment, but one that is easily forgiven."

[23] See pp. 45–49 above.

In fact, no other part of man is more truly flesh than man's highest power, his reason, because reason is the proper seat of ignorance of and contempt for God, unbelief, and other serious disorders of this kind, the fruits and works of which include all human activities. On the other hand, all the works of the saints are venial sins because they are forgiven to believers by God's mercy. God sometimes takes his Spirit from the saints with the result that they fall back into manifest sins. The Scholastics call these manifest sins mortal sins, and I do not object to this at all, so long as they understand that I call everything done by people who lack the Spirit of God mortal sins. In the past, the public outrages that the sophists now call mortal sins were generally categorized as crimes, and the sins that the sophists now call venial sins were categorized as daily sins.

I think it was especially necessary to say what I have about Law and Gospel and the Old and New Testament, though I understand that I have given a slighter treatment than the matter deserves. But I do not want to be called Teacher.[24] Becoming familiar with Scripture will supply in abundance what we have skipped over. I thought it was sufficient to show what you should especially look for in Scripture. You will look for the Law and the Gospel. The Law reveals sin and terrifies the conscience. The Gospel forgives sin and bestows the Spirit who moves the heart to keep the Law. If you should evaluate the word "testament" more closely, the Old Testament, which is a type (τύπος) of the New Testament, would not be a testament at all because the Testator did not die in it. The Testator died in the New Testament. In the Old Testament animals were sacrificed as a type of the Testator and signified the death of the Testator. But these observations are more subtle than the scope of this commentary allows. At this point, theologians usually discuss the letter and the Spirit, but I would prefer that the reader consult Augustine or Luther on this instead of me, though I did touch on this point above when I treated the nature of the law.[25]

---

[24] Cf. Matthew 23:8.

[25] See above, pp. 99–107.

SIGNS

We said that the Gospel is the promise of grace. Most closely related to the promises is this topic of signs. For in the Scriptures signs are added to the promises as seals, both to remind us of the promises and to serve as sure testimonies of God's goodwill toward us, confirming that we will certainly receive what God has promised. There has been a most terrible misunderstanding concerning the proper use of the signs. For when the schools discuss the difference between the sacraments of the Old and New Testament, they deny that the sacraments of the Old Testament had the power to justify. But they attribute the power of justification to the sacraments of the New Testament, an obvious and manifest error.[1] For faith alone justifies.[2] Moreover, the nature of a sign can be understood without any

---

[1] Cf. Lombard *Sentences* IV, dist. 1, ch. 6. See also Eck's assertion against Luther: "For the sacraments of the new law effect what they represent and for this reason are different from the sacraments of the Old Testament" (WA 1:286). Luther explains the Scholastics' reasoning in his *Assertion* (1520): "They teach this because otherwise there would be no difference between the sacraments of the new and old law. For the old sacraments justify because they were received in faith, that is, they were beneficial to those who were good, as they say. Therefore, the new sacraments should be more efficacious and benefit also those who are not good. After all, everything should be more perfect in the New Testament than in the Old" (WA 7:102; cf. AE 32:17–18).

[2] In the years leading up to 1521, Melanchthon and Luther both asserted that the sacraments do not justify. They insisted on this over against the Scholastic claim that the sacraments justify *ex opere operato*, that is, by the very performance of the act without regard to faith in the recipient. So Luther, in his *Assertion* (1520) against the bull of Pope Leo X, states, "It is a heretical though common opinion that the sacraments of the new law give grace to those who do not put an obstacle in the way. So Scripture says (Romans 1 and Habakkuk 2 and Hebrews 10), 'The just shall live by his faith,' not 'The just shall live by the sacraments.' In every sacrament is the word of God's promise, which affirmatively promises and offers the grace of God to the one who receives the sacrament. But wherever God promises, there faith is required in the hearer, lest he make God a liar by his unbelief. Therefore in the reception of the sacraments, faith, which believes what is promised, is necessary in the one who receives" (WA 7:101; cf. AE 32:12–19). Neither Melanchthon nor Luther is denying that the sacraments bestow justifying grace, that is, the forgiveness of sins. Rather, they are challenging the Scholastic doctrine that the sacraments justify outside of faith in the heart of the recipient.

COMMONPLACES: LOCI COMMUNES 1521

difficulty when we consult Paul's Letter to the Romans where, in the fourth chapter, he discusses circumcision. He argues as follows: Abraham was justified not by circumcision but before circumcision and apart from the merit of circumcision. But he received circumcision later as a seal of righteousness (σφραγίδα δικαιοσύνης),[3] that is, a seal by which God testified that Abraham was just and by which Abraham was assured that he was righteous before God, lest his conscience waver in doubt and despair.

Now if you understand this function of the signs, nothing can be more delightful. It is not enough for the signs to remind you of God's promises. The important fact is that they are also a sure testimony of God's will toward you. So Moses calls circumcision a sign in Genesis 17:[11], "So that it may be a sign of the covenant between me and you." Because circumcision is a sign, it reminds Abraham and all the circumcised of God's promise. Because circumcision is a sign of the covenant, that is, because it shows that this covenant will be confirmed, it strengthens Abraham's conscience so that he does not doubt that what has been promised will come to be, that God will provide what he has promised. But what had God promised to Abraham? Had he not promised that he would be Abraham's God, that is, that he had embraced Abraham, justified him, saved him, and so on? Thus Abraham did not doubt that all this was certain, since he was strengthened by circumcision as by a seal.

Run through all of Scripture, if you like, and discover the teaching on signs from the sacred histories, not from the godless sophists. The Lord prolongs the life of Hezekiah by Isaiah's prophecy [2 Kings 20:4–6]. So that the king might know that this promise would be fulfilled, God confirmed it by adding a sign—that the shadow of the sundial would go back ten degrees [vv. 8–11]. Gideon was strengthened by two signs so that he would not doubt that Israel would be set free under his leadership [Judges 6:36–40]. Isaiah upbraids Ahaz for despising the sign of God's will toward him [Isaiah 7:10–13]. For besides the sign, he did not believe the promise either. But there is no point in citing so many passages when Scripture is full of similar examples. I think one can learn how signs function from these examples. Signs do not justify. Just as the apostle says, "Circumcision is nothing" [1 Corinthians 7:19], so also Baptism is

---

[3] See Romans 4:11.

nothing, participation in the Lord's Supper is nothing. But they are witnesses and seals (καὶ σφραγίδες) of God's goodwill toward you, giving assurance to your conscience when you doubt God's grace and goodwill toward you.

Just as Hezekiah could not doubt that he would get better after he had both heard the promise and seen the promise confirmed with a sign, just as Gideon could not doubt that he would be victorious after he had been strengthened by so many signs, so also you should not doubt that you have obtained mercy when you have heard the Gospel and received the seals (καὶ σφραγίδες) of the Gospel—Baptism and the body and blood of the Lord. Even without the sign Hezekiah could have been restored to health if he had been willing to believe the bare promise. Even without the sign Gideon would have been victorious if he had believed. In the same way, you can be justified without the sign as long as you believe. Therefore, the signs do not justify, but the faith of Hezekiah and Gideon had to be sustained, strengthened, and confirmed by such signs. Thus our weakness is assuaged by signs so that we do not despair of God's mercy amid the constant assaults of sin. You should consider them signs of God's favor, as if he were speaking with you face-to-face and giving you a special guarantee of his mercy, such as a miracle. This is how you should think of the signs. When you receive Baptism and participate in the Lord's Supper, you should be as certain that God has had mercy on you as you would be if God himself were speaking with you or giving you some other miracle that was directed to you in particular. The signs have been instituted to excite faith. Those who question this have lost both faith and the proper use of signs. The knowledge of signs is most salutary, and I doubt whether anything consoles and strengthens the conscience more effectively than this use of signs.

What others call sacraments, we call signs, or if you prefer, sacramental signs. For Paul calls Christ himself a Sacrament.[4] But if you do not like the term "sign," you should call them seals

---

[4] So Luther in *The Babylonian Captivity* (WA 6:501; AE 36:18). The Vulgate translates the Greek word *mysterion* (mystery) in Colossians 1:27 and 1 Timothy 3:16 as *sacramentum* (sacrament). Colossians 1:27, "To whom God willed to make known the riches of the glory of this Sacrament among the Gentiles, which is Christ in you." And 1 Timothy 3:16, "Great indeed is the Sacrament of our religion, which was made manifest in the flesh . . ."

(σφραγίδας). This term describes the power of sacraments more accurately. Those who compared these signs to military symbols or signals were well-intentioned. For they reasoned that the signs were only marks by which those to whom God's promises pertain might be recognized. So Cornelius was baptized after he had already been justified so that he could be counted among those to whom the promise of the kingdom of God and everlasting life pertained. I have given this instruction on the nature of signs so that the godly use of the sacraments might be understood, and because I do not want anyone to follow the Scholastics on this point. Their attribution of justification to signs is a terrible error.

But there are two signs that have been instituted by Christ in the Gospel—Baptism and participation in the Lord's Supper. For we judge that God gave both of these sacramental signs as indications of his grace. We mortals, on the other hand, cannot institute a sign of God's goodwill toward us, nor can we say that signs are meant to signify God's goodwill when Scripture assigns a different function to them. Therefore, we wonder even more how it has come into the minds of the sophists to count among the sacraments and even attribute justification to signs that Scripture never mentions at all. For how did they come up with their sacrament of ordination? And God did not institute marriage to be a special sign of grace. The rite of extreme unction may be ancient, but it is not a sign of grace. In *The Babylonian Captivity*, Luther has discussed this matter thoroughly, and you can find a more detailed treatment there.[5] But this is the sum of the matter—grace is not signified specifically and with certainty except in those signs that have been instituted by God. Therefore, nothing can be called a sacramental sign except those signs that have been attached to God's promises. This is why the ancients said that the sacraments consisted of things and words. The thing is the sign, and the word is the promise of grace.[6]

---

[5] For Luther's discussion of confirmation, marriage, ordination, and extreme unction in *The Babylonian Captivity*, see WA 6:549–73; AE 36:91–126.

[6] Cf. Augustine's famous words: "Take away the Word and what is the water except water? The Word is added to the element, and it becomes a sacrament, becoming, as it were, a visible Word" (*Tractate on John* 80.3; *MPL* 35:1340).

Baptism

The sophists have devoted copious and superstitious discussions to the so-called material and form of the sacraments but have failed to demonstrate their use.[7] The sign is the immersion into water. The minister is the one who immerses, signifying the work of God. And this immersion is also a sign of God's goodwill as the minister says that he is baptizing in the name of the Father and of the Son and of the Holy Spirit, or as the apostles did it in Acts, in the name of Christ. These words clearly signify: "See, you have been immersed. You should receive this as a certain testimony of God's favor toward you, as certain as if God himself should baptize you." Hezekiah considered it a testimony of God's favor when God called back the shadow, an amazing occurrence.[8] The people of Israel considered it a testimony of God's favor when the waters of the Arabian Sea opened a way for them. So you should consider this immersion as a definite guarantee of God's grace. For these words, "In the name of the Father and of the Son and of the Holy Spirit," mean that the Father, the Son, and the Holy Spirit are baptizing you. The person who is baptized should understand that his sins are forgiven him by God himself, Father, Son, and Holy Spirit.

Clearly Baptism signifies a transition through death into life, the drowning to death of the old Adam and the raising to life of the new Adam. And its proper function is also understood by this signification.[9] This is why Paul calls it a "washing of regeneration"

---

[7] Popularized by Thomas Aquinas, the terms "material" and "form" began to replace the Augustinian distinction between "sign" and "word" (see previous note) in Scholastic theology. This Aristotelian distinction encouraged a philosophical treatment of the sacraments as such, with less regard for a practical discussion of their use and benefit (see *Summa* III, qq. 60–90).

[8] See above, p. 168.

[9] Cf. Luther, *The Babylonian Captivity*: "Baptism signifies two things—death and resurrection—that is, full and finished justification. For the minister's act of immersing the child in the water signifies death, and his act of taking him out of the water signifies life.... We call this death and resurrection the new creation, regeneration, and spiritual birth. And this should not be understood as mere allegory of the death of sin and the life of grace, as some like to do, but of true death and resurrection. For Baptism is not a fake sign" (WA 6:534; AE 36:67–68). See also Luther's Small Catechism: "[Baptism] signifies that the old Adam who is still in us should constantly, by daily mortification and repentance, be drowned and killed in us,

[Titus 3:5]. This definition will be understood most easily in reference to a type. Baptism was foreshadowed by the crossing of the Israelites through the Arabian Sea. They were doing nothing less than walking into death when they entrusted themselves to the waters. By faith they crossed through the waters, through death, until they escaped to the other side. In this historical account the very thing that Baptism signifies happened—the Israelites crossed through death to life. So also the entire Christian life is a putting to death of the flesh and a rebirth of the Spirit. Thus the very thing that Baptism signifies actually happens up to the day when we finally rise from the dead. Baptism properly signifies true repentance, and therefore Baptism is the sacrament of repentance, as we will explain later.

The function of this sign is to testify that you are crossing through death to life, to testify that the mortification of your flesh is salutary. Sins terrify you, death terrifies you, the other evils of the world terrify you. But take heart and believe, for you have received the seal (σφραγίδα) of God's mercy toward you, promising that you will be saved no matter how you are attacked by the gates of hell. So you see that both the meaning of Baptism and its function last throughout the entire life of the saints. I would even go so far as to say that no more powerful consolation can be given to those who are about to die than mentioning this sign and reminding them that by Baptism they have received the seal (σφραγίδα) of God's promise, so that they may know for certain that God will lead them through death and into life. Had it been possible to cross without God's help, there would have been no need for this sign. But the sign was offered so that they would not doubt that they would make it through by God's direction. If Moses had baptized the Israelites before their journey through the waters, would he not still have had to remind them while they were crossing the sea of the sign that they had received about how it all would end? Would he not have had to urge them to remember that the sign was given so that they might not doubt that they would be saved?

Baptism has the same function for us as we experience the mortification of our flesh. It reminds the terrified conscience of the forgiveness of sins and assures it of God's grace. It therefore keeps us from despairing as we undergo the mortification of the flesh.

---

together with all sins and evil desires, and further that a new man daily emerge and arise, to live before God in righteousness and purity forever" (SC IV 12).

Therefore as long as we undergo mortification, Baptism remains useful. But since mortification is not finished until the old Adam is completely killed off, this sign is always useful throughout our entire life, as it consoles the conscience in that continual mortification. Therefore, it is clear that signs are nothing but remembrances (μνημόσυνα) to exercise faith. This is how Paul discusses Baptism in Romans 6:[3], "Those who have been baptized into Christ have been baptized into his death." That is, they have been baptized so that they may be put to death, just as Christ was put to death, and so that, with Baptism reminding them, they may know that this mortification is a transition to life. This is why Paul adds, "We have been buried through Baptism" [v. 4]. He is teaching that saints are not only put to death, but also enjoy rest in this mortification and spend this Sabbath rest in Christ's grave. The godless are put to death also, but because they do not believe that there is a transition to life in Christ they despair and utterly perish. The godly are put to death so that they may spend their Sabbath rest in Christ's grave, that is, so that they may believe that there is a transition to life in Christ and may expect comfort in him. Meanwhile, the seal and remembrance (καὶ μνημόσυνον) is Baptism, as Paul says, "We have been buried through Baptism." Faith allows us to spend our Sabbath rest in peace and look forward to consolation. Baptism, as a sign of God's grace, excites this faith. I do not think that anyone could easily articulate what rich comfort this use of Baptism affords to the troubled conscience.

There have been some questions about the institution of Baptism and the distinction between the Baptisms of John and Christ. The most sensible theologians simply determined that John's Baptism was a sign of mortification while Christ's Baptism was a sign of vivification because the promise of grace or the forgiveness of sins was added to it. Therefore, the washing of John was called a Baptism of repentance, and the Baptism of Christ was called a Baptism for the remission of sins. So John preaches the Law to prepare consciences for Christ by the recognition of their sins, and Christ gives life to those whose consciences have been terrified by John's preaching of the Law. For knowledge of sin and fear of God's judgment are the first step to justification. Justification's consummation is faith and peace of conscience, which the Holy Spirit plants in the heart, as we discussed above in the chapters covering Law and Gospel.

But it seems to me that these two washings can be distinguished more simply if you understand John's Baptism as a sign of the grace that would shortly be announced in Christ, and Christ's Baptism as a sign of the grace that has already been given, so that each Baptism signifies the same thing, except that John's Baptism is a guarantee and seal (καὶ σφραγίς) of a grace that was soon to come, while Christ's Baptism is a guarantee of grace already won. Therefore, each Baptism signified the same thing—mortification and vivification. For no one is justified unless he has already been mortified. Now the reason I understand it this way is, first of all, because John's task was not simply to preach the Law but especially to bear witness of Christ and the Gospel, or the forgiveness of sins. So John 1:[7] reads, "He came as a witness, to bear witness of the light, so that through him all might believe." And Matthew 11:[11] declares, "Among those born of women no one has risen greater than John the Baptist. But he who is least in the kingdom of heaven is greater than he." This means that before the revelation of the Gospel, no one's office was superior to John's since he not only preached the Law, like Moses and other prophets, but he also bore witness of the Gospel that would soon be revealed through Christ. Therefore, Christ is greater than John even though he is the least. So also the apostolic office will be greater than John's. And since John is a witness of the Gospel, through him was instituted the sign that would afterwards be the guarantee of the Gospel and of the grace that has been secured. Then, in Luke 3:[3], the Baptism of John is called a "Baptism of repentance for the remission of sins." John says quite openly in John 1:[31], "So that he might be manifested to Israel, I came baptizing with water." In Acts 19:[4], Paul says, "John baptized the people with a Baptism of repentance, speaking of him who was to come after him, so that they might believe"—in Jesus, of course. And in Matthew 3:[11], John testifies that his Baptism is a sign of a future Baptism through the Holy Spirit, saying, "I baptize you with water, but he who comes after me will baptize you with the Holy Spirit." He also insists that he is not Christ but a witness to Christ, as in John 3:[28] when he says, "I am not the Christ."

Therefore, each Baptism signifies the same thing except that the Baptism of John testified of a grace that was still to be preached but Christ's of a grace already secured. Nor, in my opinion, did Christ's disciples baptize differently from John, since Christ had not yet been glorified (John 4:[2]). And those washed with John's Baptism had to be baptized again so that they could be assured that they had already obtained the forgiveness of sins, since up to that point they had only believed that it would come. For the signs are given to give assurance to the conscience. Neither the Baptism of John nor that of Christ justified—I am talking about the signs here—but they gave assurance. John's washing gave assurance of a grace that was still to be preached, while Christ's Baptism testified of the grace that had already been secured and the promise of grace that was already being preached. In each case, faith justified. But John baptized with water because he was not the one in whom people should believe, the one who would bring salvation. Since Christ is the Savior, he baptizes with the Holy Spirit and with fire. So those who were baptized by John were rebaptized, even though they were already justified, just as there were justified Jews in some places who had not been washed in John's Baptism. For the Baptism of Christ gives assurance of the grace that has already been secured. In fact, I do not see the difference between justified Jews before John's time and those who were baptized by John, since both were waiting for Christ, except that the latter understood the Gospel and the forgiveness of sins better.

Let this brief discussion of these matters suffice, because I do not want to keep anyone from reading Scripture with too long a discussion. It is in Scripture that these kinds of questions should be more diligently investigated.

Repentance

It is quite obvious that repentance is not a sign. For repentance is the mortification of our old man and the renewal of the Spirit. So its sacrament or sign is nothing else than Baptism. It would be quite appropriate to call Baptism the sacrament of repentance, since repentance kills us so that we might live and be renewed. And this is exactly what Baptism signifies, as we just said. So Paul testifies in Romans 6:[3], "We who have been baptized into Christ Jesus have been baptized into his death," etc. And in Titus [3:5], Baptism is called a "washing of regeneration." Nor is the Christian life anything else than this very repentance, that is, our regeneration.[10] Mortification happens through the Law, as we said above. For the Law terrifies and kills the conscience. Vivification comes through the Gospel or absolution. For the Gospel is nothing else than absolution itself.

What we call "mortification" the Scholastics have preferred to call "contrition." I will allow this terminology provided that they are not speaking of the grief simulated by the free will, through human powers. For human nature cannot hate sin. Rather, to confound and terrify our conscience is God's work. So Jeremiah 6:[15], "They do not know how to blush." Again, Jeremiah 17:[1], "The sin of Judah has been written with an iron pen; with an adamantine point it has been engraved across their heart." And Jeremiah 31:[19], "After you showed me my sin, I struck my thigh." Christ says of the Pharisees in Luke 11:[39], "Now you Pharisees clean the outside of the cup and the dish, but your inside is full of theft and iniquity." But we treated this more thoroughly above when we contrasted Law and Gospel. For repentance is nothing other than justification.[11] In the meantime, I must advise you to avoid like the plague what the Scholastics have invented about attrition and sorrow simulated by the free will. At any rate, your heart will easily be able to judge whether you are truly sorry or faking it. But you should not be trusting in your sorrow anyway, as if sin is forgiven because you are sorry, but rather in the absolution or Word of God, as I will soon explain.

But perhaps you will grant that Baptism is the sign of repentance, that is, of mortification and vivification, but only for those who persevere in the faith. But what is the sign for those who have fallen; what sign testifies to them that they are accepted back into God's grace? For the Scholastics have referred the word "repentance" and the sacrament of penance only to those who have fallen.[12] My answer is that just as we have not lost the Gospel, although we have at one

---

[10] Cf. Luther's first thesis in his *95 Theses* (1517): "When our Lord and Teacher Jesus Christ said, 'Repent, etc.,' he meant that the entire life of believers should be repentance" (WA 1:233; AE 31:25).

[11] Cf. Melanchthon in AC XII: "Repentance properly consists in these two parts. One is contrition or terrors striking the conscience with the knowledge of sin. The other is faith, which is received from the Gospel or from absolution, believes that sins are forgiven because of Christ, comforts the conscience, and frees it from terrors."

[12] That is, to those who have committed mortal, as opposed to venial, sins.

time or another fallen into sin, so neither have we lost the seal (σφραγίδα) of the Gospel—Baptism. For it is certain that the Gospel is no one-time affair but forgives our sin over and over again. Therefore, Baptism pertains just as much to the second forgiveness as to the first. For Baptism is the pledge and guarantee of the Gospel, that is, of the forgiveness of sins. So in Matthew 18, when Peter asks how many times he should forgive his brothers, Jesus answers "seventy times seven times" [v. 22]. And 1 John 2:[1–2] states, "But even if anyone does sin, we have an advocate with the Father, Jesus Christ, and he himself is the propitiation for our sins," etc. So also in 2 Corinthians 2, Paul orders the incestuous man to be welcomed back. There is also in Chrysostom and Clement of Alexandria the record of the apostle John inviting a youth who had deserted the faith back to repentance.[13]

Because they have divided repentance into contrition, confession, and satisfaction, we will speak a few words about these terms also.[14] We have said enough already about contrition. If it is true contrition, it is the putting to death of our old man, as Scripture describes it. This contrition is a far greater sorrow than anything human reason can imagine—so far from the truth is the thought that we are made contrite or mortified by the power of our free will and without the operation of the Holy Spirit.

One type of confession is when we acknowledge our sins and condemn ourselves before God. This confession is nothing else than mortification itself and the true contrition of which we just spoke. Scripture often makes mention of it, as in 1 John 1:[9], "If we confess our sins, he is faithful and just to forgive us our sins." And David declares, "For I acknowledge my iniquity and my sin is always before me. Against you alone have I sinned and done evil before you, that you may be justified in your speech and you may prevail when you are judged" [Psalm 51:3–4]. And again, "I said, 'I will confess my transgression to the Lord,' and you forgave the godlessness of my sin" [Psalm 32:5]. Sin is not forgiven without this confession. On the other hand, sin cannot but be forgiven us when we make this

---

[13] Clement of Alexandria, *On the Salvation of the Rich Man* (*MPG* 9:647–52).

[14] Luther was condemned by Rome for rejecting this tripartite division of repentance. Luther wrote, "The notion that there are three parts to repentance—Contrition, Confession, and Satisfaction—is not based in Holy Scripture or the ancient, holy teachers" (WA 7:112; AE 32:32).

confession, when we accuse and condemn ourselves and give glory to God by acknowledging his truth and righteousness.

The other type of confession is when we accuse ourselves not just at home by ourselves but before others. This used to take place in the church in the following way: Someone who was guilty of a crime would be accused privately by a brother at first and then before the church. There the offense was forgiven if he repented. But anyone who refused to hear the church was thrown out of it. You have the model for this confession in Matthew 18, where the use of the keys was given. But now there is not a trace of this confession in the church, though no other practice could be more suitable for restraining vices. Now another form of confession has replaced this one. In this confession everything is done privately and in seclusion with individual priests. And the difference between the ancient practice and ours is that the ancient practice dealt only with public and manifest offenses, while ours also deals with secret sins. The most ancient custom was that public offenses were revealed and condemned before the entire church and were absolved by the decision of the entire church. This custom was abolished long ago and instead a single priest was chosen from the presbytery and before him people could make accusations, though still only about public offenses. According to his judgment, this priest would then name a penalty for the wrongdoers in front of the church, but again this was for public offenses. The offenders were not readmitted to the congregation unless they had paid that public penalty. There still remains a trace of this practice in the public repentance of our times, when homicides are punished in the church.

Whoever is the author of the so-called *Tripartite History* describes this form of confession.[15] The author appears to be Greek, and he says that, though this practice was abolished in Constantinople, it still remained in the churches of the West. This is the form of confession often mentioned by Cyprian who informs us that it was done before a priest rather than the entire church. Though,

---

[15] The *Tripartite History* (*MPL* 69:879–1214), a compilation and translation into Latin of three Greek ecclesiastical histories, was edited by Cassiodorus (c. 490–c. 583) to serve as a church history for Latin-speaking clergy and scholars. Along with Eusebius's *Ecclesiastical History*, which had already been translated into Latin by Rufinus in the early fifth century, the *Tripartite History* served as the main resource for church history in the medieval West.

again, he is talking about the confession of public offenses. If you wish, you can look up his sermon on those who have fallen from the faith.[16] I will quote the words of the Greek *History* below:

It seemed good to the ancient pontiffs that crimes be broadcast as if in a theater for the congregation to witness. For this reason they chose a priest of good report, a wise man who could keep a secret, and to him those who had committed a crime would come and confess their sins. He named a penalty to fit the guilt of each one. Up to this day, this practice is still diligently practiced in the churches of the West, especially at Rome where there is even a special place for the penitent, where the guilty stand as if to mourn. Moreover, when the sacred celebration is completed, they, after abstaining from communion, prostrate themselves on the ground in mourning and lamentation. The bishop then runs to meet them and himself falls to the ground with tears and spiritual mourning. And all the people in the congregation weep. After this, the bishop is the first to rise. He then has those who are lying on the ground rise. Next, after a prayer is made for the penitent, he dismisses everyone. Meanwhile, the penitent torment themselves with various afflictions according to the bishop's judgment. They wait anxiously for the time of the congregational service, which is prescribed by the bishop. When this time comes they participate in the congregational service with the entire church, as if the debt has now been fully paid. The Roman pontiffs have observed this practice up to our times. But in Constantinople a priest presided over the penitent up to the time when a certain woman of the highest nobility, after making confession in the church, had intercourse several times with a deacon while doing penance. When this came out, the people rose up against the priests, alleging that they had violated the church. Then the bishop, Nectarius, removed the deacon from his office and abolished the old custom of penitents, as no priest was chosen to preside over the penitents. And Nectarius

---

[16] See Cyprian, *On those who have fallen from the faith* (*MPL* 4:465–94).

allowed everyone to participate in the Lord's Supper as he pleased according to the judgment of his own conscience.[17]

This is, for the most part, a literal rendering of the *Tripartite History*. From what we have said, you can see that there was once a twofold form of public repentance. One took place in the earliest church, where the matter was conducted before the entire congregation, and those wrongdoers who refused to repent were thrown out of communion with the believers, while those who repented were absolved. You have an example of this in 1 Corinthians 5 and 2 Corinthians 2, which deal with the incestuous man. The other form of public repentance is where the punishment is public but the confession is not. And we see traces of this practice today in the penance done by those who commit homicides. (But punishments are not obligatory by divine right. They arose, rather, from human traditions, as I will soon explain.) Of course, it is concerning this kind of repentance that the ancient canons generally speak. But the fatuous professors of pontifical law improperly twist these canons as if they dealt with private repentance.

PRIVATE CONFESSIONS

Besides public repentance, there are also private confessions. These include, first of all, our private reconciliations with those who offend us. Matthew 5:[23–24] speaks of this kind of confession: "If you are bringing your gift to the altar and there remember that your brother has something against you . . . go, reconcile with your brother." And James 5:[16] states, "Confess your sins, one to the other," which means that one should ask forgiveness for his offense from the other.

Then there are those ecclesiastical private confessions, the practice of which is so common today. It is clear that these confessions formerly took place in the following way: people whose consciences were afflicted about something consulted with other saints who were experienced in spiritual matters, and they received absolution from them. Basil made mention of this practice in his work entitled, I think, *The Ordinances of Monks*, which was reportedly translated into Latin by Rufinus.[18] I have discovered so many kinds of

---

[17] *Tripartite History* 9.35 (*MPL* 69:1151).

[18] Basil's *Rules* can be found in *MPG* 31:889–1052.

confessions, and since some of them have been handed down by divine right and others have been invented by men, we must distinguish between them carefully.

It is quite obvious from 1 John 1, which we cited above, that we must confess our sin to God by divine right. For sin is not forgiven unless we confess it to God, that is, unless we condemn ourselves and trust that our sin is forgiven by God's mercy.

There is no reason to argue about public confession of public offenses before the church, the kind of confession done in front of witnesses. Not only divine right, but the situation itself compels you to confess if you are accused. But divine right also compels you to appease your brother.

The other confessions are traditions of men. For if you come to church willingly and want to be absolved, whether your sin is secret or public, divine right does not require an enumeration of your actions. Christ absolved very many people in this way, and in Acts the apostles absolved several thousand in the same way, without demanding that they enumerate and catalogue their sins. I mention this to instruct the weak consciences of those who are just short of despairing if they pass over anything in enumerating a confession.

Private absolution is as necessary as Baptism. For although you hear the Gospel preached to the entire church indiscriminately, you are finally assured that this Gospel applies specifically to you when you are absolved privately and specifically. He does not thirst for grace who does not ardently desire to hear God's proclamation to him. For it is God's proclamation, not man's, by which you are absolved, provided that you believe the absolution. How certain was the sinful woman that all her guilt had been forgiven, since she heard Christ's voice, "Your sins are forgiven you" (Luke 7:[48])! So also you should be certain when you are absolved by your brother, whoever he may be. Only those who desire to be absolved and believe that they are absolved are truly absolved. Therefore, those are not absolved who act out confession and repentance because they are forced by the pope's requirement to confess every year. More than that, they mock Christ when they seek absolution not because they are moved by the Spirit to desire it, but because they were forced by papal law.

There is no satisfaction outside the death of Christ, as Isaiah 53:[11] makes clear: "He himself has borne our iniquities." But the satisfactions that are now imposed on the penitent are man's invention. Moreover, they originated from the penitential canons, which themselves were created to address public repentance. The satisfaction of Christ and faith in the word of absolution have been completely eclipsed by these sham satisfactions. Scripture does, of course, record the punishment of sinners in some places, but this is not recorded for all sinners. Therefore, no one could rightly call these punishments satisfactions. Indulgences, Rome's merchandise, arose from satisfactions. Indulgences originally remitted the canonical punishments imposed on public penitents. But godless men have begun to sell them as God's forgiveness so that people might trust in their word instead of God's.[19]

Therefore, to conclude this section, there are two parts of repentance—mortification and vivification. Mortification happens when the conscience is terrified by the Law; vivification happens when you are strengthened and confirmed by absolution. For absolution is the Gospel by which Christ forgives you your sin. The sign of repentance is nothing else than Baptism.

PARTICIPATION IN THE LORD'S SUPPER

Participation in the Lord's Supper, that is, eating Christ's body and drinking his blood, is a sure sign of God's grace. For this is what Christ says, "This is the cup of the New Testament," etc. And again he says, "Do this, as often as you do it, in remembrance of me" [1 Corinthians 11:25]. That is, when you do this, you should be reminded of the Gospel and the forgiveness of sins. It is not, then, a sacrifice, since it has been given only as a sure testimony of the promised Gospel. Nor does participation in the Supper take sins away. Faith does that. But faith is strengthened by this sign. Just as seeing Christ when he was about to be killed did not justify Stephen but strengthened the faith by which he was justified and given life, so neither does participation in the Supper justify but rather strengthens faith, as I said above. Therefore, all masses are godless except for those that encourage consciences and strengthen faith. It is a sacrifice when we offer something to God. But we do not offer Christ to God.

---

[19] Cf. Luther, who writes in the seventy-second of his Ninety-five Theses: "Blessed is he who guards against the lust and license of the indulgence-seller's words" (WA 1:237; AE 31:31).

He himself offered himself once and for all. Therefore, those who perform masses to do some good work, to offer Christ to God for the living and the dead, with the thought that the more often it is repeated the better it is done, these commit a godless error. In my opinion, these errors should be blamed on Thomas in large part, since he taught that the mass profited others besides the person who ate of it.[20] But the purpose of this sacrament is to strengthen us whenever our consciences waver and we doubt God's goodwill toward us. And this happens all the time, especially when we are about to die. Therefore, it is particularly those who are about to die who need to be strengthened. But the Christian life consists in our constant death.

Confirmation, I think, is the laying on of hands. Extreme unction is, I think, what Mark 6:[13] is talking about. But I do not see that these signs have been handed down in order to give assurance of grace. We have no reason to doubt that marriage has not been instituted to bestow grace. And what has entered into the minds of those who numbered ordination among the signs of grace? For ordination is nothing else than the choosing of some from the church to teach, baptize, consecrate the Supper, and distribute alms among the poor. Those who taught, baptized, and consecrated the Supper were called bishops or presbyters, while those who distributed the alms among the poor were called deacons. Nor were their duties so separated that it was sacrilege for a deacon to teach, baptize, or consecrate the Supper. Rather, these activities are allowed to all Christians. For the keys belong to all according to Matthew 18. But their care was entrusted to certain men so that there could be those who knew that the administration of ecclesiastical matters was their

---

[20] Thomas Aquinas writes, "It must be repeated, as I said before, that this sacrament is not only a sacrament, but also a sacrifice. For this sacrament possesses the nature of a sacrifice insofar as Christ's passion, by which he offered himself as a sacrifice to God (Ephesians 5), is represented in it. But insofar as in this sacrament grace is invisibly bestowed under a visible element, it possesses the nature of a sacrament. This sacrament therefore benefits those who partake of it in its capacity as sacrament and as sacrifice, for it is sacrificed for all those who partake of it. . . . But it benefits the others, who do not partake of it, only in its nature as a sacrifice, inasmuch as it is sacrificed for their salvation" (*Summa* III, q. 79, art. 7). In the same place Aquinas encourages the repetition of the sacrifice, saying, "The offering of the sacrifice is multiplied by more masses, and therefore the effect of the sacrifice and the sacrament is multiplied."

duty and so that there would be certain men to whom people could properly turn if anything came up.[21]

As long as we are on the topic, I would like to stress that the word "bishop" or "presbyter" or "deacon" have no relation to the word "priest."[22] For in Scripture the priest is called a priest (*sacerdos*) because he offers sacrifices and calls on God. And we Christians are all priests because we offer a sacrifice, that is, our body. For besides this, there is no sacrifice in Christianity. Moreover, we also have the right to call on God, no, even to placate him. Here the passage from 1 Peter [2:9] applies: "A holy nation, a royal priesthood." For we Christians are kings because we are free in Christ and rule over all creatures, life, death, and sin, as I explained above. We are priests because we offer ourselves to God and call upon him to pardon our sins. The Epistle to the Hebrews explains this more thoroughly. Bishops, presbyters, and deacons are those who teach, baptize, consecrate the Supper, and distribute alms. The priests who sacrifice the mass are prophets of Jezebel, that is, of Rome.[23]

---

[21] Cf. Luther, *The Babylonian Captivity*: "Therefore, let everyone who knows that he is a Christian be assured and understand for himself that we are all equally priests, that is, that we share the same power in the Word and in every sacrament. But it is not permissible for just anyone to use this power, except by the consensus of the community or the calling of a superior—for what is common to the community no individual can arrogate to himself, unless he is called" (WA 6:566; AE 36:116).

[22] The Latin word for priest (*sacerdos*) bears no relation etymologically (or, according to Melanchthon, semantically) to the words "bishop," "presbyter," or "deacon." In English, however, the word "priest" derives etymologically from the Greek word "presbyter."

[23] See Revelation 2:20.

LOVE

So far we have spoken of sin, Law, grace, Gospel, and especially justification, since this has been and always will be the perennial question common to all mankind: how can man be justified? The philosophers and Pharisees have taught that man is justified by his own virtues and endeavors. We have taught that we are justified by faith alone. This means that Christ's righteousness is our righteousness through faith, and that our works and our endeavors are nothing but sin. Whoever grasps this grasps the chief point of Scripture, namely, that all who believe in God's mercy are justified. Now finally, it is time for us to speak of love.

Above I stressed that love of God is the fruit of faith. For whoever lays hold of God's mercy by faith cannot help but love God in return. Therefore, love is the fruit of faith. From love of God also comes love of the neighbor, since we desire to serve God in all his creatures. And I can give no guide for this love briefer or more fitting than the following: "Love your neighbor as yourself."[1] Augustine came up with a ranking of things to be loved, so that we should love souls first and then bodies, our loved ones first, then others.[2] We always prefer faith to love. Therefore, we generally put the things of the soul over the necessities of the body. But in Matthew 5:[44] Christ commands us to love outsiders and enemies as if they were friends, and Paul gives us the same command in Romans 12:[14]. The Spirit will easily judge to which people specifically, whether friends or enemies, you should do good. Of course, Paul wanted special consideration to be paid to the household (Galatians [6:10]; 1 Timothy [5:8]).[3] But I do not want the freedom of the Spirit to be

---

[1] See Matthew 22:39; Mark 12:31; Romans 13:9.

[2] Peter Lombard *Sentences* III, dist. 29, 108–9 cites Augustine (*On Christian Doctrine*, 1.28.29) in discussing the ranking of things to be loved. Lombard notes that Augustine is ranking things not according to the affection we should feel, which should be equal for all, but according to the external obligation to aid our neighbor, in which case we should feed our children before feeding others.

[3] This is a concession to Lombard and Augustine (see previous note), who cite Galatians 6:10 to prove a ranking of things to be loved.

hampered by arguments like those of the Scholastics or of Cicero in Book III of his *On Moral Responsibility*. There Cicero discusses the moral responsibility of one who has been shipwrecked and arrived at the same plank of wood that a wise man has taken hold of.[4] Away with these stupid questions about things that rarely if ever actually happen!

---

[4] *De officiis* 3.23.

MAGISTRATES

A section on magistrates seemed especially necessary. For pedagogical reasons, we will, to start out, follow the common division. Magistrates are divided into civil and ecclesiastical. The civil magistrate is one who wields the sword and protects civil peace. Paul approves of this kind of magistrate in Romans 13. The functions of the sword include civil laws, the civil ordinances of public courts, and the punishments of criminals. The duty of the sword includes administering laws against murder, against taking vengeance, etc. Therefore, the magistrate administers the sword with God's approval. The same can be said of lawyers if they issue opinions concerning the law or defend the oppressed. But people who go to court commit an especially grievous sin.[1]

Now these are my thoughts on wielding the power of the sword. First of all, if princes command anything against God, they should not be obeyed, according to Acts 5:[29], "We ought to obey God rather than men." You have innumerable examples of this principle, perhaps the most beautiful of which is in Amos 7:[10–17]. Second, if they command what is in the public's best interest, they should be obeyed, according to Romans 13:[5], "They should be obeyed not only because of wrath but because of conscience." For love obligates us to all kinds of civil responsibilities. Finally, if they issue any tyrannical commands when nothing can be done about it short of a disturbance or sedition, we should also bear with this magistracy because of love. For this is what Christ says, "If anyone strikes you on the right cheek, turn to him also the left" [Matthew 5:39]. But if you can disobey it without scandal and a public disturbance, do so. For example, if you have been thrown into prison undeservedly and you can break out without a public disturbance, nothing forbids you from escaping. This agrees with 1 Corinthians 7:[21], "If you can be free, rather use it."

Now for our thoughts on ecclesiastical magistrates: First, ministers are bishops, not rulers or magistrates. Second, bishops do not have the right to establish laws, since they have been commanded

---

[1] For Melanchthon's later qualification of this opinion, see p. 161, n. 15.

to preach only the Word of God, not the word of men. We explained this above, and it is clear enough from Jeremiah 23.

I. In the first place, then, if they teach Scripture, they must be heard as if they were Christ. For so Christ declares, "He who hears you hears me" [Luke 10:16]. Now this pertains not to human traditions but to Scripture, as is evident from what Christ says, "He who receives a prophet in the name of a prophet" [Matthew 10:41]. For he does not mean a false prophet.

II. Second, if they have taught anything against Scripture, they should not be heard. So Acts 5:[29], "We ought to obey God rather than men." And again, Matthew 15:[6], "You have nullified the commandment of God for the sake of your tradition." Since the pope has at this time decreed contrary to divine right in issuing a bull condemning Luther, he should by no means be obeyed.[2]

III. Third, if they have issued anything outside of Scripture so as to bind consciences, they should not be heard. For nothing obligates the conscience except God's Law (*ius divinum*). Paul was speaking of this in 1 Timothy 4, where he calls the law of celibacy and the banning of certain foods "doctrines of demons" [v. 1]. Although they may not seem to be contrary to Scripture and although they are not of themselves evil (for neither celibacy nor abstaining from meat is evil), still they are godless if you think that you are sinning by doing differently. Those who think that a person sins if he does not observe the canonical hours or eats meat on the sixth or seventh day, and so on, are teaching godless things. For a bishop cannot bind the Christian conscience. So says 2 Corinthians 13:[10], "We have been given power not to destroy but to build up."

IV. In the fourth place, if you are not burdening the conscience with the law of the bishop but interpret it as an external obligation, as spiritual men do who understand that the conscience cannot be bound by any human law, you will be judging the law of the bishop as you would the tyranny of the civil magistrate. For whatever bishops command outside of Scripture is tyranny, since they have no authority to command it.[3] You will bear these burdens because of love, according to the passage: "If anyone strikes you on the right cheek,

---

[2] Pope Leo X excommunicated Luther on January 3, 1521, with the bull *Decet Romanum Pontificem*.

[3] In its classical sense, the term "tyranny" denotes power exercised outside of established law.

turn to him also the left" [Matthew 5:39]. But if you can do differently without scandal, nothing forbids you from doing so, just as nothing forbids you from breaking out of the prison in which you have been bound by a tyrant, if you can do it without public disturbance. For Scripture says, "If you can be free, rather use it" [1 Corinthians 7:21]. So also, Christ dispensed of the Pharisees' traditions in Matthew 9 and 12. But he did not dispense of civil laws. And by dispensing of pharisaical laws, we are more free, both because they are requirements for the private use of individuals rather than common obligations, and because they easily ensnare consciences. Moreover faith, love, and especially necessity rule over and manage all human laws. Necessity frees us from all traditions wherever and whenever any tradition leads the soul or the livelihood of the body into danger.

SCANDAL

You ask to what degree we should consider the issue of scandal. First of all, let me stress what I said before. Faith and love are the standards of all human activities, but faith is the more important of these.

Now a scandal is an offense by which our neighbor's faith or love is damaged. If anything is taught different from Holy Scripture, the faith of our neighbor is damaged. The Scholastics' entire doctrinal system is a scandal of this kind because it promotes satisfactions and the works of the free will, thereby obscuring grace. Christ speaks of this kind of scandal in Matthew 18:[6], "Whoever scandalizes one of these little ones who believe in me, it would have been better if a millstone had been hung from his neck and he had been drowned," etc. Love is damaged if someone does not help the poor or disturbs public peace. Christ speaks of this kind of scandal when he discusses paying the tax in Matthew 17:[27], "[L]est we scandalize them."

I. As far as those things commanded by divine right, it is God's command that we obey, do, and teach whatever is commanded by divine right without any worry about causing scandal. For faith must always be preferred to love. Here again the passage in Acts 5:[29] applies: "We ought to obey God rather than men." And Christ says, "I have not come to bring peace but a sword" [Matthew 10:34]. So Daniel did not obey the law demanding the worship of the golden idol. Nor should we obey the godless princes who condemn the Gospel in our day.

II. As far as those indifferent things that belong to human ordinances, such as the practices of celibacy and abstaining from meat, human tradition does not obligate us in cases of necessity. For Christ dispenses even of divine law in a case of necessity as recorded in Matthew 12:[1], where his disciples pick ears of grain. How much more permissible is it for us to violate human traditions if the necessity of life demands it? This is even more the case when the soul is in danger, as when a priest burns, as they say.[1] So 2 Corinthians 13:[10] states, "We have been given power not to destroy but to build

---

[1] Cf. 1 Corinthians 7:9.

up." Paul condemns laws that burden the body immoderately in Colossians 2:[16–23].

III. In the presence of Pharisees demanding observance of their traditions as if they were necessary for salvation, traditions should be violated without worrying about causing scandal. Paul did this with divine law when he refused to have Titus circumcised (Galatians 2:[3]). How much more permissible is it when we are dealing with the papists' stupid traditions? And Christ commands us to pay no attention to those who are scandalized in this way, because they are blind and leaders of the blind [Matthew 15:12–14].

IV. It is permissible to violate human traditions in order to teach Christian freedom, so that the inexperienced may understand that it is not a sin even if they do something contrary to human traditions. A clear instance of such an occasion is Paul's reprimand of Peter for yielding to inexperienced people who were foolishly observing laws in ignorance of Christian freedom [Galatians 2:11–17].

V. Around the weak and those who have not yet heard the Gospel, we should fulfill the duty of love and observe human traditions, provided that we do nothing contrary to God's command. So Acts [21:24] records that Paul had himself shaved in Jerusalem because there were so few among so many people who sufficiently understood the freedom of the Gospel. According to the same principle, Paul would rather permanently abstain from meat than that the soul of his brother should perish. Again, in Romans 14:[1], he says, "Support the man who is weak in his faith." In those times, however, they were dealing with divine law. Now, since we are dealing with human traditions, we may dispense of them more freely. In fact, it is a godless practice to obey bishops so long as they are demanding us to observe human traditions and burdening the conscience with the so-called sin of violating these traditions. For when these traditions are required of us, they are doctrines of demons. But if they are not required of us, Paul's rule should be observed: "Neither does he abound who eats nor does he lack who does not eat" (1 Corinthians 8:[8]).

You now have the most common topics of theology. You may seek a more exact account of them from the Scriptures. We are content to have shown what you should look for. Therefore, I think that I have done well in treating such things more briefly than I should have, lest by my misplaced diligence I call anyone away from the Scriptures and to my own arguments. For when it comes to sacred matters I think that the commentaries of men should be avoided like the plague, since the pure teaching of the Spirit can be drawn only from the Scriptures. For who has expressed the Spirit of God with more accuracy than the Spirit himself?

Οὐκ ἐν λόγῳ ἡ βασιλεία τοῦ θεοῦ, ἀλλ' ἐν δυνάμει.[2]

---

[2] "The kingdom of God is not in word but in power" (1 Corinthians 4:20).

SCRIPTURE INDEX

SUBJECT INDEX

The Chief Theological Topics
Loci Praecipui Theologici 1559

Translated by J. A. O. Preus; new foreword by Jacob A. O. Preus III

"One of the several most significant and influential compendia of theology written during the Reformation." —Richard A. Muller, Calvin Theological Seminary

In honor of the 450th anniversary of Philip Melanchthon's death in 1560, a second edition of his Loci Communes ("Commonplaces" or "Common Topics") has been issued. Originally published in English under the name *Loci Theologici 1543*, this book is actually Melanchthon's last Latin edition, published in 1559. This revised English edition includes several new features: a new translation of Melanchthon's "Definitions of Terms That Have Been Used in the Church," a new historical introduction, cross-references to the original Latin, a Scripture index, and an index of persons. (P) 400 pages. Hardback.

531181   9780758626875

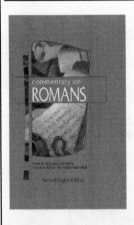

Commentary on Romans
Philip Melanchthon; translated by Fred Kramer

"Among the most significant contributions Melanchthon made to the life of the church were his biblical commentaries. This volume from Melanchthon's hand offered a model for the proclamation of the Gospel and a vital help for understanding the whole body of biblical teaching to Wittenberg students in the sixteenth century. It continues to be of value to preachers and other students of Scripture today." —From the foreword by Robert Kolb, PhD, Concordia Seminary, St. Louis

A clear, concise commentary on Romans by Melanchthon and translated into English. Written during the confessional struggles of the Reformation, the book focuses on Roman's Gospel content and comfort.

(P) 320 pages. Hardback.

155148   9780758626868

www.cph.org • 1-800-325-3040

Concordia
Publishing House

Christian Freedom

Faith Working through Love: A Reader's Edition

Martin Luther and Philip Melanchthon

In Luther's day, the message of Christian freedom was readily misunderstood by those whose focus was on worldly things rather than on Christ and the cross. Luther was not a politician; he was a pastor who found real freedom in the Gospel.

This new translation incorporates material on ceremonies not included in the text of the Weimar edition, as well as Melanchthon's summary on freedom. The book also includes a 40-day reading plan, introductory notes, illustrations, and a glossary.

(P) 272 pages. Hardback.

155184   **9780758631022**

Martin Luther: Preacher of the Cross

A Study of Luther's Pastoral Theology

John T. Pless

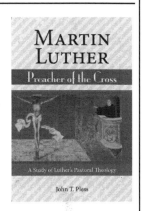

"This book is a significant contribution to pastoral theology . . . Pastors are entrusted with the task of being caretakers of people's troubled consciences and struggles in life; this book will again bring to the attention the truth and seriousness of pastoral care and ministry." —Klaus Detlev Schulz, Concordia Theological Seminary, Fort Wayne

Martin Luther was not only a theologian, but a pastor engaged in the care of souls. This new resource provides evidence for Luther's application of his evangelical theology to consciences burdened with sin, haunted by death, and afflicted by the devil.

Through the use of selected letters, *Martin Luther: Preacher of the Cross* presents compelling evidence for the reformer's application of his evangelical theology. Luther believed that above all else, the pastor offers spiritual counsel, and this is nothing less than speaking the stuff of faith.

(P) 144 pages. Paperback.

155090   **9780758611137**

Faith and Act

The Survival of Medieval Ceremonies in the Lutheran Reformation

Ernst Walter Zeeden, Translated by Kevin Walker

"Faith and Act [is] . . . a mix of exacting research and historiographical vision that may justly be viewed as one of the foundation texts of modern Reformation history."
—C. Scott Dixon, Queen's University, Belfast

"Historians of liturgy and church discipline will welcome the reappearance of Zeeden's classic monograph, gracefully translated and with updated bibliographical references." —Ralph Keen, University of Illinois at Chicago

Prof. Dr. Zeeden's classic study of how Medieval Church practices continued and developed within Lutheran Church orders offers readers a unique perspective on how faith influences the act of worship. Historians of liturgy and theology will discover insights and important continuity between the Lutheran churches of the sixteenth century and their forebears of the late medieval period. (P) 186 pages. Paperback.

531182   **9780758627018**

Divine Kingdom, Holy Order

The Political Writings of Martin Luther

Jarrett A. Carty

"Carty has wisely selected and intelligently abridged Luther's most important political writings from 1520 to 1546. His introductions to the selections are careful and insightful, written with a full awareness of the large secondary literature. . . . A highly recommended resource."
—Denis R. Janz, Loyola University New Orleans

The canon of western political theory has long misrepresented Luther's political thought, mistaking it as a forerunner of the "freedom of conscience" or the "separation of church and state," or an ancestor of modern absolutism and even German totalitarianism. These misleading interpretations neglect Luther's central point: temporal government is a gift from God, worthy of honor and respect, independent yet complementary to the purpose and mission of the Church. Spanning Luther's career as a reformer, the writings in this anthology will demonstrate his resolve to restore temporal government to its proper place of honor and divine purpose. (P) 544 pages. Hardback.

531183   **9780758627117**

www.cph.org • 1-800-325-3040

Concordia
Publishing House

Theological Commonplaces

Johann Gerhard; translated by Richard J. Dinda; edited with annotations by Benjamin T. G. Mayes

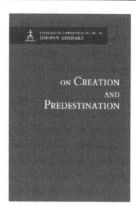

"Gerhard's Loci is the greatest doctrinal text in the entire history of Lutheranism. By putting these splendid volumes in the English language, CPH ensures access to the solid teaching of the orthodox Lutheran Church in one of its greatest expressions ever penned. And CPH is virtually the only Lutheran publishing house in the world with the capacity, fidelity, and will to produce such gems!" —Rev. Dr. Matthew C. Harrison, president, The Lutheran Church—Missouri Synod

Johann Gerhard (1582–1637) was the premier Lutheran theologian of the baroque period. Now his Loci Theologici is translated in English for the first time in seventeen volumes of Theological Commonplaces.

The Theological Commonplaces series is the most significant theological work of Lutheran orthodoxy after the Reformation and remains a classic of Lutheran theology. With skill and precision, Gerhard sets forth the Christian faith from Scripture in dialogue with the Church Fathers, medieval theology, Luther, and a multitude of contemporary theologians.

Each hardback volume includes:

- the translation of Gerhard's Loci (originally published from 1610 to 1625)
- a glossary of key theological, rhetorical, and philosophical terms
- a name index
- a Scripture index
- a carefully researched list of works cited, which presents guidance for deciphering the numerous abbreviations of the other titles from which Gerhard quotes.

For information on the newest volumes and on how to become a subscriber to Theological Commonplaces, visit cph.org/gerhard.

Concordia
Publishing House

www.cph.org • 1-800-325-3040

Luther's Works

American Edition, New Series

General Editor Christopher Boyd Brown

"This new series should delight scholars as well as engage laity and clergy." —Mark U. Edwards Jr., Harvard Divinity School

"Provides a tremendous service to historians, theologians, pastors, and students." —Amy Nelson Burnett, University of Nebraska—Lincoln

"Casual readers and those seeking to expand and deepen their knowledge of the Reformation will profit greatly from these carefully translated and edited volumes." —Robert Kolb, Concordia Seminary, St. Louis

Even now, amid the fifth century after his death, Luther remains an epochal figure in the history of the Christian Church, a prominent shaper of the religious and cultural history of the West and a provocative voice still heard and engaged by theologians, pastors, and laity around the world as a witness to the Gospel of Jesus Christ. The new volumes of Luther's Works in English will serve their readers with much that has proved and will prove its importance for the faith, life, and history of the Christian Church.

Concordia Publishing House is currently in the midst of an ambitious expansion of the American Edition to include an additional 28 volumes (now including Luther's postils). You can receive a 30% savings by subscribing to the series! Your subscription starts with the newest volume and you will continue to receive each new volume until the series is complete. Subscribers can purchase previously published, in-stock volumes at the same 30% discount.

For information on the newest volumes and on how to become a subscriber to Luther's Works, visit cph.org/luthersworks.

For information on digital editions of Luther's Works, visit logos.com/Concordia.

Concordia
Publishing House

www.cph.org • 1-800-325-3040